ESTRANGING THE FAMILIAR

ESTRANGING THE FAMILIAR

Toward a Revitalized Critical Writing

G. Douglas Atkins

THE UNIVERSITY OF GEORGIA PRESS
Athens and London

© 1992 by the University of Georgia Press
Athens, Georgia 30602
All rights reserved

Designed by Sandra Strother Hudson
Set in 10 on 13 Bembo by Tseng Information Systems, Inc.
Printed and bound by Thomson-Shore
The paper in this book meets the guidelines
for permanence and durability of the Committee on
Production Guidelines for Book Longevity
of the Council on Library Resources.

Printed in the United States of America
96 95 94 93 92 C 5 4 3 2 1
96 95 94 93 92 P 5 4 3 2 1

Library of Congress Cataloging in Publication Data

Atkins, G. Douglas (George Douglas), 1943–
Estranging the familiar : toward a revitalized critical writing /
G. Douglas Atkins.
p. cm.
Includes bibliographical references and index.
ISBN 0-8203-1452-8 (alk. paper). — ISBN 0-8203-1453-6 (pbk. :
alk. paper)
1. Essay. 2. Criticism—Authorship. I. Title.
PN4500.A89 1992
808.4—dc20   91–42648
CIP

British Library Cataloging in Publication Data available

I dare; I will also essay to be.

EMERSON, *Essays*

In most books the *I,* or first person, is omitted; in this it will be retained; that, in respect to egotism, is the main difference. We commonly do not remember that it is, after all, always the first person that is speaking. I should not talk so much about myself if there were anybody else whom I knew as well.

THOREAU, *Walden: or, Life in the Woods*

Essays belong to a literary species whose extreme variability can be studied most effectively within a three-poled frame of reference. There is the pole of the personal and the autobiographical; there is the pole of the objective, the factual, the concrete-particular; and there is the pole of the abstract universal. Most essayists are at home and at their best in the neighborhood of only one of the essay's three poles, or at the most only in the neighborhood of two of them. There are the predominantly personal essayists, who write fragments of reflective autobiography and who look at the world through the keyhole of anecdote and description. There are the predominantly objective essayists who do not speak directly of themselves, but turn their attention outward to some literary or scientific or political theme. Their arts consist of setting forth, passing judgment upon, and drawing general conclusions from, the relevant data. In the third group we find those essayists who do their work in the world of high abstractions, who never condescend to be personal and who hardly deign to take notice of the particular facts from which their generalizations were originally drawn. . . .

The most richly satisfying essays are those which make the best not of one, not of two, but of all the three worlds in which it is possible for the essay to exist.

ALDOUS HUXLEY, Preface, *Collected Essays*

Montaigne reminds all of us . . . that living is what we least know how to do and what we most need to learn for our own good.

> We are great fools. "He has spent his life in idleness," we say. "I have done nothing today." What, have you not lived? That is not only the fundamental but the most illustrious of your occupations. "If I had been placed in a position to manage great affairs, I would have shown what I could do." Have you been able to think out and manage your own life? You have done the greatest task of all. . . . To compose our character is our duty, not to compose books, and to win, not battles and provinces, but order and tranquillity in our conduct. Our great and glorious masterpiece is to live appropriately. . . .

A book is written, bound, published, lasts for centuries; but, no, says Montaigne, that is not itself the "great and glorious masterpiece." A book is only a kind of remnant, what is left over afterwards when the real composition—the work of knowing how to live—is finished. Still, these leavings do matter, for they are the chosen marks of living: here's how I do it. The doing, the writing itself, is both a path *to* knowing and a path *of* knowing; as I write, I am "forming my life," . . . which is "the greatest task of all."

LYDIA FAKUNDINY, *The Art of the Essay*

Contents

CONTENTS

Preface

THIS IS a book at once and perhaps in equal measure about the essay, criticism, and me. It is a mixed and impure thing, in tone, in structure, and not least in style. I shuttle between the personal and the scholarly. Rather than straightforward and linear, the structure is essayistic: though not exactly rambling, it circles the topic of the essay, especially the critical essay, examining it from several perspectives, repeatedly putting the matter "in other words." Some repetitiveness thus occurs, but that, I hope, won't necessarily be seen as a defect. Argument there is, but it unfolds, rather than marches in jackboots toward an all-too-predictable and definitive conclusion. The book moves toward the essay.

My starting point is also the essay, its intriguing capaciousness and artistic possibilities, wonders and delights perhaps never more apparent than now. A venerable form, the essay has been rediscovered by a remarkable array of talented writers who have restored it to a place of deserved attention and honor, if not quite of power. Whether or not it is the form of choice for our best writers, it is being courted by many of them. And readers are responding eagerly and enthusiastically. In short, according to George Core, editor of the *Sewanee Review*, "ours is the Age of the Essay." [1]

I consider part of what that means and what some of the implications might be for critical writing. Again I quote George Core: "The ordinary scholarly paper—the article—is as far removed from the essay as A. J. Liebling is from James Joyce. But both Liebling and Joyce write well, whereas your average scholar's prose, especially nowadays, is dreary at best." [2] What I hope to stimulate, my reach no doubt exceeding my grasp (but then, what is criticism for?), is a revitalized critical writing, interesting because both personal and artful, in touch with the human heart and carefully crafted, in love with sentences and humanity alike.

ix

That hope for a revitalized critical writing, I argue, may entail—though it is not limited to—a return to the essay. But not an uncritical or anti-theoretical embrace of forms magnificently exploited in perhaps simpler times. Criticism may be enervated apart from the essay and its rich and fecund traditions and opportunities, but it can only to its peril forget or ignore the difference time has made since the essay's heyday in Hazlitt and Emerson.

The result of criticism written in essay form—I insist on the difference between the article and the essay—is *personal criticism*. Part of a widespread "return of/to the personal," this practice of criticism is currently associated with feminists, whose opposition to and attacks on prevailing critical modes, styles, and exclusions represent at once impressive courage and estimable wisdom. As much as I admire them and in many ways perhaps resemble them, I differ from these "personal" critics, and not just because I'm male. I don't start with the personal but rather with the essay, in which feminist critics have shown (too) little interest and about which, to my mind, they show too little knowledge. My interest, unlike that of many advocates of "personal criticism," is thus less in the expressive than in the formal and artistic. To borrow a distinction that figures prominently in this book, I side—if we must decide—with the writers and not the critics. This book not only moves toward the essay, culminating in a series of experiments in critical writing, but it also represents my own attempt to find a voice, indeed to become *a writer,* one for whom sentences matter as does the attraction of a nonprofessional, general audience.

I am egotistical enough to suppose—in unscholarly moments—that my interests represent criticism's needs. I suppose, that is, that for criticism to reach a general readership and perhaps achieve a level of artistic attainment it must *estrange the familiar:* the venerable familiar essay may remain the basis, but its conventional openness, receptivity, and capaciousness must extend to theory, philosophy, and the candor that seems to mark the tail end of the twentieth century. "Estranging the familiar" means something else too: if we adopt the essay as our form, eschewing the perhaps outmoded, positivistic article, we have estranged what has been so familiar to us for at least a hundred years. In another sense, an important defamiliarization has always marked the essay, since its very beginnings, in Montaigne. Unfortunately, until recently the essay has been in decline, having little influence on academic criticism. But what I have in mind estranges at once the familiar that is the old-fashioned personal essay and the impersonalism of modern criticism and contemporary theory, which is itself nothing if not defamiliarizing and estranging.

The issue seems to reduce to the question of distance and the possibility of finding, in every sense, "the right distance." That is what this book is all about in its treatment of the essay, criticism, and me.

LIKE GAUL, this book is divided into three parts, each of which consists of three chapters. Part I is constituted by three different though related attempts to say what the essay is, to distinguish it from "that awful object, 'the article,' "[3] which is the goal, end, and test of our professional writing, and, finally, to assess the possible implications of the current remarkable resurgence of interest in the essay for a revitalized critical writing, no longer tied to the article, its impersonalism and narrow professional appeal. The second essay here, "In Other Words: Gardening for Love—The Work of the Essayist," is the most familiar of the three chapters, the third much more theoretical, oriented toward the *critical* essay. The problem, at least one, is somehow to bring together in one essay the personal or familiar and the critical-theoretical and to do it in a way attractive to a broad readership, in a way responsive to yet respectful of our necessary difference from earlier essayists, whose writing was magnificent and artful but often merely impressionistic when presented as critical.

In Part 2, I explore the problem further through various reflections on critical writing, the rise of the article, the influence of professionalism, the effect of theory, and the growing dissatisfaction with academic criticism and the concomitant experimentation with alternative modes. This section unfolds the issues introduced in Part I. The problem comes to be seen as one of restoring, or returning to, the personal without sacrificing artistic control. An argument is thus embedded in these explorations, these meditations.

Part 3 consists of three different, frank, and candid attempts to practice what I have been preaching, to write a personal criticism that is in a significant way autobiographical but neither indulgent nor merely expressive, an unservile and enlarged criticism "neither afraid of theory nor overestimating it."[4] These last chapters are, I hope, essays; certainly they were the hardest to write, representing a new departure for me, perhaps a turn in my career, embodying, maybe empowering, a turn in my life.

They are also, I would insist, still about the essay and critical writing, in varying degrees and different ways. They are not, in any way, intended as last words. Experimental, they are intended to open up possibilities, not close them off. The last essay, in many ways the most important, though it is dependent upon its predecessors, is clearly more memoir than criticism, even if it reconfigures the concerns and themes previously treated; it represents not so much the way toward a revitalized critical essay as a surmise for alternative professional writing, in essay form. Without too much pretension, I trust, I might say that the author here resembles the essayist Georg Lukács famously describes: "a Schopenhauer who writes his *Parerga* while waiting for the arrival of his own (or another's) *The World as Will and Idea*, he is a John the Baptist who goes out to preach in the wilderness about another who is still to come, whose shoelace he is not worthy to untie."[5]

You can't separate the essay from life—that is one of the great things about it, as Montaigne has been trying to teach us. "To compose our character is our duty," he wrote, "not to compose books, and to win, not battles and provinces, but order and tranquillity in our conduct. Our great and glorious masterpiece is to live appropriately." The essay thus becomes understood as "a medium for the art of living."[6] In the further words of Lydia Fakundiny, "The doing, the writing itself, is both a path *to* knowing and a path *of* knowing; as I write, I am 'forming my life,' which is 'the greatest task of all.'" The essay is helping me compose my life, which now seems consubstantial with it. The essay and me, living and writing—these are the major subjects of *Estranging the Familiar*.

Two of these essays have appeared elsewhere, in slightly different form: "The Return of/to the Essay," in the *ADE Bulletin* 96 (1990), and "In Other Words: Gardening for Love—The Work of the Essayist," a co-winner of the 1991 *Kenyon Review* Award for Literary Excellence in nonfiction prose, in the *Kenyon Review* (Winter 1990–91).

Acknowledgments

D URING THE COURSE of writing this book I incurred debts as great
as they are many. Here too it is, happily, impossible to separate the
professional and the personal. Friends, colleagues, and students encouraged me, assisted me, criticized me, taught me, and tried to save me from
often egregious lapses and errors in taste and judgment. Far more than
my poor efforts deserve, I have benefitted from the close attention and
sound judgment of good friends who are also severe critics, including
Robin Lehman and Ann Lowry. I took, I'm afraid, more from my graduate seminar in Personal Criticism (Fall 1989) than I gave, the best class I
have been privileged to learn from: Lori Askeland, Larry Bradfield, Frank
Doden, Becky Eason, Dan Martin, Daryl Palmer, and Brigitte Sandquist.
I cannot but acknowledge the enduring inspiration, concern, and support
of Geoffrey Hartman, nor the continuing encouragement and support of
my department chair, friend, and collaborator, Michael L. Johnson. With
pleasure I express gratitude to the University of Kansas for a sabbatical
leave during which I completed the writing of this book. I want to thank
as well Robert D. Denham, former editor, and David Laurence, editor,
of the *ADE Bulletin* and the good folks at the *Kenyon Review*, especially
Ronald Sharp, who showed faith in my work and encouraged me when I
needed it most. Then there's Lori Whitten, secretary extraordinaire, who,
with impressive skill and unflagging graciousness, typed draft after draft
after draft, written in barely legible longhand, in pencil, on yellow legal
paper. It has been nothing but a pleasure to work with the University of
Georgia Press: from the beginning Karen Orchard has been supportive
and attentive to all manner of authorial concern; the two readers, one of
whom identified himself as Jasper Neel, offered constructive and detailed
criticism, sound advice, and much encouragement; Joanne S. Ainsworth
did a meticulous job of copyediting that turned up more problems than I

care to admit; Laura Gottlieb prepared the index; and Felicia Spencer and Madelaine Cooke shepherded my manuscript through the editorial and production process with consummate skill and care. Christi Stanforth did meticulous and superb work as proofreader for the Press, ferreting out errors I could not see. For whatever infelicities, lapses, and errors that yet remain I alone bear responsibility.

Debts of a more purely personal nature deserve no less to be acknowledged, though here too mere acknowledgment by no means balances the scales. I am fortunate to labor under such debts—who would want it otherwise? I hope to be more deserving of the love of Leslie and Christopher, for whom *my* love ever increases. I dedicated my first book to my parents; and, though, God willing, this won't be my last, it is only fitting and right that I dedicate this one to them as well: with love and prayers and thanks.

PART ONE

CHAPTER ONE

The Return of/to the Essay

The essayist is—or should be—ruminative. He isn't monomaniacal. He is without pedantry; he is not, as they say in university English departments, "in the profession." The essayist might be found almost anywhere, but the last place one is likely to find him is in the pages of the *PMLA*.

JOSEPH EPSTEIN, "Piece Work: Writing the Essay"

T HE RETURN of/to the essay? With the now-familiar if not obligatory slash, my title may seem largely a bow to fashion or perhaps appear to signal yet another, perhaps predictable poststructuralist exercise in ingenuity. I hope it is more than fashionable, and at least I intend it to suggest something other than cleverness. Though my focus is the current resurgence of interest in the essay, I leave unresolved—uncontested really—the question of the power and primacy of human agency in that return: whether *we* are returning to the essay, whether *the essay* as a form possesses some power of survival and renewal, or whether certain material and cultural conditions have coalesced to effect that return, there can be little doubt concerning both general readers' growing interest in, and writers' new commitment to, this venerable genre. That growing interest and that new commitment seem so far, however, to have had little influence on academic criticism, many of us evidently being unaware of "the return of/to the essay." [1] I want to consider that return and especially some of its possible implications for critical writing.

"Essays are making a remarkable literary comeback," affirms Robert Atwan, series editor, in the foreword to *The Best American Essays 1988,* an important annual launched in 1986. In an issue of the *Sewanee Review* celebrating the essay, Scott Russell Sanders argues that more essayists are "at work in America today, and more gifted ones, than at any time in recent decades. . . . We do not have anyone to rival Emerson or

3

Thoreau, but in sheer quantity of first-rate work our time stands comparison with any period since the heyday of the form in the mid-nineteenth century."[2] Among the talented writers finding the form hospitable, and markets for it available, are Wendell Berry, Carol Bly, Bernard Cooper, Joan Didion, Annie Dillard, Andre Dubus, Gerald Early, Gretel Ehrlich, Joseph Epstein, Albert Goldbarth, Elizabeth Hardwick, Edward Hoagland, Phillip Lopate, Barry Lopez, Nancy Mairs, Peter Matthiesen, James McConkey, John McPhee, Cynthia Ozick, Noel Perrin, Samuel F. Pickering, Jr., David Quammen, Alastair Reid, Richard Rodriquez, Richard Selzer, Susan Sontag, Paul Theroux, Lewis Thomas, and Tom Wolfe. Further reflection can always turn up more names—Barbara Lazear Ascher, Bruce Berger, Joseph Brodsky, Franklin Burroughs, Philip Garrison, Donald Hall, David Huddle, Stephen Jay Gould, James Kilgo, Leonard Kriegel, Natalie Kusz, Kenneth McClane, Faye Moskovitz, Scott Sanders, Wilfrid Sheed, Susan Allen Toth, Gore Vidal, Alice Walker, and God only knows how many others, including, of course, the late Edward Abbey. Though this list is hardly exhaustive, these names suggest the range of subject matter, styles, and personalities animating the contemporary essay as it embraces nature, science, and travel writing, memoir, the familiar or personal essay, and a myriad of other, often hybrid forms. The major point, anyway, is that for the first time in a long while "many of our best essayists are writers for whom, as Annie Dillard puts it, the essay is 'the real work.'"[3] Dillard predicts, in fact, that "the narrative essay may become the genre of choice for writers devoted to significant literature." However that may be, and whether Scott Walker is right in attributing the renaissance of interest in the essay to the form's way of telling "a more directly personal sort of truth than might be told in fiction" (the essay is "a haven for the private idiosyncratic voice in an era of anonymous babble," adds Scott Russell Sanders),[4] I wonder how many readers would now dispute John Tallmadge's claim that "today's most exciting work is not being done in fiction but in essays, memoirs and travel writing."[5]

To understand this flourishing of the essay, we must make some distinctions. Though most of us no doubt think we know perfectly well what an essay is, thank you, that knowledge may prove insecure, if not actually false. As Graham Good has written in *The Observing Self: Rediscovering the Essay*, the very notion of this estimable form is linked with belles lettres, an archaism that conjures up the image of "a middle-aged man in a worn tweed jacket in an armchair smoking a pipe by a fire in his private library in a country house somewhere in southern England, in about 1910, maundering on about the delights of idleness, country walks, tobacco, old wine, and old books, blissfully unaware that he and his entire culture are about to be swept away by the Great War and Modern Art."[6] The essays being written today are different, bolder, often hard-hitting, in fact, quite candid, even risky, therefore modern in tone and content.

There is at least one other common misunderstanding. Unfortunately, essays are usually lumped together with articles, columns, reviews, pieces, themes (in composition courses), and what have you; the word "essay," in fact, has become interchangeable with each of these forms. What is enjoying "a remarkable literary comeback" is a contemporary essay that differs in quite discernible and significant ways from both the outmoded belletristic form and the article. That last difference, especially, fuels my speculations here concerning the prospects for a revitalized critical writing.

Admittedly, the essay form itself encourages some of the blurring of distinctions that often accompanies discussion of the genre, and it is true that some articles veer toward the essay, some essays toward the article. Fathered by Montaigne in the sixteenth century, or so it is rumored, the essay has always been, if not a bastard, certainly a loose and receptive form. Edward Hoagland describes it as "a greased pig," Joseph Epstein as "a pair of baggy pants into which nearly anyone and anything can fit."[7] The essay is a genre that "seems to flirt" with all the other genres;[8] it avoids marriage or even commitment to any one style, manner of presentation, or subject matter. It may be precisely this protean and loose character—with its marked if not promiscuous openness to diverse sorts of topics, "approaches," and modes of expression, indeed a receptivity and a willingness to welcome, even to embrace and consort with, many and disparate, in effect almost all, callers—that makes the essay popular and vital, which is not at all to say licentious.

Though we may not, then, be able to define the essay exactly (in a sense, it represents an implicit critique of the drive toward definition), we can point to some generally agreed-on and important characteristics and venture some preliminary distinctions. Rummaging around in essays—itself an essayistic activity—you soon discover how often, and how fondly, writers write about that fecund form, as if about a lover;

the essay *is,* I think, inseparable from love, and the essayist from an *amateur.* How better, in any case, to describe the essay than by emphasizing the way it places the loving self, which often constitutes its subject, in the foreground and incorporates the self's personal and therefore quite particular experience, including the process of thinking, even of writing. Montaigne was perhaps "the first writer to invite the reader to catch him in the act: *Watch me thinking. Watch me writing,"* and those who have come after have acknowledged, indeed exploited, in their own *essais* the centrality to the form of the thinking-writing self.[9] The plot of the essay (the genre displays that literary feature as well as others) remains the adventure of "a person's thoughts struggling to achieve some understanding of a problem."[10] As more than one student of the essay has noted, it is "*essentially* a peripatetic or ambulatory form," its activities centering on the self "traveling, pondering, reading, and remembering."[11] The essay thus produces the artistic or literary effect or illusion of witnessing thinking in progress, in process; it *is* the act of thinking through writing.

A delicate and precarious balance marks the essay: representing "the mind's natural flow, instead of a systematized outline of ideas," the essay walks a fine line between artful control and seeming random movement.[12] As William Howarth puts it, essays "fulfill but also surprise our expectations, because they are both designed and improvised. After all the preliminary study and thought, the writing process still takes unexpected turns, reveals unforeseen consequences."[13] The essay not merely allows for but actually celebrates—indeed is characterized by—surprise, interruption, meandering, and slow discovery. Refusing to be hurried, loving to ramble and explore, the essayist, being an amiable companion, caresses and nurtures ideas, observations, and emotions, allowing them time to develop and leaving the mind space and time enough to appreciate, savor, and understand the experience. It is a loving kind of attention, the essay. And the work of the essayist? Perhaps it is best described as gardening for love, planting some seeds here, cultivating some ideas and feelings there, but everywhere fertilizing and pruning the prose.

A dialectical spirit of inquiry and exploration marks the essay. Indeed, "speculative and ruminative" thinking distinguishes the familiar or personal essay, the quintessential subgenre of this ancient form, from expository writing, such as defines the article, theme, and "piece." Conversational and collegial, in contrast to the argumentative and competitive (if not downright combative) academic modes, the essay enjoys what

Umberto Eco calls an "open form," which accommodates "several view-points, even contradictory viewpoints, simultaneously."[14] Whereas expository writing, which honors "linear, sequential procedure," "abhors ambiguity and marches to a predictable conclusion," the essay can embrace the "simultaneous play of alternatives."[15]

The differences between the article and the form I have been describing are palpable. Perhaps taking their cues from Walter Pater, who (in *Plato and Platonism*) distinguishes the essay from the treatise, various writers have marked these differences, including Graham Good, Chris Anderson, and Justin Kaplan, editor of *The Best American Essays 1990*, but none more pointedly than the philosopher-novelist-essayist William H. Gass.[16] I will quote at some length from Gass's account, not because I always agree with him (while his style may be essayistic his single-minded and absolutist privileging of the essay is not), but because his sometimes-outrageous assertions point up differences we would do well to heed. The essay, he writes, is "obviously the opposite of that awful object, 'the article,' " which,

> like items picked up during one's lunch hour, represents itself as the latest cleverness, a novel consequence of thought, skill, labor, and free enterprise, but never as an activity—the process, the working, the wondering. As an article, it should be striking of course, original of course, important naturally, yet without possessing either grace or charm or elegance, since these qualities will interfere with the impression of seriousness which it wishes to maintain; rather its polish is like that of the scrubbed step; but it must appear complete and straightforward and footnoted and useful and certain and is very likely a veritable Michelin of misdirection; for the article pretends that everything is clear, that its argument is unassailable, that there are no soggy patches, no illicit inferences, no illegitimate connections; its manners are starched, stuffy, it would wear a dress suit to a barbecue, silk pajamas to the shower; it knows, with respect to every subject and point of view it is ever likely to entertain, what words to use, what form to follow, what authorities to respect; it is the careful product of a professional, and therefore it is written as only writing can be written even if, at various times, versions have been given a dry dull voice at a conference because, spoken aloud, it still sounds like writing written down, writing born for its immediate burial in a Journal. It is a relatively recent invention, this result of scholarly diligence.[17]

The form disparaged by Gass is, of course, that privileged by academic critics; it is, in fact, the standard by which professional writing is judged.

I would insist, contra Gass, however, that the article *is* valuable and necessary—it alone may be capable of effectively accommodating and communicating some historical and philological scholarship [18]—but at the same time I would hope that academic critics could not only be persuaded to distinguish between the essay and the article but also come to recognize what losses are entailed, what opportunities forgone, in privileging the article.

Now, having insisted that articles are not essays, I must acknowledge the weakness, even the tenuousness, of the distinction. Because the essay, historically and indeed generically, is a notoriously protean form, it is impossible to confine, to define precisely, and so to distinguish unequivocally from other forms, its next-door neighbors. We can often differentiate essays from articles but not always, because the essay sleeps around, has impregnated some of its neighbors, is even rumored to have begotten several offspring—all of them out of wedlock because the essay refuses to be pinned down, to be married to any one style, treatment, or subject matter. As a result of this fertility, even the article bears traces of the essay—sometimes. We can easily tell the difference between articles and personal, familiar essays, but some things that we wish to label essays, like those of John McPhee, are so far from the mode of Hazlitt, Virginia Woolf, and Samuel F. Pickering, Jr., say, that they smack of the article. Conversely, some scholarly writing, discipline-bound, systematic in approach, and seeking to advance a body of knowledge, shows personal touches, interspersing the "I" of the author with a general objectivity and on occasion at least showing signs of concern with the quality and attractiveness of expression. The published lecture by major critics, historians, and other scholars is a notable example of the latter; indeed, those at the very top of the scholarly professions typically write in a hybrid form that appears an often-pleasant union of the article and the essay, alleviating the sternness, solemnity, and neutrality of the former with potent doses of the informality, familiarity, skepticism, tolerance, openness, and grace of the latter. I think here of Frank Kermode, C. Vann Woodward, and Catherine Stimpson, among others.

Must we choose absolutely between these not-always-distinguishable forms, either, like Gass, rejecting the article or, like most academics, ignoring the essay, its rich tradition and its impressive possibilities? And what might happen if academic critics (re)turned to the essay for at least some of their work? Might essays someday appear in the pages of *PMLA*?

Not if Chris Anderson is right. In his "Hearsay Evidence and Second-Class Citizenship," Anderson wonders why "the essay as a form [has] declined in the academic world, even as it has gained in popularity outside the academic world." The response he offers is predictable (and for me unappealing): academic writing is now *necessarily* so technical, specialized, and recondite that it "excludes the casual reader," whose interests and needs often mesh perfectly, however, with what the essay is and has to offer.[19] We are left with two worlds, forms, sets of expectations, and ways of writing: they may be equal, but they are separate, and the twain shall not meet. "I mean only to account for the success of the essay in some circles," writes Anderson, "and its inappropriateness in others." This segregationist effort may, in some ways, be attractive—it avoids the privileging of either the essay or the article, and as I have said, the article allows for certain work that the essay seems ill-equipped to accommodate—but are we content merely to "live and let live," an attitude that will surely confirm and perpetuate the essay's "second-class citizenship"?[20]

Though critical writing, manifest mainly as academic articles, has not really participated in the "remarkable literary comeback" of the essay, some signs appear of new or renewed interest in the issues, desires, and needs that the essay, especially now in its more modern, tougher-minded forms, appears well equipped to engage. Interestingly, these signs often appear in the places least likely to seem hospitable to the essayistic, at least according to Anderson. In this regard, consider Geoffrey Hartman and his well-known pleas for a "creative criticism" that, at its best, might constitute the literature of "imaginative reason" that Matthew Arnold dreamed of, with the critical essay perhaps achieving the status of "intellectual poetry." Hartman's position owes much, of course, to Georg Lukács, who, in "On the Nature and Form of the Essay," seeks to establish that "the essay has a form which separates it, with the rigor of a law, from all other forms." Fundamental to the essay, according to Lukács (as well as Hartman), is *irony,* for the critical essayist is "always speaking about the ultimate problems of life, but in a tone which implies that he is only discussing pictures and books, only the inessential and pretty ornaments of life—and even then not their innermost substance but only their beautiful and useless surface." Lukács thus gives the critical essay deep and vital substance, and in "Literary Commentary as Literature," included in

Criticism in the Wilderness, Hartman elaborates on questions fundamental to the genre. Might the essay have not only "a form of its own" but also "a shape or perspective that removes it from the domain of positive knowledge (*Wissenschaft*) to give it a place beside art, yet without confusing the boundaries of scholarship and art? Is it at least possible," continues Hartman, "for the essay to muster enough vigor to institute a renewal of ideas . . . while remaining essayistic, distinct from a scientific philosophy's striving for absolute truths?" [21] Complicating our conventional but too-easy dichotomizing of literature and criticism, regarding them, in fact, as engaged in a relationship of "mutual domination" and "interchangeable supremacy," Hartman believes that the critical essay not only is about art or a work of art but is also—or at least can be—itself a work of art.

Sooner or later we will have to face the question Hartman insists on, and that concerns an "answerable style." How, he asks, "can the critic respond to the extraordinary language-event and still maintain a prose of the center?" Even if the claim is overstated, "the spectacle of the polite critic dealing with an extravagant literature, trying so hard to come to terms with it in his own tempered language, verges on the ludicrous." [22]

Deconstruction has, if nothing else, taught us to question and problematize the oppositions and hierarchies we frequently, indeed, normally, erect between literature and criticism. Wary of the closure and totality connoted by the idea of the book, deconstructionists might, in principle, be drawn, like Hartman, to the open-endedness, skepticism, and critical spirit that characterize the essay: it resists easy definition (of itself, its subject matter, its "conclusions"), avoids coming to rest in some positive truth or absolute knowledge, remains wary of systems and systematizing, and not only acknowledges but also embraces and even celebrates the uncertainty and ambiguity that deconstruction tirelessly reveals all about us. Chris Anderson has pointed to the considerable irony here, for whereas "the form of the essay, far more than the form of the article, acknowledges uncertainty and ambiguity," poststructuralist theorists "use the form of the article to make their claims about indeterminacy." The result deserves consideration, for these theorists become "involved . . . in the contradiction of arguing for gaps and uncertainties in hard and fast ways. They are dogmatic about indeterminacy, insistent. The systematic form of the article lends itself well to their scholastic demonstrations of the inadequacy of language." The essay, on the other hand, as Anderson notes, "is by definition an attempt. It is, in Emerson's phrase, a reflection of the 'Man thinking'; that is, man in the act of contemplation." Or as William Gass puts it, the essay "embodies 'activity—the process, the working, the wondering.' It doesn't pretend that everything is clear and worked out." Moreover, it "turns round and round upon its topic, exposing this aspect and then that; proposing possibilities, reciting opinions, disposing of prejudice and even of the simple truth itself as too undeveloped, not yet of an interesting age."[23]

The temperamental affinity between deconstruction in particular and the essay has been elaborated by W. Wolfgang Holdheim. Despite his own rejection of deconstruction, Holdheim acknowledges that deconstructive efforts have marked the essay from its beginnings. In Montaigne, as he notes, "the essay is less a genre than quite deliberately an antigenre, designed to flout the prescriptiveness in literary matters which had been inherited from a rationalistic rhetorical tradition."[24] In fact, Holdheim maintains, Montaigne was engaged in nothing less than "an *Abbau* of his tradition (the term has lately been translated as 'deconstruction'). It is an active deconstruction in the genuine sense: a clearing away of rubbish, of reified sedimentations, so that issues may once again be laid bare in their concreteness." Montaigne's "radical presentation of discontinuity is very much a reaction against uncritically accepted accumulations of continuity; his insistence on the uniquely diverse and particular is directed against too exclusive a concern with universals."[25] The essay and deconstruction thus share a similar agenda: what I would call *estranging the familiar*. Moreover, argues Holdheim, since the essay "presents itself, among other things, as a dialectic between developing idea and elucidated occasion," it demonstrates "the act of knowing *in flagranti*"; the essay is, in fact, "the hermeneutic genre par excellence."[26]

But there *are* differences, important ones, between deconstructive and essayistic assumptions, despite the affinities I have noted. Graham Good argues that deconstructionists, as well as other poststructuralists, are likely to dismiss the traditional essay as "a combination of the bourgeois liberal-humanist subject and a naive-realist epistemology believing in accurate linguistic construction of 'real' objects." The essay is skeptical, but its skepticism concerns accounts of reality other than "its own, which stem from personal experience. That is the essay's ultimate 'ground,'" contends Good, who notes that deconstruction rejects every idea of ground.[27] I see no necessity to accept Good's sense of the essay as locked into some naive, innocent notion about the self or of deconstructionists as inimical to the essay or to all aspects of its tradition. Nor do I understand why the essay cannot accommodate what theory has taught us about the self: that it is not an independent, unitary, and stable identity, a solitary origin of meaning, or a creature transcendent of history and culture. After all, "long before Rimbaud's discovery that 'je est un autre' Montaigne had recognized the decentered quality of selfhood. Long before Freud, he had debunked the uninterpreted self as a reliable foundation for knowledge."[28] And so the self that appears in essays? With reference to Stephen Greenblatt's theoretically sophisticated notion, O. B. Hardison, Jr., puts it this way: "Writing an essay is an exercise in self-fashioning." The essay, he adds, "is an enactment of the creation of the self. . . . We must essay to be . . . ," a point taken, of course, from Emerson and echoed by Lydia Fakundiny, who, speaking of the essay, writes that "somehow 'I' am forming myself right there in front of my very eyes: my 'self' forms itself in and as discourse" and that "it is in my every movement on paper that 'I' come into being."[29]

That poststructuralists can write in, and advance, the form of the essay is attested by the success of Roland Barthes. Barthes's later work—especially *The Pleasure of the Text, A Lover's Discourse, Roland Barthes by Roland Barthes,* and *Camera Lucida*—extends and develops the possibilities inherent in the form inaugurated by Montaigne. These texts, claims Réda Bensmaïa in *The Barthes Effect: The Essay as Reflective Text,* have "contributed more vigorously to the renewal of that 'anti-genre' . . . than [have those] of any other contemporary writer." Whether or not this is true, it seems hard to dispute Bensmaïa's claim that, thanks to Barthes, the *essai*—"the polysemic word par excellence"—(re)emerges as "an *a-generic* text or as *anti-genre*," not *a* genre at all but "rather the one from which all others are generated."[30] In any case, instead of writing in article form, Barthes "performs his argument, disposing, proposing and abandoning theories, dramatizing the processes of thought, refusing to reduce the text to a manufactured thesis."[31]

Still, despite the affinities between the essay and deconstruction, as well as the essayistic nature of at least some of Barthes's, as well as Hartman's, efforts, there remains a gap—more like a yawning chasm—between all forms of academic criticism, not just poststructuralist, and the essays en-joying a "remarkable literary comeback." *Can* the essay, with both its formal and its historical ties to the personal and familiar, to accessibility as well as grace of expression, accommodate contemporary criticism and the critic's burdens of historical and theoretical knowledge and of foreign-sounding language? Whatever happens in the future, academic criticism continues to take the form of the article, with only some isolated excep-tions (so far). These include the experimental "creative criticism" done by such different figures as Barthes, Gass, Hartman, Harold Bloom, Ihab Hassan, and Rachel Blau DuPlessis. At least some of these critics write out of an essay tradition quite different from the Anglo-American. I mean the European tradition of the speculative or philosophical essay, which sup-plies the form with an intellectual substance and insight too little known here and in England and whose practitioners include Georg Lukács, Theodor Adorno, Walter Benjamin, Paul Valéry, Jean-Paul Sartre, and Jacques Derrida. As a result, the kind of essay that Hartman praises and that he and Barthes, for instance, write seems a far cry from the familiar or personal essay we know and increasingly revere again. The paratactic style of Adorno and Benjamin, in particular, makes them appear difficult to readers accustomed to linear progression, but these writers occupy a vital position in the history of the essay. Benjamin's critical work in *Illumi-nations* and his travel and autobiographical essays represent an impressive body of reflection done in consistently artful form. Adorno, similarly, insists that his frequently open and experimental work is essayistic, and his "The Essay as Form" is a powerful assertion of the essay's claims to critical and philosophical significance.

As much as I would like us in this poststructuralist age to be aware of and to appreciate the essay and its rich tradition, I grant that the critical essay cannot hope or expect to return to the simpler state and comely form practiced in the nineteenth century; "the amount of positive histori-cal knowledge we are expected to carry along is too great." Like Hartman, I cling, however, to the possibility that the "dignity" given the critical essay by Hazlitt, Pater, Ruskin, and others need not be lost "in its more specialized and burdened form."[32] Might there be, I want to suggest, the possibility of a *familiar (essay) estranged*—a reorientation of the essay in English: not a flouting of its rich artistic heritage or of the dignity it has earned—no concession to the article, in other words—but a return to the

13

essay that acknowledges, maybe even embraces, the unavoidable burden of knowledge both historical and theoretical?

The "personal criticism" sought, and to some degree made available, by feminist theory provides both hope for and one direction toward the achievement of such a possibility. Such a possibility, at the moment frankly experimental and groping for a form, would not separate the professional and the personal, the autobiographical and the critical. The essay may well be the form sought and needed.

At any rate, a commitment to the essay, no less than to personal criticism, represents an implicit critique of professional values. Given the profession's privileging of the article, of "objectivity" and neutrality, such a decision may be seen, in fact, as a political act of no mean consequence. Of course, the essay, historically, is related precisely to such *critical* activity. Indeed, the essay arose as "*commentary* . . . yielded to *criticism*," at the time, that is, when the medieval procedure of merely compiling information gave way to a skepticism and a questioning of authorities.[33] Whereas, then, the scholarly or critical article has, as a modern form, been marked by a stance of noncritique (to apply Robert Scholes's term from a different though related context, it is "hermetic"), the essay has both implicitly and explicitly commented on matters cultural. Think of the essay from Arnold to Lukács, Adorno to Joseph Epstein. For all their differences in political perspective and cultural assumptions and aspirations, such essayists—and you could add here Kenneth Burke, Derrida, and Guy Davenport, among others—look not merely at a text but through it to contexts that that work engages and to the large social, political, and cultural issues on which it impinges and that impinge on it. Evaluation, judgment, and critique thus return, by no means limited to a balancing of aesthetic values or to a ranking of texts but extending, in the way theorists like Scholes and Edward Said wish, to a questioning and indeed a *criticism* of a text's own perspectives, assumptions, values, and implications. A return to the critical essay today, while involving a resumption of a more personal kind of commentary than has recently been privileged, need not, in other words, portend either a new aestheticism or yet more isolationism. On the contrary, the essay provides the form, as well as the history and so the encouragement, for the practice of a criticism culturally engaged as well as socially and politically responsible.[34] It is as hard to refrain from cultural critique as from personal expression when one writes an essay.

Freedom is crucial to the essay, as Adorno remarks, and perhaps a certain negativity as well. For the essay, historically and generically, has opposed not just systems and systematizing but all forms of packaged thinking. It is speculative, thoughtful, whether the thinking concerns matters ordinary and quotidian (as in E. B. White and Samuel F. Pickering, Jr.) or intellectual and philosophical (as in Adorno and R. P. Blackmur). In its resistance to forms of totalitarianism, its respect for diversity, heterogeneity, and impurity, the essay can represent a significant critique of what Adorno calls administrative thinking. It also (thereby?) offers an implicit critique of professionalism.

If my experience is any indication, graduate students and faculty members alike, many of them, are eager for some such "revolution" as a return of/to the essay entails. This loaded term "revolution" is not mine but one that keeps coming up when, in classes and at conferences, I talk about the essay and the kind of criticism that it encourages. I seldom have had such warm responses as when I venture, in conference presentations, to mix the personal and the theoretical, attempting the essayistic, more precisely the *familiar (essay) estranged*. Similarly, students in my bibliography and methods course and seminars in criticism jump at the chance I now routinely provide to write essays as their final "papers." I have even written an essay on, as well as taught, *essayistic teaching*. The essay is, it seems to me, nonphallocentric and so is the kind of writing best suited to an open, humane teaching such as that sought by feminists, psychoanalytic critics, and educationists like Paulo Freire.

My aim in my classes, as here, is not to replace the article with the essay. Pace William Gass, as I have indicated, the article *is* valuable; it provides opportunities perhaps, or sometimes, unavailable to the essay. But the latter also represents opportunities and encouragement too long unavailable to us or repressed because they are largely unappreciated by the profession. I am not monistically arguing for only one kind of critical writing; I *am* arguing that to slight the essay is damaging: such disdain not only risks, if it does not actually encourage, a monolithic approach to critical writing but also reduces the possibility for both cultural critique and personal criticism, as well as promotes writing that emphasizes a certain kind of clarity at the expense of grace and art, and thus the essay's disparagers are too willing to forgo the chance of reaching general, non-academic readers. I would, then, like to restore the essay to a place of prominence. For that reinstatement to occur, I maintain, the essay cannot exist in ignorance or avoidance of theory and its demands; nor can the essay isolate itself from social, political, and cultural investments and so from those concerns and expressions that touch "ordinary" people in their everyday lives. I look toward an essay theoretically informed and artful. Is that too much to hope for, too much to expect?

Let me, in conclusion, briefly describe the kind of critical essay I encourage. (I should emphasize that what follows represents only one of several possible and desirable orientations.) Reestablishing contact with the Anglo-American tradition of the personal or familiar essay, without (this is the hope, anyway, as well as the aim) sacrificing intellectual rigor or forgoing the insights and accomplishments of recent theory, such an essay would place the experience of reading in the forefront, relating it to the writer's experience. Such a criticism could be considered a kind of travel writing: no longer enslaved to explication but moving back and forth between textual considerations and familiar experience, it would feature the spectacle of the critic's mind (and heart) struggling with texts and by means of them charting "the course of interpretive discovery," and at the same time narrating a journey toward (some) understanding of a textual, personal, cultural, or political problem.[35] As in other forms of literature, *character* matters in criticism, where neither commentator nor text commented on should be subordinated one to the other. And so the critical character moves on stage (or returns to it): not just in the tone of the speaking voice, the quality or capaciousness of mind, the depth of engagement, the extent of human-heartedness—important as they are— but also in what happens to the critic *in* the drama that constitutes imaginative critical reading and writing. Bringing theory to life and life to theory, this new criticism, possibly unthinkable apart from the essay, might thus depict the relation of books and reading to the making of a soul, as well as record "the adventures of the soul among masterpieces" (Anatole France). It might, productively, be the attempt to find a voice as well as "the right distance."

The full potential of the mutually supportive relation between criticism and the essay we can at present only glimpse, perhaps barely imagine.

One result of the union could be better, more vigorous, more interesting, critical writing, commentary at once richer and more culturally responsible—a result devoutly to be wished. Whether this close relation would also help to bridge the gap between academic criticism and a general reading public, God only knows. But why bind the imagination, confine our efforts, or continue to repress our desire?

CHAPTER TWO

In Other Words: Gardening for Love— The Work of the Essayist

God Almighty first planted a garden. And Indeed it is the purest of human pleasures.

BACON, Essays

If you would know the power of character, see how much you would impoverish the world, if you could take clean out of history the life of Milton, of Shakespeare, of Plato,—these three, and cause them not to be. See you not, instantly, how much less the power of man would be? I console myself in the poverty of my present thoughts, in the paucity of great men, in the malignity and dullness of nations, by falling back on these sublime recollections, and seeing what the prolific soul could beget on actual nature;—seeing what Plato was, and Shakespeare, and Milton,—three irrefragable facts. Then I dare; I also will essay to be.

EMERSON, Essays

[Essaying to be] is the fundamental conceit of this greatest of American essayists. He too dares, endeavors, tries, attempts, essays . . . to create himself in the very process, in the very act, of setting words on paper or uttering them aloud. In order to exist, he must speak, for the speech validates itself—brings into being that which is envisioned or hoped for and gives Emerson a solid platform on which to stand.

JOEL PORTE, Representative Man

Like Mem, a character in *The Third Life of Grange Copeland*, my mother adorned with flowers whatever shabby house we were forced to live in. And not just your typical straggly country stand of zinnias, either. She planted ambitious gardens— and still does—with over fifty different varieties of plants that bloom profusely from early March until late November. Before she left home for the fields, she watered her flowers, chopped up the grass, and laid out new beds. When she returned from the fields she might divide clumps of bulbs, dig a cold pit, uproot and replant roses, or prune branches from her taller bushes or trees—until night came and it was too dark to see.

Whatever she planted grew as if by magic, and her fame as a grower of flowers spread over three counties. Because of her creativity with her flowers, even my memories of poverty are seen through a screen of blooms—sunflowers, petunias, roses, dahlias, forsythia, spirea, delphiniums, verbena . . . and on and on. . . .

I notice that it is only when my mother is working in her flowers that she is radiant, almost to the point of being invisible—except as Creator: hand and eye. She is involved in work her soul must have. Ordering the universe in the image of her personal conception of Beauty.

ALICE WALKER, "In Search of Our Mothers' Gardens"

E SSAYISTS, teachers, or both, we typically, indeed unavoidably, use various metaphors in attempting to describe this baggy, perhaps unwieldy, seemingly (but only seemingly) shapeless, in any case lovable, thing, the essay. We keep trying to capture it in words, this slippery, elusive shape, though as Elizabeth Hardwick says, it's a little like trying to catch a fish in the open hand.[1] That we keep trying, posing new metaphors, putting the matter in other words, says something, though I'm not sure quite what, besides that a virtual subgenre exists of essays on the essay. "In other words": essayists put it *otherwise*—that's what essayists do, when, so often, they write about the essay, trying on one, then another metaphor in an effort to describe, to capture, its handsome, comely, beckoning, teasing, essence. It is impossible to do, of course, and that is one reason, a major one, for the continuing, happy, respectful effort. I am obviously implicated in the attempt, this essay in one sense acknowledging the failure of the previous chapter. "In other words": I'm adding mine to the conversation, to the stream of voices that have spoken for so long so well about the form they love.

It's hard to do better than Joseph Epstein, in "Piece Work: Writing the Essay," collected in his *Plausible Prejudices* and significantly positioned last in that volume of essays on American writing. At the risk of simplifying and reducing the importance of his rich and informed if somewhat surly account, I want only to suggest how much is packed into Epstein's title, which even he doesn't fully exploit: "piece work." How appropriate for the essay, for, thinking of its openness and amiableness, I hear "peace work"; and of course "piece work" alludes to everything from the irregular and poorly paying, temporary jobs sometimes available in factories and print shops to the art and craft of quilting, the province of women in the last century and continued, by women, largely in rural areas in this century as at once an outlet for their artistic skills and often a necessity for survival. Essay writing is certainly irregular and poorly paying work; in a number of ways the form seems (to me at least) feminine, and writing it resembles the piecing together of rags and remnants from hither and yon, discarded, thought to be no longer of any use. As in so much else concerning the essay, Montaigne led the way, cleared the path, asking in "Of Friendship," "And what are these things of mine, in truth, but grotesque and monstrous bodies, pieced together of divers members?" and elsewhere (in "Of Vanity") referring to his *essais* as "only an ill-fitted patchwork."[2] The essay often seems, in fact, more a crazy quilt than an organic growth (which may help to account for its disfavor during the heyday of the New Criticism). And like quilting, the essay dropped out of fashion (though I sense that quilting too is enjoying a renascence, surviving mainly as a self-conscious craft and appearing in such phenomena as Whitney Otto's best-selling novel *How to Make an American Quilt*).

Applied to essays, the metaphor of piece work as quilting points up just how dependent these things are on quotation, cut from the full cloth of other text(ile)s. Here William H. Gass, philosopher-novelist-essayist, is best:

> Born of books, nourished by books, a book for its body, the essay is more often than not a confluence of such little blocks and strips of texts. Let me tell you, it says, what I have just read, looked up, or remembered of my reading. Horace, Virgil, Ovid, Cicero, Lucretius meet on a page of Montaigne. Emerson allows Othello and Emilia words, but in a moment asks of Jacobi, an obscure reformer and now no more than a note, a bigger speech. A strange thing happens. Hazlitt does not quote Shakespeare but Henry VI, whose voice is then lined up to sing in concert with the rest: the living and the dead, the real and the fictitious, each has a part and a place. Virginia Woolf writes of Addison by writing of Macaulay writing of Addison, of whom Pope and Johnson and Thackeray have also written. On and On. In this way the essay confirms the continuity, the contemporaneity, the reality of writing. The words of Flaubert (in a letter), those of Madame Bovary (in her novel), the opinions of Gide (in his *Journal*), of Roger Fry, of Gertrude Stein, of Rilke, of Baudelaire (one can almost imagine the essay's subject and slant from the racy cast of characters), they form a new milieu—the context

of citation. And what is citation but an attempt to use a phrase, a line, a paragraph, like a word, and lend it further uses, another identity, apart from the hometown it hails from?[3]

Like those once-familiar things, quilts, essays offer comfort and warmth.

Continuing with Gass: the essay, he says, in the way it pieces together quotations "convokes a community of writers" and "uses any and each and all of them like instruments in an orchestra." (Metaphors abound.) The essayist plunders texts—like a quilter rummaging around in a treasured bag of remnants, scraps left over or cut from other serviceable items: shirts and sheets, pants and tablecloths, dresses and curtains, the fabric in which we live our daily lives. Why? why do essayists plunder texts? "Precisely because they are sacred." Thus the essayist's work of quoting (or quilting) needs to be distinguished from that of the article writer, who also quotes. The method of the essayist, "we are essay-bound to observe," writes Gass,

> is quite different from that of the Scholastics, who quoted authorities in order to acquire their imprimaturs, or from that of the scholar, who quote[s] in order to provide himself with a set of subjects, object lessons, and other people's errors, convenient examples, confirming facts, and laboratory data. However, in the essay, most often passages are repeated out of pleasure and for praise; because the great essayist is not merely [!] a sour quince making a face at the ideas of others, but a big belly-bumper and exclaimer aloud; the sort who is always saying, "Listen to this! Look there! Feel this touchstone! Hear that!" "By necessity, by proclivity,—and by delight, we all quote," Emerson says. You can be assured you are reading an excellent essay when you find yourself relishing quotations as much as the text that contains them, as one welcomes the chips of chocolate in those celebrated cookies. The apt quotation is one of the essayist's greatest gifts, and, like the good gift, congratulates the giver.[4]

Quoting . . . quilting—they *do* sound somewhat alike, don't they?

Remembered, picked up, and dropped or sewed in, these bits and pieces, these strips and shards, of texts may, Gass seems to suggest, grow, even take on a life of their own, not overwhelming an essay the way weeds take over a flower bed or untended land, but nonetheless sometimes coming to be relished almost as much as the text in which they have been planted. The language thus shifts; our metaphors turn, almost in spite of ourselves, like flowers toward the sun (helio*tropes*), toward nature as ground. If the essay seems pieced and patched together like a quilt, it also seems natural—in several important ways. It appears at once as both a natural growth and a constructed thing. It is, in more than one respect, a threshold being, an "in-between" thing, hanging indeterminately—but not unhappily—between knowledge and art, creation and cognition, thought and things, writing and living, nature and cultivation, involving a little of both and all. Maybe *that's* one reason why it evades our grasp, is so difficult to describe. Could it also help to account for its staying power, its appeal?

A COUPLE OF YEARS AGO a lady friend gave me a book entitled *Gardening for Love: The Market Bulletins*. The book, handsome in design and full of rich surprises, is a posthumously published collection of the writings of one Elizabeth Lawrence on a variety of topics having to do with gardening, compiled by Allen Lacy, himself the author of such books as *Ground Work: A Gardener's Miscellany*. Lawrence writes, simply but often gracefully, of her love affair with plants, of the "market bulletins" she eagerly sought (a product of another age, these are classified ads in which gardeners hawk their herbs and ornamental perennials), of the letters she received in response to her replies to those ads.

Not until several months had passed, the seeds perhaps having had time to germinate, did I really come to appreciate the title of Elizabeth Lawrence's book. And then all at once it struck me that "gardening for love" nicely describes the work of the essayist: the essayist's labor resembles gardening in part because both proceed from love, bodied forth in their very manners. Alice Walker makes the point movingly in the passage from "In Search of Our Mothers' Gardens" that I adduced as an epigraph. And I think, too, of Sir William Temple's tender "Upon the Gardens of Epicurus; or, of Gardening, in the Year 1685," a virtually paradigmatic essay on gardening.

Love links gardening and essay writing. You don't rush love—we, at least many of us, have the scars about our hearts to prove it. Tiresome platitudes concerning "love at first sight" and romance versions of tempestuous "love" notwithstanding, love, which certainly involves hormonal response though without being identified with it, takes time, develops over time, requires time for hearts, minds, and not least bodies to become finely attuned, atoned, at-oned. It grows "slowly, precariously," not unlike the tender peach trees I grew up with in South Carolina, susceptible to early frosts that can destroy an entire crop. In a relationship between two people, always fragile and far more delicate than we care to admit to each other and to ourselves, chance or accident is important: some relationships blossom and grow to maturity, others fade, wither, and die. We all know that. Love requires not only time but also nurture and cultivation: it doesn't just develop on its own, free of attention and work. You don't maintain and develop a relationship, any more than you grow full-bodied, variegated, and delicately scented American Beauty roses, by ignoring the coloration of response to your caress, the almost-imperceptible whisper of need, the appearance of dis-ease, or signs of boredom, the strength of attachment, the nature and depth of roots. Love*making,* so central to love even if slighted in our contemporary (over-)emphasis on sex, figures the problem (and opportunity): slow, careful nurturing, marked by attention, concern, and response, produces the best yields. Time matters: it bodies forth respect—for the other. You have to take the time, be patient, and *love*. Love is incommensurate with haste, inseparable from nurture. The same may be said of the essay.

Nature and nurture: they belong together as much as quilting and quoting. What *is* there about the essay as form that links it to nature? Many of the great nature writers, of course, have been essayists, many of the great essayists nature writers: I think not just of Emerson and Thoreau, John Muir and John Hay, and before any of them William Bartram, but also of Noel Perrin, David Rains Wallace, Ann Zwinger, Wendell Berry, Peter Matthiesen, Barry Lopez, Sue Hubbell, Gretel Ehrlich, Robert Finch, David Quammen, Edward Abbey, Edward Hoagland, John McPhee, Annie Dillard—the list is not endless but certainly long and distinguished. Sometimes technical, this nature writing is also artful (I think too of Richard Selzer, writing about that aspect of nature that is the human body under conditions of surgery); it is, as a matter of fact, as respectful of the reader, language, and form as it is of the earth and the creatures that populate it. There is, in other words, represented in much of this writing stewardship of both land and language.

To repeat: What *is* there about the essay that links it to nature?

In *The Observing Self: Rediscovering the Essay* Graham Good opens a path toward an answer. Good distinguishes four "principal types" of the essay:

the travel, the moral, the critical, and the autobiographical, which, he admits, are neither mutually exclusive nor exhaustive categorizations. Corresponding to these types or forms are "the main essayistic activities: traveling, pondering, reading, and remembering." Often the travel essay, notes Good, simply narrates a *walk,* and he goes on to claim that "the essay is *essentially* a peripatetic or ambulatory form. The mixture of self-preoccupation and observation, the role of chance in providing sights and encounters, the ease of changing pace, direction, and goal, make walking the perfect analog of 'essaying.' "[5] The history of commentary on the essay, by essayists (whose opinions weigh heavily), confirms Good's thesis.

Unhurried, taken by all the flora and fauna fortunately come upon, more interested, in fact, in the journey, in journeying, than in any destination finally reached, the essay *is* a walk (and at the same time a garden of delights made of its adventures). Hazlitt's "On Going a Journey" is a classic example of the peripatetic nature of the essay, an account of a walk that itself meanders, that truly offers the reader the experience of journeying. In a *Sewanee Review* celebration of the essay, a tribute collectively entitled "Sallies of the Mind," William Howarth elaborates on this notion (and motion). Though all texts are journeys, Howarth suggests, without quite saying it, the essay seems paradigmatic, even quintessential writing. At any rate, the essay's itinerancy is a matter of process, indeed natural process, subject to the vicissitudes of chance, entailing accident and thriving on serendipity. Such writing—according to Howarth, who has written so well elsewhere of McPhee's writing way—is "motion, a journey through constantly recurring cycles. The circuit spins repeatedly, through steps of gathering material, compiling and arranging it, then synthesizing a draft. Successive revisions follow, a learning process that reveals what to say and how to find a form—often a form that rehearses the writing journey. This faith in continuity values loose and imprecise forms, devoted to an ecological web of relationships rather than strict hierarchies."[6] Constituted by movement, the essay is related to the cycles of nature, rooted in an awareness of the ebb and flow of life, constructed in accordance with seasonal change, planting seeds here, carefully nurturing saplings there, harvesting at some point, lying peacefully limp and fallow at another. It paces, but the essay also knows *about* pace, how to pace itself. Probably thought of most often as an autumnal, even mature creature, the essay is not always bursting with life, it is true, yet alive it certainly is, redolent of the stages and processes of natural growth and the life cycle.

Discussing Montaigne's "originating" efforts, Graham Good shrewdly notes, "The starting-point of the essay was the mind's *natural* desire for knowledge. The task is to bring that desire back to Nature in a wiser and more accepting condition. To do this, thought has to stay close to life, rather than constituting a separate world." Rooted in the world, the essay is anti-Gnostic: thought "has to be reapplied to the experience in which it originates and of which it is a part. Thought should enhance the process of living rather than erode or ignore it."[7] Since Montaigne, the essay has been physical, material, taking the body very much into account. For Montaigne, of course, "the body's existence in time is the very basis of existence. . . . Montaigne rejects asceticism or any other view" that Gnostically "emphasizes the split in man between divine and earthly, rational and irrational, virtuous and sinful."[8]

LET ME TRY to make all this a little clearer, the link between nature and the essay a little more secure. I will do so via Wordsworth and Geoffrey Hartman's understanding of the poet whose early career (leading up to *The Prelude* in 1805) represents an attempt to understand the relation of mind or imagination and nature. By the time of his great autobiographical poem, according to Hartman, Wordsworth "took literally the concept of *culture* as *cultivation,*" having moved beyond a certain radicalism, having returned, in fact, "from revolutionary schism to the idea of a ground out of which things grew slowly, precariously; where accident was important, some grew and some didn't, but where there were, for humanity generically considered, infinite chances of birth and rebirth. The literalism of 'Fair seed-time had my soul' (*Prelude* I 301) shocks us into a view of culture as nature."[9] In describing this relation to nature, Hartman uses the Hebraic term *akedah,* which literally means "binding" and which he opposes to the (Christian) notion of "apocalypse." The latter term denotes the haste and impatience manifest in the *uncultivated* mind or imagination.

Implied, maybe even made explicit, by "culture as nature" is the idea of *slow* growth, careful and responsive nurturing—what has to be respected, then, because it deserves no less, and cultivated: fertilized, weeded, watered, caressed, even pampered, brought along at its own pace, which must be discovered and can only be by a heart responsive, a soul prepared. For Hartman, such ideas link up with the essence of the humanities, with due process, and with what he calls "delay time," voided in our mad rush toward communication, meaning, and intimacy. He says it best, I think, in *Easy Pieces*. Describing the humanities as "always in 'slow motion' compared to the sciences or to the immediate demands of the practical world," Hartman writes of their "calendar" as might the *Farmer's Almanac* of the seasons: the humanities calendar, he says, "allows the store of experience to come before us once again, as we incline—fast and forgetful—into the future. Here and there contact is made between these calendars or wheels moving at different speeds; and the meshing that occurs, which can be very powerful indeed, not only at the point of contact but as it provides a design for mutual and coordinated work, is what we call experience." As usual, Hartman has reference to Wordsworth, and as we read him, we may find springing to mind such contemporary naturalists or, better, environmentalists as Wendell Berry, Wes Jackson, and Gary Paul Nabhan. Wordsworth attacked, writes Hartman, "in what he named *lyrical* ballads, the very concept of the newsworthy event, composing lyrics that were anything but sensational. They displaced the avid reader's attention from the unusual or fantastic incident to the sensitive response that an ordinary life might elicit. His almost plotless ballads are our first instance of minimalist art. But they are not yet abstract like that art: they surround familiar thoughts and happenings with an imaginative aura. The strange subtlety of Wordsworth's poems was intended to retain ear, eye, and imagination, to wean them from the age's degrading thirst after 'outrageous stimulation.' " [10]

Enter, then, the quotidian or "ordinary," familiar existence. At the heart of Wordsworthian realism lies what? Respect for time, the capacity to abide time, *and so* the ability to find in everyday life the materials of romance. No vampish rush after immediate gratification, either. It's a *negative* capability, like what Keats described as the ability to abide "uncertainties, Mysteries, doubts, without any irritable reaching after fact and reason" and therefore to rest content "with half knowledge." The impulse clearly resembles that which prompts the realistic novel. In perhaps the *locus classicus* of apologies for that effort, George Eliot (in *Adam Bede*) allegorically expresses her preference for Dutch "genre" paintings: "I turn without shrinking," she writes, "from cloud-borne angels, from prophets, sibyls, and heroic warriors, to an old woman bending over her flower-pot, or eating her solitary dinner, while the noonday light, softened perhaps by a screen of leaves, falls on her mob-cap, and just touches the rim of her spinning-wheel, and her stone-jug, and all those cheap common things which are the precious necessaries of life to her." Graham Good, who quotes this passage, comments as follows: "The sensibility described here, with its ability to find significance and beauty in the detail of a small world and little-regarded people and things, is often found in the essay, which also turns aside from the grand design and the imposing statement for minor truths."[11] Minor truths perhaps from some transcendent perspective, but major ones for those of us embroiled in the inevitable pains and frequent pleasures of day-to-day living.

Lacking the muscle, strength, girth, and power of a novel or the wound tightness and intensity of a poem, the essay is modest, unpretentious, often all too willing to acknowledge, even to accept, what E. B. White called its second-class citizenship. Which is not to say that it gives up on being artful. On the contrary, the essay is secure enough in its own being to be artful on its own terms, in its own admittedly limited, fragile way, of inviting its readers to share in its artistry, not marvel at or stare in awe and amazement, but instead to feel reassured that its maker was an artisan who, precisely in the lack of show, showed her art. That's part of what is meant, I gather, by the term *"familiar* essay": not only are its subjects ordinary, quotidian, but its tone and mode of address, the nature of the voice heard in the narrative and along the rise and fall of the sentences, are such that you know a good deal about that of which the essayist speaks. He or she speaks to you, moreover, as someone known, recognized, familiar. The familiarity bred is, however, neither quick nor vampish: as in all good, effective, loving relationships the essayist preserves an identity while allowing you yours; the essayist engages in conversation with you and though, like Edward Hoagland, Phillip Lopate, and—even more—Nancy Mairs, he or she can be open, candid, and at times brutally frank, there is usually no lust for intimacy. If it comes, fine, but only after you've gotten to know each other. Rather than in bed, you feel more like in a garden, walking and talking with someone you know, like, and respect, teasing a little, perhaps flirting some, but also discussing situations and ideas and perhaps admitting emotions that matter to you in both your everyday and your inner life.

Whether or not it is quite yours, the essayist's garden through which you both stroll, sometimes arm in arm (the essay *is* a dia-logue), the garden that *is* the essay is marked by those qualities Alexander Pope famously prescribed for gardens (and writing!)—utility rather than show, and "naturalness," not excessive order or signs of manipulated diversity and apertures. "Unaffected simplicity"—that was Pope's goal (and achievement in both his own garden at Twickenham and his best poetry), and it is the goal of the essay as well as its achievement in the hands of those who well (at)tend the form. This is Pope "On Gardens" in the *Guardian* no. 173 (29 September 1713), edited by the essayist Joseph Addison: "There is certainly something in the amiable Simplicity of unadorned Nature, that spreads over the Mind a more noble sort of Tranquility, and a loftier Sensation of Pleasure, than can be raised from the nicer Scenes of Art." In stark contrast, Pope claims, to such simplicity "is the modern Practice of Gardening; we seem to make it our Study to recede from Nature, not only in the Tonsure of Greens into the most regular and formal Shapes, but even in monstrous Attempts beyond the reach of the Art it self: We run into Sculpture, and are yet better pleas'd to have our Trees in the most awkward Figures of Men and Animals, than in the most regular of their own."[12] The garden is, thus, artful precisely in its imitation of nature. It is a product of cooperation between us forked creatures and nature, not so unlike the way the essay appears as both a natural and a constructed thing.

LISTEN to E. B. White on the essayist. He's writing in the foreword to his collected essays. In what he says, you can hear many of the themes threading their way through the foregoing account. White *exemplifies,* in fact, the work of the essayist. Catch the rhythm of the thought, the cadence of his sentences. Note how White lingers over notions, caresses them in the structure of his language, stays with language, in fact. He's in no hurry: he's gardening for love. "The essayist is a self-liberated man, sustained by the childish belief that everything he thinks about, everything that happens to him, is of general interest. He is a fellow who thoroughly enjoys his work, just as people who take bird walks enjoy theirs. Each new excursion of the essayist, each new 'attempt,' differs from the last and takes him into new country. Only a person who is congenitally self-centered has the effrontery and the stamina to write essays."[13] Perhaps, we say in response to White's quietly joyful and perambulating self-criticism, which is quite attractive, if not positively seductive. It is affirmative, perhaps egotistical, in its very criticism of self-centeredness. What a strange effect! What a wonderful thing, the essay!

Continuing, not exactly rambling on, White turns to the work of the essayist, meaning himself, of course. "There are," he begins, "as many kinds of essays as there are human attitudes or poses, as many essay flavors as there are Howard Johnson's ice creams. The essayist arises in the morning and, if he has work to do [!], selects his garb from an unusually extensive wardrobe: he can pull on any sort of shirt, be any sort of person, according to his mood or his subject matter—philosopher, scold, jester, raconteur, confidant, pundit, devil's advocate, enthusiast." Immediately White becomes more personal, all the more engaging—the turn from the general to the personal is neither sharp nor modulated and is, therefore, exemplary. "I like the essay," he writes (and then proceeds to indict himself for imposing his love, even as he details the effects of that love), "have always liked it, and even as a child was at work, attempting to inflict my young thoughts and experiences on others by putting them on paper. I early broke into print in the pages of *St. Nicholas*. I tend still to fall back on the essay form (or lack of form) when an idea strikes me, but I am not fooled about the place of the essay in twentieth-century American letters—it stands a short distance down the line."[14] And it does, of course, still does, but since White wrote in 1977 the essay has advanced some distance in popularity and prestige, even as Howard Johnson's myriad flavors of ice cream have given way to Baskin-Robbins as a cultural landmark.

Still, White is clear-sighted, not really plaintive, certainly not resentful of the essay's status. It is, after all—or so it pretends, as White does here so beautifully—a slight thing, almost a trifle. Thus the essayist, "unlike the novelist, the poet, and the playwright, must be content in his self-imposed role of second-class citizen. A writer who has his sights trained on the Nobel Prize or other earthly triumphs," advises White, "had best write a novel, a poem, or a play, and leave the essayist to ramble about, content with living a free life and enjoying the satisfactions of a somewhat undisciplined existence."[15]

White goes on to claim—"argue" is not quite the right word—that what matters most is the essayist's honesty. "There is one thing the essayist cannot do, though—he cannot indulge himself in deceit or in concealment, for he will be found out in no time. Desmond McCarthy . . .

observes that Montaigne 'had the gift of natural candour. . . .' It is the basic ingredient. And even the essayist's escape from discipline is only a partial escape: the essay, although a relaxed form, imposes its own disciplines, raises its own problems, and these disciplines and problems soon become apparent and (we all hope) act as a deterrent to anyone wielding a pen merely because he entertains random thoughts or is in a happy or wandering mood." [16]

The candor we experience in essays, including White's here, is a matter of integrity, of being honest with and faithful to what one is writing. The honesty is artistic, and the ironic self-deprecation is that virtually endemic to the essay—it is already there in Montaigne, and it persists through the centuries, though with modifications in form. In Edward Hoagland's words: "an essayist soon discovers that he doesn't have to tell the whole truth and nothing but the truth; he can shape or share his memories, as long as the purpose is served of elucidating a truthful point." [17] And that fact advances somewhat, at least in my judgment, the essay's status along the line of art forms.

At the end of his brief account, White circles back to what has exercised him from the beginning, the matter of the essayistic ego. Whether he did then, White now understands how much it is precisely a question of the essayistic ego, even if he does not (of course) use that rather unessayistic term. If he remains critical of his own self-involvement, the presumption appears in perspective; the essayistic now seems special, as indeed it is— both modest and presumptuous, self-denying and affirming, critical of self and *thereby* assertive of self. A delicate balance is needed, and justice is nothing if not a complex and problematic thing:

> I think some people find the essay the last resort of the egoist, a much too self-conscious and self-serving form for their taste; they feel that it is presumptuous of a writer to assume that his little excursions or his small observations will interest the reader. There is some justice in their complaint. I have always been aware that I am by nature self-absorbed and egotistical; to write of myself to the extent I have done indicates a too great attention to my own life, not enough to the lives of others. I have worn many shirts, and not all of them have been a good fit. But when I am discouraged or downcast I need only fling open the door of my closet, and there, hidden behind everything else, hangs the mantle of Michel de Montaigne, smelling slightly of camphor.

The voice we hear here, and in essays generally, may be a construction rather than the unalloyed representation of the flesh-and-blood human being, but still, something genuinely good, warm, human and humane, generous of spirit, and good-hearted can be heard in that voice, felt in the prose. No matter how created the pose, you want to believe the man or woman wears it comfortably. Who but one attentive to others and interested in people, affairs, feelings, geese, a dying pig, yellow roses, Kansas sunsets (had he the privilege of observing them), the sun, the moon, and the stars can be so critical as White is of not attending enough to the lives of others? The essayist is so involved in life—Joseph Epstein says, "love of life . . . is one of the qualities that all the great essayists hold in common"—so sensitive to the balance that makes it good that he or she feels intensely when the scale is tipped ever so slightly and so must attempt to redress the balance, even if the terms of the attempt seem to us, who are less sensitive, unbalanced.[18]

In "Being Familiar" Sam Pickering joins the effort to describe the essay, suggesting that it is a product of both wander and wonder: "Scholarly writing and the familiar essay are very different. Instead of driving hard to prove a point, the essay saunters, letting the writer follow the vagaries of his willful curiosity. Instead of reaching conclusions, the essay ruminates and wonders. Rather than being right or informative, it is thoughtful. Instead of being serious, it is often lighthearted, pondering subjects like the breeding habits of beetles, and, alas, of people. Of course as a person ages it becomes increasingly difficult to be scholarly or definitive." Of course, "being definitive" is the goal of article writing; "being familiar," the heart, never merely the goal, of essay writing. Pickering goes on: "Truth seems beside the point, or at least amid the many doings of a day it seems to have progressively less to do with living. Years have passed since I have read a study advertised as definitive. Being definitive, and perhaps even clever, is an activity for youth. Certainly it was in my case." "Being definitive" is also a matter of reaching conclusions. It contrasts with the skepticism and what I have called the "negative capability" of the essay. Being particular in the way the essayist is, Pickering helpfully illustrates: "Not long ago a university press that just reprinted an academic book I wrote in fresher days rejected a new manuscript. 'You don't reach enough conclusions,' the editor explained; 'writing essays seems to have affected your scholarship.' The editor was right; I now have trouble reaching conclusions. Instead of cudgeling stray dogs along the route I travel . . . I stop and pet them. If they could talk, I'd probably sit down, start chatting, and forget about the race." [19]

Reading Sam Pickering, I recall E. B. White describing an ideal reader of *Walden*, probably the quintessential nature book in our literature. As Susan Allen Toth has written in her tribute to White, included in *How to Prepare for Your High-School Reunion*, his essay "A Slight Sound at Evening" works because, a mix—I might say, a quilt as well as a garden—of Thoreau, *Walden*, and White, it embodies the commentator's excitement about the author and his work and in so doing provides reason sufficient why "our hearts beat faster when we read him." [20] White's response to Thoreau is human—that's what it comes down to.

Here is White on *Walden*'s ideal reader, one who has approached perhaps Sam Pickering's "negative capability": "I think it is some advantage to encounter the book at a period in one's life when the normal anxieties and enthusiasms and rebellions of youth closely resemble those of Thoreau in that spring of 1845 when he borrowed an ax, went out to the woods, and began to whack down some trees for timber. Received at such a juncture, the book is like an invitation to life's dance, assuring the troubled recipient that no matter what befalls him in the way of success or failure he will always be welcome at the party—that the music is played for him, too, if he will but listen and move his feet." [21] The essay may *be for* those who have achieved some age, maturity, and judgment (many commentators think so), for whom "outrageous stimulation" is neither required nor desired. (If it is, and I doubt that the essay's real appeal is limited to us middle-aged folk, but *if* it is, then we're obviously and sadly mistaken in making it the cornerstone of freshman comp.) *In any case,* and age is no necessary prerequisite for maturity, the essay persists as "an invitation to life's dance." It represents, in other words, neither quiescence nor acquiescence in the face of increasing age, sagging breasts, and graying hair. It is, instead, a celebration and a thanksgiving, figured by both May and November: an invitation to life's *dance.*

"INVITATION" also deserves emphasis, for essays smile. Being familiar, they welcome, enjoin you. They are not always happy, of course (think of Dr. Johnson's *Rambler* essays or, differently, Hazlitt's), though they manage, somehow, to remain affirmative, affirmative in the way Keats's "negative capability" is affirmative: that affirmation, if not joy, derives from and perhaps only by means of experienced pain. The essay is thus experienced, though—pace Sam Pickering—not sad.[22] It recalls the Wordsworthian knowledge that "lies too deep for tears."

I repeat: essays smile. The skin around the eyes crinkles (a sign of age?); the eyes, soft and warm (probably brown), may not dance, though they can twinkle. And the smile appears genuine; the face makes you feel comfortable. It offers recognition, and you feel positively invited to respond.

Whether or not they make you smile in turn, essays can make you feel good, comfortable, at ease. They're familiar and personal. It's impossible to be with them long and remain tight or glum. You want, in fact need, to spend time with them, more and more time. You can become dependent. It's like with a lover.

You and essays: a relationship develops. If, as has often been claimed, the essayist is an *ama*teur, it is surely in the root, the most basic sense of the word: the essayist is one who loves, who understands the value of nurture and cultivation. The smile that creases the face of the gardener-essayist betokens love.

CHAPTER THREE

Critical Writing
and the Burden of History

The more "creative writing" runs amuck in fiction, the more we find ourselves
indecisive before it: now stupidly admiring, now donnishly supercilious. The literary essay can avoid that split; it knows itself as both creative and receptive, a
part of literature as well as about literature. True, we can't go back to Pater or
Ruskin, or the best Hazlitt or Coleridge; the amount of positive historical knowledge we are expected to carry along is too great. But they gave the essay a dignity
which it need not lose in its more specialized and burdened form.

GEOFFREY HARTMAN, *The Fate of Reading*

T HE LITANY is all too familiar: since its fall *into* theory (and *from*
glory), criticism has become so ethereal and recondite, so riddled
with technical terms, laced with foreign words, and confused by philosophical abstractions, that it has lost contact with its essence, whoring
after lesser gods, selling its birthright, being unfaithful to and turning
its back on its reason for being, generally understood as the explication
of acknowledged masterpieces and the demonstration of the relevance of
their formal beauty and significant meanings to the conduct of human
life. It was not, of course, theory that severed the suppositious positive
relationship between criticism and the interests and needs of a "general
reading public." Though something *has* happened to critical writing to
reduce its general appeal or relevance even further, blame does not lie
with theory. The roots of the problem go much deeper.

I have no desire to incriminate our time as yet another age of scribbling
pedants and small-minded critics such as Pope lambasted as characteristic
of his. The appeal to and of crisis is recurrent in—perhaps, after all, a de-

fining feature of—*criticism*. If we inhabit an Age of Criticism, as Randall Jarrell proclaimed almost half a century ago, or of Theory, as you might well suppose now, the "we" described are professors as well as the students for a short time held captive and subjected to professional opinions and judgments. "Ordinary" men and women, in the meantime, go their own way, and when they read, it is certainly not criticism. And why should they? But if it was ever thus, must it continue to be? Is it too much to ask, too much to hope for, that criticism might touch the hearts and minds of ordinary women and men, or at the very least be of potential interest and value to them by virtue of addressing issues relevant to their daily lives? Why shouldn't criticism be of general, rather than merely professional, interest?

CRITICISM currently labors under a considerable burden, part of it—to be sure, a significant part—being theory and the responsibility to grapple with Sigmund Freud, Friedrich Nietzsche, Karl Marx, Martin Heidegger, Jacques Derrida, Jacques Lacan, Michel Foucault, Julia Kristeva, Hélène Cixous, and others. Such thinkers we must somehow "digest," for all their difficulty, and incorporate in our response to individual poems, novels, plays, and essays. They will not be ignored, their voices make up too large a part of our cultural heritage.

There is, in addition to the unavoidable demands of theory, the burden of history and now so much knowledge to be carried, including that of literature. With so much information, so much *positive* knowledge available, accessible, and at least partially absorbed, how can we do critical writing that is other than highly technical, specialized, and accessible to only a few initiates? The burden of history is not merely quantitative, however, limited to the massive amount of knowledge to be borne; the burden of history is also qualitative, including the obligation to preserve the pastness of the past, the difference or otherness of history, in the face of ever-accelerating pressures toward synchronicity stemming from the positive knowledge that historical studies provide. To let the past have its say, to preserve the voices of the dead, means that we *thereby* sustain the present—that is, ourselves—in our difference; the burden of history, therefore, is neither to close the historical gap nor to widen it.

The past of criticism constitutes precisely *its* Other, thus adding to the history to be borne that of critical writing, a history still too little known.

Critical writing from Dryden and Johnson, through Hazlitt and Pater, to Wilde and Woolf is so different from that done today in the academy that, in some circles, the earlier sort is dismissed as amateurish and in others, ironically enough, classified and read as literature rather than as criticism! Such critics as I have named, lived, so the argument runs, in simpler times; they did not slink and stumble under the burden of knowledge we have to carry—and they did not have theory to infect their prose.

What I am interested in here, the small but significant part of the history of commentary that I want briefly to reflect on, concerns its form, style, or mode. How contemporary criticism differs in that respect from the sort done earlier is my subject; my focus is the medium, or vehicle, of commentary. Critical writing today, which for almost all practical purposes *is* academic, appears either as (scholarly) monographs or, when shorter, as articles (the monograph functions as the article writ large, expanded to book length). The difference between the article and the essay, the form that critical writing formerly took, is a distinction I continue to insist on.

We say, rather blithely and unthinkingly (I know I have done so), that we write articles, and in the very next breath we call them essays. We use these very different terms interchangeably. The practice or habit of lumping them together, and treating them as equals, begins as early as freshman comp, in which those texts we call "readers" indiscriminately combine essays like those of Montaigne and E. B. White, Alice Walker and Annie Dillard, with articles, reviews, columns, and just about anything else reasonably short and written in prose (it doesn't even have to be nonfiction); the writing our students produce, having imbibed this mixture, is called themes, also known as essays. What our *teaching* practice thus shows is that we are, as a profession, remarkably cavalier about the differences between the essay and other, admittedly related, prose forms. What our own *writing* practice shows is that, as a profession, we clearly privilege the article, which has become the standard by which our writing is judged: again, it is the goal, end, and test of our scholarly and critical efforts (significantly, we cannot quite allow ourselves to say "art"). Taken together, our professional practices evince our massive disregard, even disdain, for the essay as form and its very rich and fecund traditions. We may give lip service to the essay in our comp courses, but we positively ignore it elsewhere, and what we write shows precious little affinity with, or appreciation of, the essay, its interests, tones, and art.

The point is, "an essay is *not* an article; it is not a thorough, scholarly treatment of an isolated subject"; instead, it is, by definition, "an exploration, a journey out that frequently becomes . . . an inward journey, too, a picking at the thread which finally unravels the garment of the writer's particular concern and scrutiny."[1] Whereas the essay thus appears "tentative, continuously self-reflective, structured, yet informal," the article is definite, strutting toward definitiveness, in fact, formal, pretending mastery, neutral or objective in stance and tone, marshaling evidence, quoting authorities while establishing often-minute differences from previous commentators, moving ineluctably and in strict linear fashion toward a conclusion proudly announced in its opening paragraph or introductory section.[2]

The distinctions I insist on cannot be absolute, hard and fast (such insistence would be decidedly unessayistic). And I repeat: I do not wish to deny the article's own particular achievements or our need for information that it may be uniquely adapted to convey. Still, there are aspects of the essayistic that we would do well to recall—and to return to.

Essayists typically, indeed, characteristically, "reflect on contemporary life from the standpoint of [their] own experience or . . . engage in autobiographical narrative which ultimately leads to commentary on the social [or literary or critical] problems of the time."[3] These are important points. "In a direct line [from Montaigne] descend essayists who remain essentially autobiographers, all explorers of the self, who seek clues to that self directly in their own lives and the trivial details of their daily routines."[4] The idea of the essay is simply inseparable from that of personal engagement. As the history of critical commentary makes clear, this idea is neither a wen on the scalp of criticism, to be removed as a form of unfortunately lingering Romantic expressivism, nor a hermetic individualism unconcerned with culture and politics. Far from entailing aestheticism or isolationism, insistence on the personal has historically meant for criticism an active engagement with culture and a substantial investment in politics: no shirking of larger responsibilities, in other words, but, on the contrary, an embrace of them deriving from awareness of the socially as well as psychologically constituted nature of selfhood.

37

Even at the height of romanticism, there is, in Hazlitt, for example, a sense of both history and contemporary culture that is not eclipsed by the touted focus on individual personal experience.[5]

THE KIND of *criticism,* with a strong emphasis on "critical," virtually endemic to the essay, which Adorno calls "the critical form *par excellence,"* is a state of being "in-between," "a free play of the mind on all subjects which it touches," such as we find in Henry James, Sainte-Beuve, and of course Matthew Arnold. Such criticism proceeds, and succeeds, says Arnold, "by steadily refusing to lend itself to any of those ulterior, political, practical considerations about ideas, which plenty of people will be sure to attach to them." Arnold famously illustrates this independence of mind with reference to Edmund Burke. He most admires in Burke a certain negativity, an ability to move beyond and even counter to his own engaged and invested position, that is, "when one side of a question has long had your earnest support, when all your feelings are engaged, when you hear all around you no language but one, when your party talks this language like a steam engine and can imagine no other,—still to be able to think, still to be irresistibly carried, if so be it, by the current of thought to the opposite side of the question, and, like Balaam, to be unable to speak of anything *but what the Lord has put in your mouth."* W. Wolfgang Holdheim called the essay "the hermeneutic genre par excellence," and "hermeneutic reflection," argues Geoffrey Hartman, disables "the one-dimensional, progressive claims of conqueror or would-be conqueror" interested only in winning and subscribing to "a simple location of historical meaning."[6]

The essay but not the article is marked, accordingly, by a certain *reserve* and a certain *negative capability.* As we saw in the previous chapter, for Keats such *negative* ability constitutes the highest art, forming "a Man of Achievement especially in Literature and which Shakespeare possessed so enormously."[7] The essay shares in such ability, being patient, respectful of time and of the need to let things happen at their own pace, of the mind's need for time and space, and respectful, too, of other persons, their minds, bodies, and privacy. So the reader of essays, as much as the writer, must evince some "negative capability"; otherwise, he or she will consign these "loose, baggy monsters" to the trash heap of history or dismiss them as effete, indulgent, and inconsequential. The essay understands the art of cultivation, of caress and nurture: gardening for love, the work of the essayist.

I will try to connect this "negative capability" with the essay's reserve. Art always resists; it resists our drive to master it, plumb its depths, make it yield up its secrets, its meanings, to our voracious desire. Reticent though not shy, art holds back, keeping something in reserve. The essay exhibits this kind of reserve. Not only does it resist, in its wariness, doctrines and dogmatism, being skeptical of all systems and systematizing, impatient only with abstractions, but in its tentative, exploratory, and inevitably inconclusive manner it also opposes the lure of mastery, ever mindful of complexity and interimplication, including that of the self and any object or subject observed and written about. There is more to the essay's reserve than appears in its skepticism, however, notably including the irony Lukács identified with it.

Reticent and reserved, essays are a part of literature. Even critical essays are a part of literature when they body forth the deep human engagement with issues, situations, and emotions, the capaciousness of mind and soul, the imaginative power, and the passion that spark the more prestigious forms. Who is to say that the creative spirit cannot infuse critical writing, as it did in Pope's *Essay on Criticism*, Johnson's *Lives of the Poets*, various essays by Hazlitt, Emerson, Pater, Woolf, Benjamin, Barthes, and Hartman? Even when it doesn't approach such a level, critical writing done essayistically shows the artisan's care for sentences, their shape and rhythm, for figures seemingly tossed off but actually woven very carefully into the crazy quilt or piece work that also rather well describes the form, for the character of the "speaking voice," for a structure that is often anything but linear and so inches up on artfulness almost in spite of itself. Critical essays are at once critical and committed— including being committed to literature as a passion, which necessitates surveillance, evaluation, and, when necessary, forthright rejection, repudiation, and condemnation. Unlike that done in article form, which is characteristically not evaluative or judgmental, literary commentary done essayistically reflects the critic's passionate engagement and expresses his or her involvement *in* the commentary. A sense of drama accompanies the critic's investment in opinions, judgments, and assumed positions— risky business.

The change in critical writing is of fairly recent vintage; it has coincided with the displacement of the essay as the form literary commentary takes, and it is responsible, to a large degree, for the gulf separating criticism from general relevance. The ascendancy of the article coincides, of course, with the professionalization of literary studies, which began late in the last century and which enthroned the professor as savant and high priest, keeper of the keys to the kingdom of those masterworks before which "ordinary" readers are supposed to (can merely?) genuflect. Professionals are engaged, of course, but their commitment is more to a discipline than to literature or criticism, their stance and tone analytical rather than passionate.

So lightly regarded by the profession are literary *essays* that those who embrace and practice the form risk early dismissal as impressionistic or journalistic or both—in short, as amateurs. We have effectively given over the essay to reviewers and an occasional novelist, for whom the essay hardly constitutes the work of choice (it doesn't pay, after all). With only a few exceptions (must they always be British?) these folks are not now doing distinguished work or bringing honor to the essay.

Despite those predicting even bleaker days for the critical essay, due to the prominence of theory, signs are beginning to appear of renewed interest in the essay as form, a return that I traced in Chapter 1 and that has the potential to exert a positive impact on critical writing. Interest in the *critical* essay so far remains modest, though there are reasons for hope, such as those I have mentioned. If critical writing returns to the essay, it can't be at the expense of our knowledge, our apparent theoretical sophistication, or our (post)modernity—that is part of its burden. We cannot, I argue, forget the positive knowledge we have amassed and adopt the lighter tones and unspecialized, relatively unburdened form of the eighteenth- or nineteenth-century essay. But I am idealistic, perhaps romantic, enough to cling to the admittedly tenuous hope of writing a critical essay that evinces the familiar touch characteristic of the essay tradition in English while bringing theory and history to bear on texts rigorously considered and evaluated. I believe, strongly, that we need to know the essay, its traditions, achievements, and possibilities. At present, the essay represents strangeness; estranged, it is contemporary criticism's Other. As with other differences, we cannot, must not, simply adopt that strange form, somehow forgetting or wiping out what currently separates our writing from it; nor should we reject the essay, as we are inclined to do now, as an alien other that, if we are going to consort with it at all, we'll have to remake in our own image, another version of the story of difference Tzvetan Todorov tells in *The Conquest of America*. The burden of history, I repeat, is neither to close the historical gap nor to widen it. The burden is, instead, to effect a relation.

I propose, in fact, that we turn to the cherished and venerable tradition of the familiar or personal essay but without forgoing either theory or the positive historical knowledge we are obliged to shoulder. Though we can't simply take on the form of the earlier, unburdened essay, which in its difference now appears strange to us, we can try to adapt it to our theoretical sophistication and historical awareness *as* we adapt to its style, structure, and perspective. This dialogic encounter may breed the *familiar (essay) estranged*. We won't be collapsing the differences between us and those "easier" times when a familiar style was relatively unproblematic, but by returning to the past we will at once acknowledge its production and indicate respect for and response to those contributions. Yet the way we return to the past means no effacement of ourselves and our historical situation. *Estranging the familiar* thus entails respecting and preserving both the past and the present.

It also means a return to the personal that would not be *merely* personal. The negative factor must be respected: "to see only the human . . . is like seeing only the personal God: it must produce an apocalyptic self-consciousness, a too-human or superhuman image and so fix the person to one self-image."[8] Unlike, then, the (old-fashioned) familiar or personal essay, the one I am proposing for criticism would include otherness, theory, history, and mystery, but unlike the article and the various kinds of commentary—formalist, historical, and poststructuralist—that embrace it, it would not cease being personal. It would be neither merely personal nor merely critical-theoretical.

Perhaps—who knows?—the day will come when not only will *PMLA* accept essays but general readers will turn to the critical essay because, in responding imaginatively and with impressive human power to literature, it will exist *as* literature and so touch, in a unique, layered, and resonant way the hearts and minds of ordinary women and men in our daily lives. To accept that possibility as a responsibility would be a considerable burden, indeed.

PART TWO

CHAPTER FOUR

Criticism, Theory, and the Essay: Strange Bedfellows?

I've speculated a lot lately on the decline of the poet-critic—the person of letters who (in the tradition of thinkers from Sidney, Coleridge, Emerson and Arnold to D. H. Lawrence, T. S. Eliot, Allen Tate and John Crowe Ransom) was both a practitioner and an analyst of literary art—and I've come to the tentative conclusion that the specialized structures of the university have fostered a schism between the right brain (the creative writer) and the left brain (the critic), which leaves both halves of the communal mind engaged in activities that often seem partial, passionless, even pointless.

SANDRA M. GILBERT

"Feminist Criticism in the University: An Interview"

HARD—above all, hard—fast-paced (no room for "slow hands" here), determined, and definite, the article has always aped scientific rigor. Because—to play on Guy Davenport—every form evolves from a force, the rise of the article as the medium of literary scholarship and criticism followed upon the emergence of what Gerald Graff calls the "secularized professional" in the second half of the nineteenth century. This was the academic who, invested with "positivist ideology," engaged dispassionately in "the search for impersonal truth." Specialized research, which rather quickly became the goal of professional literary study, entails "hard investigation" and the rigorous application of quasi-scientific methodology, pointedly distinguishable from the "soft appreciation" that guided the efforts of unreclaimed generalists and amateurs. This model of literary professionalism, which effectively converted the critical—certainly the evaluative or judgmental—into the scholarly, was designed to remove

45

the aura of effeminacy clinging to the study of literature: thinking especially of the "large universities of the Midwest," Irving Babbitt lamented that "the men flock into courses on science, the women affect the courses in literature. The literary courses, indeed," he went on, "are known in some of these institutions as 'sissy' courses. The man who took literature too seriously would be suspected of effeminacy." In response, the new professionals formed the Modern Language Association (1883), and soon appeared journals seeking and publishing scholarly articles (e.g., *Modern Language Notes*, founded at Johns Hopkins University in 1886). The first university press, an institution with the mission of publishing scholarly monographs, had sprung up at Hopkins in 1878. Dedicated to the production of research scholars, and determined to instill and promote rigor, graduate study in English, which in this country originated with that same institution in 1876, established the (masculine) article as the form—almost immediately the only form—acceptable, until you graduated to the monograph, understood as a longer, better, more virile and potent version of the article. Not much has changed since those heady, formative years—unless it be a hardening of distinctions and a clearer defining and drawing of lines. As a result, says Joseph Epstein, editor of the *American Scholar*, "the essayist might be found almost anywhere, but the last place one is likely to find him is in the pages of the *PMLA*."[1]

THE HISTORY, condition, and fate of criticism are tied up with the essay. The essay has given place to the article, and criticism has become virtually limited to the academic variety. To add the qualifier "*academic* criticism," say Gerald Graff and Reginald Gibbons in the preface to their *Criticism in the University*, is redundant, "since no other kind is . . . even generally considered as a possibility." Graff and Gibbons's volume is important because it goes against the grain of our (academicist) assumptions, pointing to the losses involved in the professional revolution. Though they do not, unfortunately, treat the situation of the essay, they do touch on form and style and their importance in a consideration of criticism's condition and responsibilities:

> The rhetorical trope by which the word "criticism" is narrowed to mean what is written and taught by professors involves the "forgetting" of what was once thought important—that criticism was formerly part of a "literary culture" much broader than the university and, indeed, scarcely involving

the university; that literary critics were once journalists and men (and too rarely women) of letters, usually outsiders to the university; that they wrote either for general readers or for the community of imaginative writers, rather than for a coterie of specialized professors and graduate students, and thus delivered their findings and opinions in an accessible style rather than in an esoteric jargon of methodological terms.[2]

The diminution—if not demise—of the journalistic critic, whom Graff and Gibbons mention, represents an impoverishment of critical form and style of which we in the academy are too little aware. Even though packing little clout nowadays, the journalist-critic was once a power-ful, respected, and influential figure. But how many of us professors and literary scholars recognize, let alone turn to for elucidation and evalua-tion, reviewers like Peter S. Prescott or Michiko Kakutani? Writing in *Criticism in the University*, Morris Dickstein elaborates this point that the journalist-critic represents values we have sadly lost, values worth trying to reclaim. As a model of the journalist-critic, Dickstein offers Henry James, whose reviews "demonstrate how the needs of the common reader encourage the journalist-critic to be especially vivid and dramatic. Writ-ing constantly about new works to readers unlikely to have read them, the reviewer must try to flesh them out as effectively as a fictional char-acter. James goes further," Dickstein continues; "he tries, as all the great critics have traditionally done, to catch the essential flavor of a writer, to discern the figure in the carpet and lay bare the essential project." Such critical writing as Dickstein describes, "the New Criticism and academic criticism have shunned. It seems old-fashioned for being so impression-istic and lyrical," but modern—that is, academic—criticism, "by veering towards either the explication of themes or the analysis of formal struc-tures, loses the intimate, experiential dimension that we feel in James and his forebears, and that"—for Dickstein and some others, though their numbers continue to dwindle—"survives best in journalistic criticism."[3] I quote this academic critic's moving elegy for an alternative tradition now barely alive, his hopes in the face of that decline for a return: "The almost forgotten journalism of a century ago remains a model of what criticism might yet become, a totality of response to works of art that is both scrupulous and committed, intensely private yet intensely public. James in 1868 gave some of the purest formulations of the critic's func-tion when he wrote that 'the critic is simply a reader like all the others—

a reader who prints his impressions.' 'Nothing will ever take the place of the good old fashion of "liking" a work of art or not liking it. The most improved criticism will not abolish that primitive, that ultimate test.'"[4] No matter how theoretically sophisticated or analytically acute we become, we cannot avoid, nor should we minimize, impressions and personal response; literary experience stems from the former and is arid and insignificant without the latter. Nor can we afford to continue to neglect something else that once made journalistic criticism powerful and important: the quality of the writing itself. Even in its failure to attain the level of art, journalistic criticism showed a respect for craft perhaps belied by the name we give it.

However embattled, and scanted by academic criticism, the tradition survives (barely) of a confrere of the journalist-critic. The "poet-critic" is an analyst of literary art who is primarily a writer, a poet, and a basic premise of this tradition is that the fit critic is one who first of all writes well him- or herself. Pope perhaps said it best in *An Essay on Criticism*, itself a magnificent poem as well as an important critical document: "Let such teach others who themselves excell,/ And *censure freely* who have *written well*." Pope, of course, means by "criticism" something evaluative and judgmental, not primarily analytical and interpretive, which is what (impoverished) academic criticism means by the term. Sandra M. Gilbert associates the decline of the poet-critic with "the specialized structures of the university," which have, she argues, "fostered a schism between the right brain (the creative writer) and the left brain (the critic), which leaves both halves of the communal mind engaged in activities that often seem partial, passionless, even pointless." As a result, she finds, "in America today, the major 'theoretical' names—Bloom, Fish, Hartman, Miller, Culler et al.—are as divorced from what has traditionally been considered 'the mysterious power of creativity' (that is, the power to write poetry) as the major poetic names—Bly, Rich, Levertov, Ashbery, etc.—are from so-called critical theory."[5]

The impressive line of poet-critics to which Pope belongs has, maybe without exception, written in essay form, preferring this short form to the book and showing little patience with the detachment, impersonality, and strained rigors of the article. As James Engell reminds us, "in the ordinary way we now understand it Johnson never wrote a book of criticism. Neither did Dryden, Addison, Hazlitt, Keats, Shelley, or Wilde."

48

Until the advent of the scholarly journal and the university press, devoted to the service of the "secularized professional," in the 1870s and 1880s, the essay was the vehicle of critical expression: Arnold, of course, wrote "essays in criticism," as did Emerson, Poe, James, and, closer to our time, T. S. Eliot, whose "one systematic book-length study he determined to write, on Elizabethan and Jacobean poets and playwrights, remains scattered in essays and shorter pieces." Such facts should give us pause, who blithely privilege both the article and the book. "It remains to be seen," as Engell has written, whether criticism "has found its most accommodating length in the [book]. . . . The book of criticism or even of literary scholarship is a relatively recent genre, the creation of which is in part institutional and professional. Attaching reverence to it as the highest, most comprehensive critical genre entails assumptions worth questioning."[6]

Length is an issue, to be sure, but it is not the only one, nor the most important. The article is, after all, relatively short, much like the essay in length, though different in tone, form, direction, implicit relation to its subject, character, and implied values. What marks the essay, distinguishing it from related forms, notably includes "a multiplicity of perspectives presented in an engaging form designed to awaken and maintain reader interest even after the piece has been 'completed.' If a piece of writing . . . is not a living event as genuine literature should be," then "we should think twice about labelling it essayistic."[7] Precisely such *literary* values draw poet-critics to the essay.

Also barely surviving is a figure related to the poet-critic and the journalist-critic, one who shares their literary values. I mean the essayist-critic, an essayist by trade—rather than a journalist, though in particular instances the distinction may well be supersubtle, even impossible to maintain—who on occasion turns his or her attention and perspective to the job of commenting on literature. One productive contemporary essayist-critic is Joseph Epstein, the earlier-mentioned editor of the *American Scholar* and author of the collections of familiar essays *Familiar Territory, The Middle of My Tether, Once More around the Block,* and *A Line Out for a Walk.* Epstein is also author of the collections of critical essays *Plausible Prejudices: Essays on American Writers* and *Partial Payments: Essays on Writers and Their Lives.* In "Piece Work: Writing the Essay," Epstein describes the essay as "in large part defined by the general temperament of

49

the essayist." Who and what the writer is may be central to the essay, but it is of little if any consequence, of course, to the article. Epstein proceeds to define the essay in terms of the impression it creates of "a strong or at least interesting character."[8]

Epstein—or at least the character who appears in his critical essays—certainly is "strong." Opinionated and proudly prejudicial (criticism, according to his hero H. L. Mencken, is merely "prejudice made plausible"), Epstein adopts the self-appointed role of sheriff, parading in *Plausible Prejudices* his anger at "what one deems literary injustice" and announcing that he "stand[s] ready to apprehend delinquent writers." Committed, as an essayist, to the notion that "good books can sustain us and make life better, while bad books wrongly praised can cause real harm in life," Epstein understands the critic's role as not merely evaluative but also persistently skeptical and insistently negative, ever alert to unwarranted praise and genuinely discontented.[9] A curmudgeon rarely pleased and never swayed by either popular or "critical" opinion, he stands tall as a conservator of *literary* values.

Epstein's authority derives, not just from the strength of personality he projects, the firmness with which he holds to his beliefs, opinions, and prejudices, the breadth of his reading, and the ease with which he seems to write, but also from the assumed character of a "literary man." Epstein describes his "point of view" as precisely that, which he defines in the following way, unusually saccharine for this generally raspy voice:

> What it means to have the point of view of a literary man, I believe, is that one is above all impressed with the immense variety of life, its multi-facetedness, its unpredictability, its extraordinary richness. What literature teaches, what it has taught me, is that life is more various than any intellectual or political system can ever hope to comprehend. Life, one learns from literature, is filled with sadness and joy, tragedy and splendor, despair and dignity in despair, hatred and laughter, and more doublets of this kind than any single sentence can hope to contain. Literature is about life, which is a commonplace; yet literature is also on the side of life, which, if it too is a commonplace, is frequently forgotten.[10]

With some adjustment, this statement might pass as the essayist's credo.

The implied counter to Epstein's argument is an ambitious and uncritical professionalism that prizes the systematic, theoretical, and ethereal, neglectful of quotidian, cultural, and human interests. Epstein, in fact, lambastes the professionalization of literary studies ("One of the results of legitimizing criticism in the university has been to professionalize it. Much literary criticism today is written for colleagues, not for people interested in books"[11]) and proceeds to animadvert against the emergence of theory in the academy, which he promptly reduces to boring nonsense. Not surprisingly, Epstein's subsequent collection of critical essays, *Partial Payments*, in treating authors and their lives, pointedly represents a reversion to earlier, "purer," biographical criticism, presented as the one, true critical endeavor.

For Reginald Gibbons, among others, the problem reduces to an opposition between criticism and imaginative writing, academics and writers. The former, he asserts, "tend to be interested in the play of ideas rather than in the exploration of existence"; thus when it comes to literary commentary, they are wont "to focus on *ideas* of form rather than material artistic effects, on semiphilosophical notions rather than thought or emotion."[12] Though his terms are general and evanescent, the point is, I think, clear enough. At any rate, like Epstein, Gibbons argues for literature because of its connection with "life," which is rigidly distinguished from literature and preferred to it.

The lines are thus drawn. Nothing short of war is in the offing, according to Peter Stitt, a former teacher of creative writing at the University of Houston and now editor of the *Gettysburg Review*. Stitt recently offered his militaristic account in the *Newsletter* of the Associated Writing Programs. Pulling no punches, Stitt urges "creative writers" to circle the wagons against the savage, marauding theorists "gradually taking over the departments of English, thereby making the life of writers and writing students miserable."[13] Stitt offers little evidence in support of his large claims (which, in my experience, he has all wrong: the problem is not so much opposition of one "camp" to the other but the failure of each even to recognize, let alone communicate with, the other). Instead of supporting his claims, Stitt merely laments the misery theorists supposedly wreak, concentrating on reasons "why there seems such a deep dislike for literary criticism among creative writers." These include, he says, theorists' arrogance, greed, and lust for power, from which, I take it, (other) writers are somehow exempt. But there is also, and more to the point, the fact—at least for Stitt it is fact—that "not only do theorists seldom refer to texts, but they seem to take no pleasure in them when they do." The first charge here is so blatantly preposterous and false as to deserve no serious attention, but the second carries some weight, augmented when placed beside such points as Epstein's, quoted earlier, and Gibbons's that literary value is somehow inseparable from life and hope. The threat, for Stitt, in any case, is as palpable as it is immediate, and so he attempts to rally the forces of good against the poised, determined, and unscrupulous forces of evil. It's going to "grow worse," he warns, "if we do not place ourselves on alert." [14]

In calmer, less militaristic, if still oppositional terms, Stitt describes his ideal, what or who stands tall in and is exemplary of "traditional literary studies in America." That ideal derives from the nineteenth century, from before the emergence of the "secularized professional," and it echoes both Epstein's depiction of the "literary man" and Dickstein's praise of Henry James. Stitt's model is even more directly essayistic. Here is his nostalgic, romanticized account of Oliver Wendell Holmes, barely remembered anatomist, poet, and author of "piece work" collected as *The Autocrat at the Breakfast Table*: "Dr. Holmes was a literary critic whose jottings were published regularly in the *Atlantic Monthly*, then gathered into the book. His critical method was the most traditional one imaginable; he—an articulate and well-educated connoisseur of all types of literature—offered a perfectly balanced and good-natured commentary on the books that came his way. In print, it is the sort of conversation about literature that happens every day, in thousands of proper New England homes, over cocktails and brie or bacon and eggs, as the case may be." Referring more specifically to Holmes's manner of reading and doing commentary, Stitt avers: "There is no science to it, scarcely any organized method, just some person we find likeable and intelligent telling us what he thinks. This kind of thing went on for years, and still goes on today, and it is maddening to those of a more analytical cast of mind." [15]

Stitt's ideal is the "teatotalling" style against which Geoffrey Hartman has long been animadverting: friendly and familiar, polite and graceful (recall Somerset Maugham: "To like good prose is an affair of good manners. It is, unlike verse, a civil art").[16] For Hartman, this ideal, though admittedly alluring, seems inevitably to entail unwarranted readerly accommodation and avoidance of both philosophy and archaic, enthusiastic, and mysterious residues and so to reduce to "sublimated chatter," willing to take on only what can be discussed at the breakfast table or over cocktails. It is an ideal tied, Hartman acknowledges, to both the historical development of English prose and the tradition of the personal or familiar essay.

Put so boldly and reductively as Stitt does, this ideal will appear antiquated to those of us with an "analytical cast of mind," the result of defensive nostalgia. Yet it deserves attention. Hartman may too quickly dismiss the conversational style; he may miss something substantial, certainly persistent, perhaps strikingly American in the repeatedly expressed commitment to familiar experience, offered in a voice accessible and personal: commonsensical, committed to the practical and the particular, the concrete and the quotidian, impatient with (if not intolerant of) abstractions and analytical reasoning, perhaps preindustrial and agrarian in sensibility, more interested in cultivating a garden (and maybe strolling through one with a sweetheart) than in reading the crabbed sentences of German idealistic philosophy or in deconstructing reality. This is the essayistic ideal. For all the posturing, bravado, defensiveness, and intemperateness of the various accounts we have considered, and despite their simplicity and reductiveness, maybe because of the common sense involved, we—or at least I—cannot but be attracted.

Moreover, in the accounts we have noted of a forgotten, supposedly passé criticism appears a common thread of sense and sensibility, which sometimes quietly asserts the primacy of simply liking what you read and, if not, letting your distaste be known and in no uncertain terms. To make what James called "the good old fashion of 'liking' a work of art or not liking it" the "ultimate test" smacks, obviously and no doubt uncomfortably (but oh God, so attractively), of another, greener world that we are invited to think we have lost but might regain. The attraction is familiar.

THEORY is said to have driven a monumental wedge between criticism and art, between critical endeavor and the general reader, whose interests and concerns differ radically from those of the professional. However unconsciously, the common reader insists on good or at least interesting, carefully crafted prose, whereas the latter, the professional, seems increasingly neglectful of the quality of his or her own writing. More's the pity. The quality of the prose seems to say it all or nearly all.

Although some moments in recent theory "might seem conducive to the development of the essay" (for example, an entailed dehierarchization of genres, the questioning of canon, the blurring of distinctions among kinds of discourse), theory is generally felt to be no friend of the essay.[17] In Europe, the situation is different. There, as one of our best familiar essayists, Phillip Lopate, has observed, a "fragmented, aphoristic, critical type of essay-writing," owing something to Nietzsche no doubt, "became used as a subversive tool of skeptical probing, a critique of ideology in a time when large, synthesizing theories and systems of philosophy are no longer trusted."[18] Practitioners of such essay writing include—and I mention only some prominent examples from several countries—Ortega y Gasset, Adorno, Czeslaw Milosz, Josef Škvorecký, Adam Zagajewski, Nicola Chiaromonte, E. M. Cioran, Sartre, Camus, and Barthes. Like their Anglo-American counterparts, writers in this tradition have produced some important discussions of the essay. But whereas writers in America speak lovingly of the form they court, in Europe the essay receives a quite different treatment, in line with the intellectual, cultural, and critical responsibilities associated with it. In Europe, in fact, the essay is a very ambitious form, not at all a second-class citizen, but a genre recognized as making a literary and a cultural difference. Thus European discussions offer a *theory* of the essay, something that seems alien, indeed anathema, to essayists like Pickering and Epstein, who seek only (!) to describe the form's essential features and to account for its special effects and pleasures.

Though certainly more philosophical, intellectual, and speculative, European discussions of the essay make it clear that, for all the differences, we are indeed talking about a single form. In the "Epistemo-Critical Prologue" to *The Origin of German Tragic Drama*, Walter Benjamin offers some brief but salient comments on the essay as form. Like Georg Lukács before him and Theodor Adorno after (see below), Benjamin understands the essay as speculative, philosophical, and critical. He refers to "the esoteric essay" and describes the postulates of "philosophical style" as follows: "the art of interruption in contrast to the chain of deduction; the tenacity of the essay in contrast to the single gesture of the fragment; the repetition of themes in contrast to shallow universalism; the fullness of concentrated positivity in contrast to the negation of polemic." Benjamin's own style is, obviously, difficult. In the "Epistemo-Critical Prologue" he emphasizes the digressiveness and fragmentariness of the essay, but, he argues, "the absence of an uninterrupted, purposeful structure is its primary characteristic." He adds: "Tirelessly the process of thinking makes new beginnings, returning in a roundabout way to its original object. This continual pausing for breath is the mode most proper to the process of contemplation. For by pursuing different levels of meaning in its examination of one single object," Benjamin continues, "it receives both the incentive to begin again and the justification for its irregular rhythm."[19] The similarities to, but, more important, the differences from, the Anglo-American familiar essay are manifest.

Similarly, in "Über den Essay und seine Prosa," published in 1947, Max Bense describes, in terms reminiscent of William H. Gass and others, how the essay "distinguishes itself from a scientific treatise He writes essayistically who writes while experimenting, who turns his object this way and that, who questions it, feels it, tests it, thoroughly reflects on it, attacks it from different angles, and in his mind's eye collects what he sees, and puts into words what the object allows to be seen under the conditions established in the course of writing." But if in such passages Bense anticipates the descriptions of Gass, Hoagland, and Pickering, in others the differences are palpable. For Bense, as for the European tradition generally, the essay is not merely an intellectual form, but it is also inseparable from notions of the *critical*. As Bense puts it, "the essay is the form of the critical category of our mind. For whoever criticizes must necessarily experiment; he must create conditions under which an object is newly seen, and he must do so in a fashion different from that of a creative author. Above all the fragility of the object must be probed, tested; this is precisely the meaning of the small variation that an object undergoes in the hands of the critic."[20]

Ever so quietly, Bense lays down the gauntlet in describing the essayist as one distinct from "a creative author." It would not be quite fair (however tempting it is) to say that this issue divides the European from the Anglo-American tradition, the latter regarding the essay, even if it be thought of as a second-class citizen, as a form with some pretension to art whereas European writers are less concerned with suggestiveness, evocative features, and grace of expression than with the quality and especially depth of thought represented. Actually, these questions are *within* European accounts of the essay, or at least they lie at the heart of arguably the two most important theories of the essay. I refer to Lukács's "On the

Nature and Form of the Essay" (1910) and Adorno's counterstatement "The Essay as Form" (1958).

Lukács's famous and pivotal account, addressed as "a letter to Leo Popper," from the outset pointedly links up with familiar and personal writing. It is, in fact, though, a speculative, richly philosophical attempt both to define the critical essay and to establish its importance by revealing its distinctive features and contributions. For Lukács, as later for Bense and Adorno, the essay is inseparable from criticism. But unlike theirs, Lukács's concern lies primarily with the essay "as a work of art, a genre." Thus he begins, as so many others have, with the attempt to say what an essay is. In his estimation, "the essay has a form which separates it, with the rigour of a law, from all other art forms." As he struggles with the essay's protean nature, Lukács writes at one point, with unusual figurality: "Let me put it briefly: were one to compare the forms of literature with sunlight refracted in a prism, the writings of the essayists would be the ultra-violet rays."[21]

This subtle, penetrating discussion entails plastic distinctions between the tragic and the essayistic, the poet and the essayist, life and living, image and significance. It glides back and forth between the essay and criticism, arguing, for example, that "form *is* reality in the writings of critics; it is the voice with which they address their questions to life."[22] From the issue of the questions addressed to life, which itself suggests the essay's seriousness, its difference from mere chatter or polite conversation over "cocktails and brie or bacon and eggs," Lukács moves to the notion that "the writings of the essayists are produced only in order to explain books and pictures, to facilitate their understanding."[23] For Lukács, irony marks the essay, lying at its very heart, indeed constituting its nature; it appears, he says, "in the writings of every truly great essayist":

> The irony I mean consists in the critic always speaking about the ultimate problems of life, but in a tone which implies that he is only discussing pictures and books, only the inessential and pretty ornaments of real life—and even then not their innermost substance but only their beautiful and useless surface. Thus each essay appears to be removed as far as possible from life, and the distance between them seems the greater, the more burningly and painfully we sense the actual closeness of the true essence of both. Perhaps the great Sieur de Montaigne felt something like this when he gave his writings the wonderfully elegant and apt title of "Essays." The simple modesty

of this word is an arrogant courtesy. The essayist dismisses his own proud hopes which sometimes lead him to believe that he has come close to the ultimate: he has, after all, no more to offer than explanations of the poems of others, or at best of his own ideas. But he ironically adapts himself to this smallness—the eternal smallness of the most profound work of the intellect in the force of life—and even emphasizes it with ironic modesty.[24]

If, then, "poetry takes its motifs from life (and art)," Lukács believes that "the essay has its models in art (and life)"—a subtle but by no means a sophistic distinction. "Perhaps this is enough to define the distinction" between poetry and the essay, Lukács believes.[25]

Like Anglo-American apologists for the essay, Lukács goes on to emphasize the form's respect for openness, its characteristic skepticism, and its recognition of the arbitrariness of any ending: "A question is thrown up and extended so far in depth that it becomes the question of all questions, but after that everything remains open; something comes from outside—from a reality which has no connection with the question nor with that which, as the possibility of an answer, brings forth a new question to meet it—and interrupts everything."[26] This kerygmatic sense, if I may use that religious term, appears as well in Lukács's concluding account of the essayist's vital role as critic, "sent into the world . . . to judge every phenomenon by the scale of values glimpsed and grasped through [the] recognition that poetry is older and greater—a larger, more important thing—than all the works of poetry." The critic, in other words, understands that "the idea is there before any of its expressions," that "the idea is the measure of everything that exists." And yet the critical essayist, as important as his or her work is and though it be in touch with the *idea,* is only a herald, precursor, and threshold figure, for, according to Lukács, "the essayist is a Schopenhauer who writes his *Parerga* while waiting for the arrival of his own (or another's) *The World as Will and Idea,* he is a John the Baptist who goes out to preach in the wilderness about another who is still to come, whose shoelace he is not worthy to untie."[27]

Ultimately, then, aesthetic considerations, and especially the essay's own claims to be art, constitute the heart of Lukács's theory of the essay: the critical essay treats art, judges it by the absolute standard of the "idea," and is itself, however modest its pretensions, an instance of the very art on which it comments. As Geoffrey Hartman has written, elaborating on Lukács's account, "the essay lives off a desire that has an in-itself, that is more than something merely waiting to be completed, and removed, by absolute knowledge." Lukács himself puts it this way: the essay "stands too high, it sees and connects too many things to be the simple exposition or explanation of a work. . . . The essay has become too rich and independent for dedicated service."[28] No longer willing to lie submissively at the feet of the work of art considered, the critical essay has, in Hartman's terms, crossed over and become art.

And *that* proved a matter of no small concern to Theodor Adorno, determining, in fact, "The Essay as Form," a subtle, complex piece whose difficulty stems from the dialectical nature of Adorno's thinking and his nonlinear, paratactic style of writing. These are the very qualities he identifies with the essay, his own contribution consisting of both its particular argument and its effective demonstration of that argument. Indeed, the both/and thinking that Adorno posits as crucial to and characteristic of the essay is much in evidence as he argues, pace Lukács, that this particular form "acquires an aesthetic autonomy that is easily criticized as simply borrowed from art, though it distinguishes itself from art through its conceptual character and its claim to truth free from aesthetic semblance. Lukács," he continues, "failed to recognize this when he called the essay an art form." The value, even the validity, of the essay, I understand Adorno as saying, consists neither in its resemblance to art nor in its distance from it (for it is by no means absolutely distinct from art). "The positivist tendency to set up every possible examinable object in rigid opposition to the knowing subject remains—in this as in every other instance—caught up in the rigid separation of form and content: for it is scarcely possible to speak of the aesthetic unaesthetically, stripped of any similarity with the object, without being narrow-minded and *a priori* losing touch with the aesthetic object."[29] Though he grants that the essay "labors emphatically on the form of its presentation," it resembles art only in the respect that "the consciousness of the non-identity between presentation and presented material forces the form to make unlimited efforts. . . . Otherwise, on account of the concepts which appear in it and which import not only their meaning but also their theoretical aspects, the essay is necessarily related to theory."[30] Whereas, then, the issue for Lukács remains the essay as "a work of art," for Adorno, quite differently, it is the essay in its conceptual character and theoretical base.

Adorno's focus is essayistic form, and as he explores the essay, he considers at some length those features unappreciated and frequently criticized because misunderstood. In this revisionist effort, faults become, many of them, virtues. To the charges of "objectionable transitions in rhetoric, . . . [mere] association [of ideas], ambiguity of words, neglect of logical synthesis," for instance, Adorno responds thoughtfully, penetrating deeply into what the form is all about and distinguishing its procedures from those of discursive logic. The essay's transitions, for example, he writes, "disavow rigid deduction in the interest of establishing internal cross-connections, something for which discursive logic has no use. . . . Here as well," he contends, "the essay verges on the logic of music, the stringent and yet aconceptual art of transition; it aims at appropriating for expressive language something that it forfeited under the domination of a discursive logic which cannot be circumvented, but may be outwitted in its own form by the force of an intending subjective expression." Because the logic operating in the essay is musical, rather than discursive, the form is "not situated in simple opposition to discursive procedure." The relation is far more complicated; it is dialectical, in fact. Contrary to what some may think, insists Adorno, the essay is thus "not unlogical; rather it obeys logical criteria in so far as the totality of its sentences must fit together coherently. Mere contradictions may not remain, unless they are grounded in the object itself. It is just that the essay develops thoughts differently from discursive logic. The essay neither makes deductions from a principle nor does it draw conclusions from coherent individual observations. It co-ordinates elements, rather than subordinating them; and only the essence of its content, not the manner of its presentation, is commensurable with logical criteria."[31]

In "The Essay as Form," as I have suggested, Adorno practices what he preaches (my exposition is literally straightening out what exists as pointedly roundabout): his writing "shrinks back from the over-arching concept under which particular concepts should be subordinated."[32] For Adorno, "the rhetorical function of essaying is not merely to transmit the essayist's thoughts but to convey the feeling of their movement and thereby to induce an experience of thought in the reader." R. Lane Kauffmann is right: "To read Adorno's essays is to be compelled to think dialectically."[33]

Behind discursive logic, founding it perhaps, stands Descartes's *Discourse on Method*. Philosophy has embraced its recommended procedures, which are also those characteristic of "objective," professional writing in article form. For Adorno, Cartesian method is all wrong, and so he lambastes "the adult pedantry that admonishes thought with a threatening finger to understand the simple before risking the complexity which alone entices it. Such a postponement of knowledge," he asserts, "only prevents knowledge." The essay reverses this procedure, abjuring, in fact, the very notion of method; it "insists that a matter be considered, from the very first, in its whole complexity; it counter-acts that hardened primitiveness that always allies itself with reason's current form. . . . Shak[ing] off the illusion of a simple, basically logical world that so perfectly suits the defense of the status quo," the essay has little truck with "things as they are"; in fact, claims Adorno, it "remains what it always was, the critical form *par excellence*. . . . It is the critique of ideology."[34] A major part of that critical effort remains directed at "method," as it always has been: method, which created and services the "administrative" thinking of the post-Enlightenment bourgeoisie, and which operates oppositionally, *dividing* the world, freezing differences. "Doubt about the unconditional *polarity* of method was raised, in the actual process of thought," argues Adorno, "almost exclusively by the essay. It does justice," he goes on, "to the consciousness of non-identity, without needing to say so, radically non-radical in refraining from any reduction to a principle, in accentuating the fragmentary, the partial rather than the total."[35] Just as he rejects absolute difference, so Adorno opposes the reduction that mirrorlike produces identity and totality, for the result is the same: loss of elasticity, complexity, and openness—in short, of truth.

Adorno is arguing that "the need arises in the essay as form to annul the theoretically outmoded claims of totality and continuity and to do so in the concrete procedure of the intellect."[36] That effort, in turn, redirects thought toward what has been scanted and undervalued, "the changing and ephemeral," the experiential and the historical, the fragmentary and the partial—on which the essay thrives. About the essay's concentrated attention to both the ephemeral and the concrete, Adorno writes: "It revolts above all against the doctrine—deeply rooted since Plato—that the changing and ephemeral is unworthy of philosophy; against that ancient injustice toward the transitory, by which it is once more anathematized, conceptually. The essay shys [*sic*] away from the violence of dogma, from the notion that the result of abstraction, the temporally invariable concept indifferent to the individual phenomenon grasped by it, deserves ontological dignity."[37] The frequently heard reproach—that the essay is "fragmentary and random"—becomes here a measure of its value. That character is also connected to the essay's "desire." For Adorno, differently from Lukács, who also noted the essay's desire, it has little to do with art understood as beauty of design and grace of expression, and everything to do with thought: "the desire of the essay is not to seek and filter the eternal out of the transitory; it wants, rather, to make the transitory eternal. Its weakness testifies to the non-identity that it has to express, as well as to excess of intention over its object, and thereby it points to that utopia which is blocked out by the classification of the world into the eternal and the transitory. In the emphatic essay, thought gets rid of the traditional idea of truth." Suspending the idea of method, thought, as it works itself out in the essay, "acquires its depth from penetrating deeply into a matter, not from referring back to something else."[38] When Adorno identifies "the bad essay" as one that simply "chats about people instead of opening up the matter at hand," we cannot now but think of the Anglo-American essay—though the latter at its best reveals the dramatic, substantial, and even the eternal *in* that "chat."[39]

Adorno's own penetration is perhaps nowhere greater than in what I take to be his most direct and straightforward exposition of essayistic procedure and insight. You feel quite unmistakably in Adorno's (musical) composition the rise to a crescendo—he is, of course, also describing his own densely textured writing in this essay—though the passage comes roughly halfway through, not at the end:

> Not less, but more than the process of defining, the essay urges the reciprocal interaction of its concepts in the process of intellectual experience. In the essay, concepts do not build a continuum of operations, thought does not advance in a single direction, rather the aspects of the argument intervene as in a carpet. The fruitfulness of the thoughts depends on the density of the texture. Actually, the thinker does not think, but rather transforms himself into an arena of intellectual experience, without simplifying it. While even traditional thought draws its impulses from such experience, such thought by its form eliminates the remembrance of these impulses. The essay, on the other hand, takes them as its model, without simply imitating them as a reflected form; it mediates them through its own conceptual organization; it proceeds, so to speak, methodically unmethodically.[40]

The next paragraph brings to a climax the effort that is under way—a sectional break follows it in the English translation. Unusually figurative, and intense, it proceeds to discuss, all the while performing its argument, the important notion of *Kraftfeld* ("force field"), which Martin Jay identifies as a crucial figure in the weave of Adorno's thinking and writing. I quote the paragraph entire:

> The way in which the essay appropriates contexts is most easily comparable to the behavior of a man who is obliged, in a foreign country, to speak that country's language instead of patching it together from its elements, as he did in school. He will read without a dictionary. If he has looked at the same word thirty times, in constantly changing contexts, he has a clearer grasp of it than he would if he looked up all the word's meanings; meanings that are generally too narrow, considering they change depending on the context, and too vague in view of the nuances that the context establishes in every individual case. Just as such learning remains exposed to error, so does the essay as form; it must pay for its affinity with open intellectual experience by the lack of security, a lack which the norm of established thought fears like death. It is not so much that the essay ignores indisputable certainty, as that it abrogates the ideal. The essay becomes true in its purposes, which drives it beyond itself, and not in a hoarding obsession with fundamentals. Its concepts receive their light from a *terminus ad quem* hidden to the essay itself, and not from a *terminus a quo*. In this the very method of the essay expresses the utopian intention. All of its concepts are presentable in such a way that they support one another, that each one articulates itself according to the configuration it forms with the other. In the essay discreetly separated elements enter into a readable context; it erects no scaffolding, no edifice. Through their own movement the elements crystallize into a configuration. It is a force field, just as under the essay's glance every intellectual artifact must transform itself into a force field.

As a "constellation," the essay, Adorno explains, is far from arbitrary; it seems such only to "a philosophical subjectivism which translates the exigencies of the object into those of its conceptual organization. . . . The essay's openness," he reiterates, "is not vaguely one of feeling and mood." Instead, that openness, than which hardly anything is more important, "obtains its contour from its content."[41] The essay, then, as a mode of and a means toward intellectual discovery takes its form from the very process of thought; it is the *movement* of ideas that creates structure and form.

The "truth" of the essay is inseparable from this focused "mobility" of intellect. Without that openness and resulting movement, there is no truth. Truth is something that the static and merely discursive (article) cannot effect. Adorno says it best in the following lines, which return attention to our familiar if unfortunate way of thinking in oppositional terms: "If the truth of the essay gains its momentum by way of its untruth, its truth is not to be sought in mere opposition to what is ignoble and proscribed in it, but in these very things: in its mobility, its lack of that solidity which science demands, transferring it, as it were, from property-relationships to the intellect. . . . Intellect itself, once emancipated, is mobile. . . . Truth abandoned by play could be nothing more than tautology." [42]

A powerful brief for emancipated thought, one deserving of our closest consideration in this "administrative" age, "The Essay as Form" stakes large claims, investing the essay with almost-limitless powers and responsibilities. I come away from Adorno's account inspired and hopeful (despite his own expressed pessimism), moved alike by the argument and the presentation. I would not call Adorno's "manner of presentation" artful, but of course he doesn't want or intend it to be such. In fact, I find the prose itself dismaying, seemingly careless, certainly lacking ease and grace. And therein lies the crux of the matter we're struggling with in this chapter—not just the differences between Adorno and Lukács but nothing less than what the (critical) essay is, somehow or to some degree familiar, as Adorno acknowledges, and yet thoughtful, speculative, genuinely critical, and artful or at least carefully crafted. In the final analysis, Adorno's essays are no more personal than conventionally artful; it may be that reading them we sense an unmistakable persona, but "the speculative freedom and playfulness of Montaigne's essays, and their unabashed self-reference, are implicitly proscribed in Adorno's essays as breaches of philosophical protocol." [43]

In a massive, posthumously published book entitled *Beautiful Theories: The Spectacle of Discourse in Contemporary Criticism*, Elizabeth W. Bruss adds an interesting twist to the situation I have been describing. With detailed attention to William H. Gass, Susan Sontag, Harold Bloom, and Roland Barthes, Bruss argues that theory has begun to assume the attributes and function of art, even if, by conventional standards, it appears anything but beautiful. Precisely what Adorno prizes as conceptualization, open intellectualism, and the free play of mind, which he distinguishes from the aesthetic, Bruss finds beautiful. For her, in fact, those qualities Adorno must defend in the essay ("objectionable transitions in rhetoric, . . . [mere]

63

association of [ideas], ambiguity of words, neglect of logical synthesis") become the very foundation of a new art.

To begin with, Bruss regards theoretical literature (that *is* how she understands theory) as "part of a larger prose 'revival' "—even though it is "typically," she acknowledges, excoriated for its "crabbed or circuitous expression, its fugitive impersonations and impersonalizations, its wandering paragraphs, jointless sentences and the abstract, undercooked, 'translationese' that haunts its diction." These would appear to be major and damning faults—for many of us, they certainly are. But having acknowledged them, Bruss proceeds to claim that conventional criticism of theoretical prose is misguided, deriving from the imposition of alien standards, in this case from the limited "decorums of polite scholarship and the familiar essay."[44] With theory, argues Bruss, we are dealing with a new and "unestablished" genre, whose very purpose seems to be "to strip familiar objects and commonplace practices of their obviousness."[45] A consideration of *Beautiful Theories* will clarify my rather different sense of "estranging the familiar."

Bruss presents theory as a hybrid with unique potential for addressing and satisfying postmodern readers (she evidently means academic readers of a particular slant). It "preserves," she maintains, "all that is best and most authentic in contemporary skepticism, our 'lost capacity for naive response.' "[46] Now, she argues, those "schematic or reductive qualities" for which theory has been condemned "seem liberating, allowing imagination to be suggestive when it cannot be concrete, to sketch with broad strokes what cannot yet be rendered in any great detail, and to open a conceptual space where we might someday learn to dwell. Theory is also free, as fictions and lyrics usually are not, to mount extended explanations and to engage in elaborate argumentation without provoking charges of digression. Such leisure for development, so much more room for exposition and defense relative to what is actually posited or claimed, are precisely what the present situation, with all of its uncertainties, its diffidencies, its necessary hesitations, calls for." Bruss is surely right that "there is less assurance now that literary theory *is* strictly ancillary to the real business of literature, or that argument and explication must be mechanical and artless, with no compelling interest or exhilaration of its own."[47] Theory of literature has become theory *as* literature.

Engaged more, it seems, in *creating* an audience for theoretical literature than in *describing* an existing situation, Bruss says that "what theory seems to feed is a new appetite for difficulty (the inverse, perhaps, of the increasingly facile entertainment industry), a new appreciation for the problematic and the speculative as aesthetic categories." Although it does not ignore aesthetic satisfaction, theory places greater weight on "other considerations—plausibility, logical consistency, applicability, and falsifiability." These now, somehow, become associated, if not identified, with the pleasing and even the beautiful. According to Bruss, theory simply "provides a new quality of satisfaction," for example, "when an explanation suddenly realizes the elements of a familiar scene or a series of questions slowly reveals to us the precariousness of the ground on which we stand." [48]

Principally, Bruss bases her argument for the beauty of theory on its "conceptual design": "how it constructs its explanations and prescriptions (by model or metalanguage, by laws or narratives, by taxonomies or simple procedural recommendations), as well as what these operations do to resituate or reconstrue the object of analysis (and how drastically), and for what purposes—to master that object, to estrange it, to glamorize it, or to denude and demystify it." Bruss trains her sights on more than reader recognition and response, as important as they are; she is interested, above all, in effect. "There is," she maintains, "a penetrating pleasure in the scope, the starkness or the intricacy, the sheer ingenuity of a conceptual design, and in the thoroughness or eccentricity of its application, the surprise (even the incongruity) of its operations compared to operations that we already know of." [49]

Theory's powerful effects and supposed appeal stem directly from the defamiliarizing that results from carefully reading theory. Bruss insists, in fact, that among "the chief excitements in reading theoretical prose" is an inevitable and disturbing "sense of disorientation." Part of this effect she attributes to the nature of the prose itself: "legible phrases that cluster in unpredictable and unnerving ways, or syntax that forms a solid and respectably sane frame around a verbal lunacy of dismembered syllables and awkward neologisms." [50] In support of this (unstinting) praise of the unconventional and even tortuous, Bruss offers a critique of the prose we normally prize, much as she elsewhere dismisses the familiar essay as part of a limited and misguided, essentially retrograde, "decorum": "To establish and remain with a regular margin, to mark the endings of one's sentences, to provide conventional footholds . . . for readers suddenly has a different meaning—perhaps more than one. One reads in these a concern for proper etiquette, a nascent classicism, a desire to guide or control the entrances to the text."[51]

Bruss is exuberant, unflinching, if not heartening or convincing: "the pleasures of accommodation and immediate assimilation are the first that theory asks us to forgo," she rather proudly announces.[52] Tossed out along with them are "the pleasure of simple recognition, identification, absorption, and appropriation." But rather than lament their passing, we should be glad, for these values too have become "guilt-ridden of late, more hysterical or forced." In their stead, happily, come "the compensatory pleasures" of defamiliarization, here called "the jolt of interruption: the sharp but interesting pangs of estrangement and disorientation, the receding of comfortable acquaintance and the approach of an entirely different mode and magnitude of apprehension—oblique, denatured, yet thrillingly pellucid."[53]

Conventionally, of course, literary artfulness has been attributed to an accomplished, individual *maker,* or artisan, whose voice, personality, and character, as well as skills, are felt in the prose. But in theoretical literature, as Bruss represents it, "the logical subject" becomes nothing more than "a bare propositional function," by now a familiar enough argument, in this poststructuralist age. The "drive" of theoretical writing, "the passion itself," says Bruss, is accordingly "impersonal" or at least nonpersonal, "a compulsion without fixed location or private identity. Thus," she continues, "the theoretical text may more closely approximate the sort of pure discursive force, exceeding any particular authorizing subject and irreducible to any individual personality."[54]

Impersonal force replaces creative personality. The fallible, fumbling, bungling, engaged human voice gives way to the "beauty" of conceptual design. And crabbed sentences, made of barely legible phrases and awkward neologisms, yet somehow reflective of "syntax that forms a solid and respectably sane frame around a verbal lunacy"—these now draw the praise once reserved for grace, elegance, and eloquence. In *Beautiful Theories* Bruss assumes the unenviable position—I at least regard it as such—of honoring what others lament and decry, labeling as beauty and art what many of us find merely mechanical, pedestrian, or careless. Can we not find something worthier to honor, without giving over theory, without forgetting the lessons taught by Lukács and Adorno, and without accepting "sublimated chatter" as the substance and object of the essay?

The critic who best seems to fit Bruss's conceptual framework is Geoffrey Hartman, whom she barely mentions even though he both argues for and practices (theoretical) criticism as literature. As early as *The Fate of Reading* (1975), Hartman was arguing that criticism is "creative," a position he elaborated elsewhere and developed at length in *Criticism in the Wilderness* (1981). As he has insisted—I could also say "shown"—that criticism forms a not-insignificant part of literature, Hartman has written critical essays that at their best at least approach the level of "intellectual poetry," a borrowed phrase that he uses to describe the strongest work in essay form of writer-critics like Ortega y Gasset and Paul Valéry. In a mixed, therefore impure, and paratactic style that may owe something to Adorno, Hartman writes thoughtful, evocative, and demanding essays that we have trouble with because they don't develop in the usual linear fashion of the academic article. They often seem to ramble, though never aimlessly, representing the divulgations of Hartman's well-stocked and fertile mind as it broods, shuttling between text and idea. As Paul H. Fry has remarked, "The roundabout course of [Hartman's] allusiveness represents the course of interpretive discovery. His criticism is the most *realistic* record we have of what literate reading is like." In an age that has proclaimed and even celebrated "the death of the author," Hartman understands, with Milton, that the great text or masterpiece is "the pretious life-blood of a master-spirit."[55] Janus-faced, he thus looks both forward to a theoretically informed future and backward to a past still big with possibility.

Hartman is important for many reasons, not least among them being his recognition that the nature and function—and indeed, the fate—of criticism are inseparably linked to questions of form and style: in other words, to the essay. "The central question," he writes, in agreement with Lukács, "is criticism, the essay as work of art, as art genre." And the critical essay, the form of commentary, insists Hartman, "is an essay above all: a literary and experimental work rather than a dogmatic pronouncement." No matter what may have happened to them in recent years, criticism and the essay go hand-in-glove: like Lukács, to whom he confesses to being "drawn strongly," Hartman rejects "subordination as a defining characteristic of the essay," just as he does the subordination of criticism to the literature on which it comments.[56]

The question of the essay's power, strength, and place is inseparable from considerations of style. The essay is important, perhaps central, to criticism not least because it represents a form and a style *answerable* to the literature on which it comments, no matter how independent it may appear to become. Hartman has long sought in criticism an "answerable style," for "the spectacle of the polite critic dealing with an extravagant literature, trying so hard to come to terms with it in his own tempered language, verges on the ludicrous."[57] And yet the "plainstyle" critic, Hartman wrote in 1975 (and the situation remains essentially unchanged today), produces texts "called articles, merchandized in the depressed market place of academic periodicals, [that] conform strictly to the cool element of scholarly prose. They are sober, literate, literal, pointed." The critic—you know him, his or her name is legion—"will not violate the work of art by imposing on it his own, subjective flights of fancy, however intriguing these may be. He has put off personality except for the precise amount it needs to animate his prose."[58] And, asks Hartman, "who can fault him? Is anyone against objectivity, integrity, and the scrupulous distinction of functions?" More specifically concerning prose style, Hartman writes in *The Fate of Reading* (like Adorno, he won't simplify, his thinking, too, being of the both/and, or dialectical, type):

> Is criticism a yea yea, nay nay affair, best conducted in as dry a prose as possible? This admirable ideal has its shortcomings. It establishes too often a schizoid rather than useful distance between art and criticism. Under the pressure of such an ideal writers divide into a class of artists and a class of adjudicators, each with its own prerogatives. Surely a bureaucratic or managerial, rather than a human and persuasive solution. Why shouldn't the critic be "divers et ondoyant," in the essay form at least? (Perhaps we need a distinction between literary review and literary essay, though this too should hardly be absolute.) In any case, to prescribe the separateness of literary-critical genres, and put down all mixed criticism as bad art, does not resolve the contradiction faced by those who want criticism to be a rigorous testing of interpretive hypothesis or clarifying of the artist's intention. How will they reconcile the notion of essay—tentative, continuously self-reflective, structured, yet informal—with the rigor that evaluative or historical criticism should ideally bring to its subject?[59]

Unfortunately, Hartman does not, so far as I can tell, venture an answer, though a clue may reside in such a statement as the following, which acknowledges criticism's perhaps inherent links. It is, he says, "a relatively free, all-purpose genre, and closely related to the personal or familiar essay. It is a literary genre of a special sort, although I mean by this not that it should aim to be prose-poetry, but simply that it shares its text-milieu with other genres of literature while struggling with its own generic pressures of style."[60]

But Hartman does not carry very far that acknowledgment of criticism's close relationship to the personal or familiar essay. He remains interested primarily in the critical essay as "intellectual poetry," a notion that he takes from A. W. Schlegel and that links up with Lukács. By "intellectual poetry" Hartman means something more than, and in fact different from, artful prose or charm and grace of expression applied to intellectual questions. Like Adorno, he has in mind writing severe and demanding, as well as genuinely critical: philosophical, probing, and speculative. In such writing, the poetry inheres in the depth of penetration achieved and the quality of insight offered rather than in "the manner of presentation." Consequently, the examples Hartman cites of "intellectual poetry" (the commodity is "scarce")—certain essays of Friedrich Schlegel, Valéry, Ortega, Freud, and Heidegger—are, as he puts it, not only "less distinguished in their decorum," but they are also much more "exacting than the 'familiar' prose which aimed, in the previous century, to expand the family of readers. Hazlitt makes you feel equal to, or different only in degree from, Wordsworth."[61] No such familiarity, accommodation, or accessibility obtains in the "intellectual poets" Hartman names.

Whether or not Hartman's own essays consistently reach some such level of "intellectual poetry," they are, at the very least, essays; they do not, to invoke his own terms, "conform strictly to the cool element of scholarly prose." Instead, they are peripatetic, highly allusive, richly metaphorical, stylistically mixed and impure, and unpointed ("point" is a technical term, which Hartman defines as denoting "concentrated reality or concentrated verbal meaning" and suggesting the attempt to "encapsulate something," which he reads as implying "a fixed locus of revelation or a reified idolatrous content").[62]

As a critic, Hartman remains his own person, practicing what he describes as needed: "an unservile, an enlarged and mature, criticism, neither afraid of theory nor overestimating it." He uses whatever is at hand, but he won't allow himself or his judgment to be taken over by any theory, text, or person. Though often linked with deconstruction and described as a "Yale critic," Hartman frequently writes against deconstruction, just as he does against psychoanalysis, semiotics, and hermeneutics, even as he admires them and on occasion writes from within their insights. He is as critical as he is individualistic, as wary as he is patient. What he practices as a critic is never systematic: "modern 'rithmatics'— semiotics, linguistics, and technical structuralism," he maintains (never forgetful that "though a text is discontinuously woven of many strands or codes, there is magic in the web"), "convert all expression into generative codes needing operators rather than readers." [63]

These and other qualities would seem calculated to appeal to a large audience, a broad readership, extending well beyond the merely academic. Yet Hartman remains an academic critic, in terms of both his evident intentions and his appeal. Even the writing collected as *Easy Pieces* and self-described as journalistic is difficult and demanding, refusing in various degrees to engage in reader accommodation. In this regard Hartman differs pointedly from his fellow (academic) critic Northrop Frye. However we may feel about their meaning and significance, Frye's efforts have earned him a considerable general audience; he remains an academic critic, to be sure, but his writing has enjoyed impressive commercial success. And that must be attributed in large part to an accommodation and a demystification Hartman forgoes in favor of estrangement and defamiliarization.

As attractive as he is, with the *potential* to reach a large readership, Hartman also suffers from an uncertain, uneven prose style. More than one reader has expressed frustration not only with Hartman's refusal to come to "a point" but also with an occasional insouciance in his sentences. Sometimes they are playful and therefore engaging, even charming, but at others they appear wayward and willful. At still other times one may feel, if not a pedestrian sense, at least a prosaic one. But then, as you are about to write him off, Hartman turns a neat phrase or offers an insightful, compelling statement, and you're back in his grip.

What might Hartman, or any other academic critic for that matter, achieve with the prose qualities we find in William H. Gass? Consider this *pointilist* passage from *On Being Blue*, which both discusses and performs "the art of the sentence":

If any of us were as well taken care of as the sentences of Henry James, we'd never long for another, never wander away: where else would we receive such constant attention, our thoughts anticipated, our feelings understood? Who else would robe us so richly, take us to the best places, or guard our virtue as his own and defend our character in every situation? If we were his sentences, we'd sing ourselves though we were dying and about to be extinguished, since the silence which would follow our passing would not be like the pause left behind by a noisy train. It would be a memorial, well-remarked grave, just as the Master has assured us death itself is: the distinguished thing.[64]

And this passage from Cynthia Ozick, describing *her* commitment to sentence making and exemplifying its art and craft:

Nothing matters to me so much as a comely and muscular sentence. It is my narrow strait, this snail's road; the track of the sentence I am writing now; and when I have eked out the wet substance, ink or blood, that is its mark, I will begin the next sentence. Only in treading out sentences am I perfectionist; but then there is nothing else I know how to do, or take much interest in. I miter every pair of abutting sentences as scrupulously as Uncle Jake fitted one strip of rosewood against another. My mother's worldly and beautiful hand has escaped me. The sentence I am writing is my cabin and my shell, compact, self-sufficient. It is the burnished horizon—a merciless planet where flawlessness is the single standard, where even the inmost seams, however hidden from a laxer eye, must meet perfection. Here "excellence" is not strewn casually from a tipped cornucopia, here disorder does not account for charm, here trifles rule like tyrants.[65]

To cite Ozick, or Gass, is unfair, of course, and I don't want to be unfair; they are masters of the English sentence, whom none can touch and few approach. Still, it is my contention that the critical essay will thrive only to the degree that it relearns "the art of the sentence"; only then can it hope to earn the attention, and respect, of a wide audience.

But of course, sentences alone won't turn the trick. Here too the example of Hartman is instructive. An essay included in *The Fate of Reading*, "The Interpreter: A Self-Analysis," opens with some autobiographical references, but despite the title we learn very little about the critic. Similarly with *Criticism in the Wilderness*, despite some titillating remarks by Hartman, who describes this text as "a book of experiences," avers that in the face of systematizations and rationalizations he prefers to *"confess* what art has meant to me," and quotes with evident relish Anatole France's definition of the critic as "one who relates the adventures of his soul among masterpieces."[66] The "I" sometimes appears, but more as rhetorical strategy than sustained account or revelation. Hartman very rarely speaks about himself. He is never distanced, objective, clinical; he is, on the contrary, always deeply engaged with texts, and you certainly cannot mistake the play of this particular, agile, amazing mind with ideas, texts, and emotions. And yet perhaps the main effect on Hartman that we feel from his adventures with texts is that he has been moved to share his interpretive discoveries with us ("one difference that reading makes is, most generally, writing").[67] There is no self-revelation, very little *self*-analysis. Were Hartman willing to be more confessional, more personal, more willing to speak directly and openly to the reader about himself, I wonder if he might achieve a broader audience, the kind of readership that criticism ought to be in the business of addressing and attracting.

CHAPTER FIVE

The Return of/to the Personal

Why personal criticism now? Is it another form of "Anti-Theory"? Is it a new stage of theory? Is it gendered? Only for women and gay men? Is it bourgeois? postmodern? A product of Late Capitalism? Reaganomics? Post-feminism? . . . One of the resistances already mounted against personal criticism is the specter of recuperation: what if what seems new and provocative just turned out to be an academic fashion, another "congealed" genre . . . ? What if everyone started doing it?

NANCY K. MILLER, *Getting Personal*

WHETHER OR NOT Geoffrey Hartman achieves in his critical essays the level of the "intellectual poetry" that he honors—he will strike many as a voice crying in the wilderness rather than an artist sculpting prose—neither he nor those he praises as intellectual poets engage the personal. Occasionally in his work, to be sure, as in that of Schlegel, Valéry, Ortega, and Derrida, the "I" appears, and, more rarely, an autobiographical reference is dropped. But in the main, the essays of the "intellectual poets" eschew the personal. In this, they are not much different from scholarly and philosophical treatises, even if they avoid the detached, objective, almost scientific stance of "that awful object, 'the article'" (William H. Gass). This nervous avoidance impoverishes and, in my view, enervates critical writing. I am like Jane Tompkins: "when a writer introduces some personal bit of story into an essay, I can hardly contain my pleasure"; I too "love writers who write about their own experience"—as we may have reason to believe Hartman will do when he announces on the very first page that *Criticism in the Wilderness* is "a book of experiences."[1] Of *his* experiences "in the realms of gold" that define literature, however, we hear next to nothing and thus miss out on what Tompkins and I and, I'm convinced, so many other readers crave.

"I feel I'm being nourished by writers who write about themselves and their own experience," she declares. I feel as she does that in that case "I'm being allowed to enter into a personal relationship with them, that I can match my own experience with theirs, feel cousin to them, and say, yes, that's how it is." [2] Such an admission no doubt appears unprofessional; it smacks of the affective, certainly of the emotional, and *that,* we have come to accept, has no place in critical commentary. But not to engage the personal in critical writing, whether out of unfamiliarity with its possibilities or nervousness and fear concerning professional conventions, increasingly seems out of step; it is also unnecessary, as well as unwise. Not to engage the personal, moreover, consigns critical writing to a narrow, professional audience and assures it of merely academic interest.

One "intellectual poet" who *does* engage the personal is Roland Barthes. And not surprisingly his work has gained wide notice, his many books attracting readers that not even the most entrepreneurial of academic scholar-critics dream of. In his last, most essayistic "phase," Barthes focused on himself, unabashedly and brilliantly. He declared, as a matter of fact, that, though having "long wished to inscribe my work within the field of science—literary, lexicological, and sociological—I must admit that I have produced *only* essays, an ambiguous genre in which analysis vies with writing" (my italics). [3] Barthes seems to have grown closer and closer to Montaigne, the "father" of the essay, who famously declared himself and only himself to be the subject of his *essais.*

My concern in this chapter is not, however, directly with Barthes, who has been well served by a host of recent commentators, including Elizabeth W. Bruss, whose *Beautiful Theories* I treated earlier, and Réda Bensmaïa, in a challenging book entitled *The Barthes Effect: The Essay as Reflective Text.* Like Michèle Richman, who introduces that book, Bensmaïa is unreserved in his claims for Barthes as worthy successor to Montaigne. Rather than debate the issue at this point (Barthes writes out of the European essay tradition that I discussed earlier and that is more philosophical than familiar), I want to consider and elaborate on what I take to be crucial, at least for an Anglo-American audience, and that is the much larger question of "the return of/to the personal" strikingly manifest in Barthes's last works.

Signs of that return are everywhere, by no means limited to a growing preference for a certain kind of writing, though it is surely important that writers seem increasingly interested in a "directly personal sort of truth," which the essay warmly accommodates.[4] That interest I understand as part of a larger return. In what follows I make no pretense to exhaustiveness of treatment, nor do I seek to be authoritative. My effort is neither documentary nor really argumentative. If pressed to define my aim, I would describe it as suggestive: I take up some facets of "the return of/to the personal," neglect others, but hope to make clear that a constellation of results is now appearing with a brightness that cannot go unnoticed. I have little to say about the causes of this return; and about that failure, I can only plead that such concerns are the province of the historian rather than the *amateur* of the essay.

THE RETURN of/to the personal would be unthinkable and impossible without a strong interest in and commitment to the truths of the human heart. We seem almost ravenous for such verities, trapped in a world grown bewilderingly complex and widely impersonal; taught that language speaks (*Es gibt,* claims Heidegger), that the author is dead, and that the subject is merely a historical anomaly or accident, a mere site or cipher, a grid where power relations cross; and fed on films, stories, and art, minimalist in perspective, that depict the person as an automaton, the victim of blind forces, who, if he or she is capable of thought, seems incapable of feeling, a shrunken, shriveled bag of bones, muscles, and neurons—but, alas, no heart.

I suppose our current condition is accountable for fueling interest in the humanistic writing of men and women of medicine, those who should know the body best; witness the popularity of Lewis Thomas, Oliver Sacks, Richard Selzer, Perri Klass, Gerald Weissmann, John Stone, and others. We crave assurance from professionals, despite seemingly incontrovertible evidence and loud proclamations to the contrary, that a metaphorical heart beats somewhere in us, along with that literal one that we can actually hear pumping. In *The Country of Hearts,* John Stone cites Pascal's learned recognition that "the heart has its reasons which reason knows nothing of" and himself writes in similar fashion, "All fully rational people presume that our emotions spring from the electrical and biochemical corridors of the *brain,* but for many writers (incorrigible as they are) and cardiologists, this proposition is difficult to accept." Wasn't it Faulkner, he asks, "who said that the writer must leave 'no room in his workshop for anything but the old verities and truths of the heart . . . love and honor and pity and pride and compassion and sacrifice' "?[5]

These truths require story, take root in, blossom, and bear fruit as story, argument and demonstration evidently lacking the arable and fertile soil necessary for the cultivation of the heart's truths. These last require personal narration. Annie Dillard believes that "the narrative essay may become the genre of choice for writers devoted to significant literature." The essayist, she writes, "does what we do with our lives; the essayist thinks about actual things. He can make sense of them analytically or artistically. In either case he renders the real world coherent and meaningful."[6] Increasingly, it seems, in an effort to understand our world and ourselves, we are, neophytes and established writers alike, professionals as well as "ordinary" men and women, writing, telling stories, no longer just reading what others have written, though we do that, too, with perhaps unmatched rapacity. Discussing a "personal-essay course" she offers each summer, Phyllis Theroux writes that by the end "each woman"—her students are almost always women, an interesting if predictable and lamentable fact—"has come to the realization that writing can be a crucial skill, like cartography. Everybody lives in the middle of a landscape. Writing can provide a map." The opportunity thus provided for self-expression may suggest that its value is mainly therapeutic. Not so, claims Theroux: "It would be wrong to imply that a personal-essay course is really a consciousness-raising session in disguise. Something other than self-awareness is involved here: the work itself." And that work is the essay, which "has a strict form, and while the experience of the essayist fuels it, there are rules that one breaks at one's peril."[7] The essayist's experience—that is key, but so is loving attention to and successful courting of that strict if protean form.

As writers are more and more turning to the essay to tell a "directly personal sort of truth," journalists are, many of them, embracing "the new art of personal reportage." These are practitioners of "literary journalism." In an anthology bearing that title, Norman Sims includes John McPhee, Joan Didion, Tom Wolfe, Richard Rhodes, Jane Kramer, Mark Kramer, Tracy Kidder, Sara Davidson, Richard West, Mark Singer, Barry Newman, Ron Rosenbaum, and Bill Barich, most of whom are associated with the *New Yorker*. Their work obviously resembles, and is indebted to, that of the "new journalism" of the 1960s, which "self-consciously returned character, motivation, and voice to nonfiction," but the "literary journalism" being practiced today seems less flashy than that done earlier (according to Sims, "the younger literary journalists have calmed down"), with arguably greater interest in transcending "mere" reportage at least to approach the level of art.[8] At any rate, as Sims puts it, "literary journalists bring themselves into their stories to greater or lesser degrees and confess to human failings and emotions." Because they are "concerned with finding the right voice to express their material," these writers may no longer be "worried about 'self,'" but they do, in Sims's words, "care about tactics for effective telling, which may require the varying presence of an 'I' from piece to piece."[9]

Whatever the form, whatever the discipline, and no matter the issue, there can be no gainsaying the power of personal narration or confession. To this judgment appears increasing assent. Take religion, for example, where you could expect the personal to play an uncontested and prominent role. But even here, Harvey Cox laments, "the loss of the personal voice" has, at least until recently, been felt, with incalculable damage. In *Many Mansions: A Christian's Encounter with Other Faiths*, Cox addresses the issue in the context of discussing the relations between Christianity and other religions and ideologies. For dialogue to occur, whether on this or any other issue, the personal may have to be foregrounded and staked. Honoring what smacks of the essayistic, Cox puts it this way: "I believe a certain careful and modest restoration of personal narrative—call it 'testimony' if you will—can help restore some of the life-giving particularity to the dialogue among religions. After all, it is never the religions themselves that converse but individual people who embody those religions. I have seen more than one interfaith colloquium that was drifting toward death by tedium restored to life when someone had the courage to speak personally rather than in general terms." Cox's own procedure is highly personal. "The essays" in his new book, he writes, "grow almost entirely from my own encounters with actual people of other faiths. . . . They are unified by the lived experience of one person. *Many Mansions* is not about 'the' Christian dialogue with other religions but about one Christian's encounters with particular people of other faiths."[10]

AND in literary criticism? Has *it* experienced, let alone benefited from, this "return of/to the personal"? To those of us by now inured to claims insistent upon "the death of the author" and so to the gutting of the self, the answer may seem sadly obvious. Actually, though, it is not nearly so clear-cut as we might suppose. Structuralism, it is true, and in its wake poststructuralism, both of them smitten with linguistic operations, went far toward redefining the traditional, humanistic notion of the singular, personal self as "a subordinate function or 'site' of impersonal significations," structures, and codes.[11] Inevitably, however, a reaction set in. And of course, the structuralist victory was never complete. In pockets of resistance, people continued to believe in, because they experienced, the wonder-workings of the human heart, stirrings undreamt of in linguistics.

Though his influence has so far been little felt in this country, the French philosopher Emmanuel Levinas some time ago offered an alternative to structuralist and poststructuralist impersonalism. In *Fragments of Redemption: Jewish Thought and Literary Theory in Benjamin, Scholem, and Levinas*, Susan A. Handelman delineates that alternative. In such books as *Totality and Infinity* and *Otherwise Than Being*, she shows, Levinas has been engaged in a "passionate search" for a way out of what he calls the "multiplicity of allergic egoisms."[12] Opposing "the structuralist priority of sign-function over sign-giver," Levinas engagingly writes against those who depose the subject, making it, in Handelman's words, "no longer a self-controlling unified center of meaning" but instead relocating active force in something like "discursive practice" (Foucault), the play of difference (Derrida), the unconscious (Lacan), or the interplay of codes or "strategies of subversion."[13] Levinas roundly rejects what Handelman calls "all the contemporary talk in the 'human sciences' about the way in which the subject is conditioned by impersonal structure." His critique of those positions becomes "a defense of subjectivity as irreplaceable uniqueness."[14] He shares with them, however, a rejection of the narcissistic ego and its claim to identity and autonomy. Rejecting as well (he is apparently thinking of Buber) the romantic fusion of two selves in exclusive reciprocal relationship, or "a love born of some free will or purely subjective attraction to another," according to Handelman, Levinas "deconstructs the subject but saves the person."[15]

For Levinas, the idea of a self autonomous and free of all constraints, is, in being bound to itself, negligent and dismissive of the other, whom it in fact denies. Levinas, however, defines the self precisely by and in terms of its relation with the other, a relation irreducible to that of subject/

object; in Handelman's words: "the 'other' is disproportionate to all 'the power and freedom of the I,' and precisely this disproportion between the other and I is 'moral consciousness.' "[16] As he puts it in *Otherwise Than Being*, "difference" becomes nonindifference to the other. Levinas, in fact, makes the ego a *subject to*. The subject is "a unique self" "called upon to respond to the appeal of the other" and precisely "constituted as responsible for the other."[17] With Levinas, therefore, ethics replaces ontology. In his words: "To utter 'I,' to affirm the irreducible singularity in which the apology is pursued, means to possess a privileged place with regard to responsibilities for which no one can replace me and from which no one can release me. To be unable to shirk: this is the I."[18] In *Otherwise Than Being*, Levinas defines the subject as "the very *substituting of oneself* for the other."[19] By this, Levinas means something concrete and physical: "the duty to give the other even the bread out of one's own mouth and the coat from one's shoulders."[20] In opposing what Handelman calls "the logic of identity which denies the other (A = A. A cannot be other than itself . . .)," Levinas is engaging in another kind of reason altogether, one where " 'difference,' the difference between A and B, becomes the ethical non-indifference of the one to the other: A is for B in responsibility. On the level of '*either* A *or* B,' the difference between A and B can be resolved only through dissolution, conflict, war, or the violence in which one subordinates or obliterates the other." The result is a different kind of subject altogether, flesh-and-blood, nonegoistic, constituted as "for the other": "In place of the self-enclosed Cartesian ego is the Levinasian ego disrupted, exiled from itself, contracted, exploded, but yet singular. It is now defined as a 'recurring to itself' in the very assignation to the other, as inescapable responsibility, 'ill at ease in one's own skin,' vulnerable, exposed—and thus also opened and capable of *giving*. 'Maternity' characterizes this 'for the other,' and it is sensibility as signification as material 'nourishing, clothing, lodging, in maternal relations, in which matter shows itself for the first time in its materiality' [*Otherwise Than Being*, 77]. Maternity, then, is the 'matrix,' the immediacy of the ethical, the very sense of 'the material.' "[21]

Levinas speaks from outside the structuralist/poststructuralist orbit. But even in the most hardened theorists, weaned on poststructuralism, now appears a return to "things silently gone out of mind and things violently destroyed." For example, in "Blues and the Art of Critical

Teaching," Jim Merod writes against a perceived sacrifice of "modes of feeling" and endorses R. P. Blackmur's essayistic contention that "criticism . . . is the formal discourse of an amateur." As he proposes the blues as an effective means of deconstructing "the master's commanding voice," Merod argues for due recognition of the passionate and its place in critical discussion: "Nearly doctrinal in its unspoken tenacity has been the sense of separation or exclusion by which 'things intellectual,' things related to theory and critical practices, have been detached from things seen and heard passionately. I mean not so much that intellectuals in our era have not written about the arts; they have. I mean that the force of music and film and painting and dance have seldom been allowed to collide, and intersect surprisingly, with conceptual and critical activity." [22]

In such discussions, however, the basic orientation remains poststructuralist. Even so, there appears renewed interest in the subject (if not yet the self) and especially its agency. Take, for instance, John Schilb's "Poststructuralism, Politics, and the Subject of Pedagogy." Schilb goes so far as to praise both feminism for its stress on lived experience and autobiography as "a mode of classroom interaction." Declining to embrace an uncritical or pretheoretical notion of an independent, autonomous, and unmediated self, he nevertheless effects a return to an empowered subject. Thus he writes, for instance: "Trying to slough off the more deterministic tendencies of Foucault and Althusser, many theorists are in fact now emphasizing how resistance to hegemonic regimes and discourses is always present and at least potentially efficacious. This claim will not entail a romantic view of human beings as autonomous shapers of their own destiny, ultimately capable of surmounting all forces that hamper them." Schilb cites Paul Smith, author of *Discerning the Subject*, who proposes that "continued adherence to the notion of 'subject position' can on its own terms breed hope, since thinking of the various subject positions comprising one's identity can help one learn from their conflicts." [23] Schilb proceeds to a long critique of deconstruction's alleged simplification of "students' agency, background, and authority," singling out a book I coedited with Michael L. Johnson, *Writing and Reading Differently: Deconstruction and the Teaching of Composition and Literature*. He illustrates his objections via reference to several of the included articles, beginning with Vincent B. Leitch's "Deconstruction and Pedagogy." Zeroing in on one passage, Schilb objects that although it calls for revolutionary deconstructions of habitually accepted phenomena, it curiously fails to invoke human subjects who might perform these maneuvers. Although it cites many actions, it does not really specify their agents. Only once does the passage even allude to human beings, when it declares that "this teaching . . . must pass to students." Even here, though, it portrays students as recipients or objects of an action, not as agents of one. . . . [Moreover,] Leitch valorizes the "classroom discourse" of "deconstructive teaching" at the expense of attention to the particularities of context—the wide spectrum of purposes and situations and degrees of agency that students may experience during this discourse. . . . He in effect posits a generic student as well as a passive one.[24]

Schilb's points are telling, I feel their sting, having myself only recently returned to the personal.

In psychoanalytical criticism, the situation is clearer, as might be expected. Psychoanalysis has, of course, always acknowledged the analyst's interestedness and involvement in a structure that can only pretend to be objective. But now critics inspired by Jacques Lacan are foregrounding their personal engagement. In *Jacques Lacan: The Death of an Intellectual Hero*, Stuart Schneiderman, the only American ever to undergo training analysis with Lacan, recounts, with impressive narrative skill, his sessions with "the French Freud." He explains his book's form this way, referring to his decision to leave behind a career as an English professor and become a Lacanian psychoanalyst: "My transition, or passage, or translation, is the subject of this book. Rather than offer a critical commentary on Lacan's texts or an elaboration of his theory, I want to re-enact my experience of psychoanalysis with Jacques Lacan, rhetorically." Those who focus on Lacan's texts and elaborate on his theory similarly emphasize personal involvement. Shoshana Felman thus begins *Jacques Lacan and the Adventure of Insight* with this sentence, "I will start by recounting the peculiar story of my first encounter with Lacan's work," and goes on to say, "The very fact that I have started by telling you a story, to which I will return, the fact that in this introduction I will from time to time address the reader as 'you' while referring to my own voice as 'I,' itself partakes of a question that is meaningful with respect to crucial analytic issues that Lacan is specifically concerned with: issues such as dialogue and the performative psychoanalytical character of understanding and of knowledge as itself an act, a process of narration."[25] But having declared the primacy of storytelling, Felman qualifies the place of the personal, striking poststructuralist chords: "It should be understood, however, that the pronouns 'I' and 'you' are not merely personal but also metaphorical or allegorical. If 'I' and 'you,'" Felman continues, "are here, in practice, a pragmatic entryway into a theoretical (analytic) problematics, what they talk about should be approached with caution." Not surprisingly, then, we hear very little more about Felman. In *Reading Lacan*, we learn a good bit more, however, about Jane Gallop, who is not infrequently quite candid, the book refreshed and enlivened by a personal air throughout. Gallop discusses, for example, the "great impression" made on her by a reader's (negative) report on an earlier version of her book, includes an "Interstory" describing her own experiences in analysis, and concludes with a "Postory" that has to do with a dream about Lacan and his response to her work.[26] For psychoanalysis, the personal thus asserts itself, and the story of its doing so must be acknowledged as a constitutive part of any analysis, critical or otherwise. That is, in fact, what all the fuss is about.

This seems to be the point that Tzvetan Todorov now embraces. Todorov has been since the 1960s perhaps the preeminent structuralist working in the field of literary criticism, the author of such acclaimed books as *The Fantastic: A Structuralist Approach to a Literary Genre*, *The Poetics of Prose*, *Theories of the Symbol*, *Symbolism and Interpretation*, and *Introduction to Poetics*. Having come under the influence of Mikhail Bakhtin and dialogical criticism, Todorov has undergone a significant change in perspective. That change, or development, he makes a subject of *Literature and Its Theorists: A Personal View of Twentieth-Century Criticism*. Not the first to do so by any means, Todorov now understands criticism as dialogue. As he explains it, in language unfamiliar to structuralism, certainly phonocentric and "metaphysical," and echoing Martin Buber: "Dialogic criticism speaks not about literary works but to them, or rather with them; it refuses to eliminate either of the two voices involved. The text under study is not an object that must be taken in hand by a 'metalanguage,' but rather a discourse that is met by the critic's own; the author is a 'thou' and not a 'he,' an interlocutor with whom one discusses human values." Paralleling Geoffrey Hartman's longstanding call for a critical style "answerable" to the author's, Todorov now believes—surely it is an understatement—that "the form of one's writing is . . . not without importance, since this form must authorize a response, and not mere idolatry."[27] He describes the form of his own book as "nothing but a *Bildungsroman*," suggesting a certain if tentative near-crossing of critical text into the realm of "the primary" or art: his book is, he says, provocatively, "a novel of apprenticeship—and moreover one that remains unfinished." All nine chapters, he claims, for all their differences in subject matter "relate my own personal history." And indeed what the dustjacket blurb calls Todorov's "personal, self-reflexive method" produces one chapter that consists of correspondence with the historian of the British novel Ian Watt and another presented as a conversation with the *écrivain* Paul Bénichou. Avoiding the dogmatism that he rightly ascribes to simple monologic commentary, Todorov thus achieves the dialogic, at least in these chapters. As with so many other critics, the personal is another matter. The "I" certainly appears—the exchange of letters with Watt and the dialogue with Bénichou, as well as in the crucial last chapter, where, Todorov writes, "I take myself as its object"—but the autobiographical impulse is restrained.[28] And there is, to be sure, the self-realization that comes of certain critical or theoretical discoveries, but the focus resides in the criticism or with the trajectory that marks the development of Todorov's *thinking* (emphasis on this last term, not the man). No hint appears of what lies close to Todorov's heart, beyond—and this is important, of course—his deep and earnest commitment to truth as possible only via the dialogic. We have trouble, Europeans and Americans alike evidently, in talking about ourselves in our critical writing. And that critical writing, no matter how much it *argues* for the personal, remains pointedly unessayistic in form.

To their credit, feminists have for years been engaged in a personal criticism that is truly personal and confessional, often quite candid in its self-revelations. However you choose to date the irruption of feminist criticism—the short view might take 1968, with the publication of Mary Ellman's *Thinking about Women*, followed two years later by Kate Millet's *Sexual Politics*, though a longer view would trace those beginnings at least as far back as Virginia Woolf's classic *A Room of One's Own*—feminist criticism has enacted a return to the personal. It is no less true for being commonplace to say that for feminists the professional *is* the personal; that is, "the professional can't be separated from the personal."[29] The personal, therefore, also becomes the political, the ground on which the struggle for recognition and equality is to be fought, as well as the ground to be fought for, the personal being the arena of deepest value and meaning. No matter how undervalued and devalued, sometimes dismissed, discounted, and even subjected to ridicule, personal experience counts for something. And we may only now be beginning to awaken to the fact, though feminists have long known it, and though in their hearts women have always known it.

The admitted difference between the personal and the professional we (males) have turned into an opposition, and where there is opposition, there is hierarchy, a lesson taught by Derrida and deeply felt (because experienced) by women. The personal is not merely associated *with* women, it is widely regarded *as* feminine: domestic perhaps, certainly smacking of emotion if not of passion, and private—but more, of little or no significance in the worlds of criticism, learning generally, business, politics, and so forth. Almost—or so you can get this sense—an unmentionable, like that monthly visitation, the personal had best be kept out of serious discussion, where the coolness and supposed objectivity of reason can be expected to hold sway. Associated with women, the personal can spot, contaminate, ruin. It has no business being injected into serious discussion. It's okay in its place, and that place is clearly and tightly circumscribed. It is not serious criticism.

This separation of the personal from the professional is strictly maintained by academic conventions. Frances Murphy Zauhar draws an accurate picture of the situation. "I and many other women have been taught that the heightened sensitivity, the heightened feeling, the sense of relationship developed through our girlhood reading," she begins, "have no place in our professional lives."

> Many of us—when we decided to leave the world of the leisurely reader to become English majors and then English professors—learned that the way we responded to literature as professionals ought to be authoritative, objective, and engaging, but that we should not focus on ourselves as readers or on the way that a particular book may have affected us personally. The language of enthusiasm, of heightened sensitivity, had no place in our professional writing and was not involved in an articulate, perceptive analysis of/response to literature. We might write in strong words about our subject, we might even be enchanting in the arguments we make, but if we are personal, intimate, if we try to create for our readers, or between our readers and ourselves, the affiliation we feel with texts most important to us—we will be emoting, we will not be working, we will not be writing criticism.[30]

Whether or not it was the first such effort in the mode Zauhar hankers for, Rachel M. Brownstein's *Becoming a Heroine: Reading about Women in Novels* (1982) is an impressive, sophisticated attempt to bring together the personal and the professional; it is, in fact, sometimes said to have set the standard, if it did not exactly provide a model, for all such further attempts. It is also apparently the first book-length attempt in criticism to return to the personal. Treating the various ways women take to heart the experiences of fictional heroines, Brownstein relates her own engagement with the heroines of Jane Austen, *Villette*, *The Egoist*, *Daniel Deronda*, *The Portrait of a Lady*, and *Mrs. Dalloway*, an involvement that prompted her critical effort. As Brownstein puts it, she has

> chosen novels that develop the ideas about heroines that interest me. And I
> talk about myself, to begin with, so as to admit outright that that interests
> me, and to suggest that some of my interpretations have been determined by
> my life at least as much as my life has been determined by novels. My first
> chapter acknowledges what Freud nicely termed "the family romance"—the
> fantasy of being the son or daughter of royalty, in other words a more spe-
> cial person of a higher social class—is involved in the appetite for romances.
> By starting off with a sketch of where I came from, I also want to emphasize
> that the idea of becoming a heroine is private and personal, and to insist that
> just as realistic novels depend on real life, life may depend on novels.[31]

The starting point is, in fact, an essay entitled "My Life in Fiction," a beautifully woven quilt of autobiography and genuine critical reflec- • tion, nuanced, rich in detail, and suggestive if not exemplary for personal criticism.

What Brownstein perhaps inaugurated, Blanche Gelfant pursued, in *Women Writing in America: Voices in Collage* (1984). Though hers is by no means a slavish imitation—her interests, evidently much more than Brownstein's, lie in subverting "traditional standards and forms" and opening the canon—Gelfant shares Brownstein's assumption that "the reader's 'personal involvement' with the text is central."[32] Her book con-sists of twelve chapters, offering engagements with American women writers as diverse as Ann Beattie and Meridel Le Sueur, Willa Cather and Margaret Mitchell, Anzia Yezierska and Jean Stafford. Each of these chap-ters is prefaced by an autobiographical note in which Gelfant "reiterates the personal importance of each writer to her and the empowering effect that the personal sense has on her reading." This sense of the personal, far from "clouding her perspective or dimming her vision," the effect feared or at least claimed by proponents of impersonal criticism, actually "sharpens her perceptions of what each writer attempts," and so she "sees evoking relationship rather than maintaining detachment as an alternative and positive way of reading well."[33] The individual critical discussions themselves mingle the personal and the critical, in the main successfully.

Judith Fetterley takes the reader's response further than do either Gelfant or Brownstein. I refer not to Fetterley's well-known *The Resisting Reader* but to her *Provisions: A Reader from Nineteenth-Century Women* (1985), an anthology that appends her own history of reading the included texts. What I mean is that in introducing each of the sixteen anthologized selections, ranging from the unfamiliar to the neglected (Maria W. Stewart to Rebecca Harding Davis, Harriet Prescott Spofford to Harriet Beecher Stowe), Fetterley talks about them by talking about herself *in relation to* them. This surely constitutes the direction critical writing will take in the years just ahead—and must if it is to maintain even professional interest: repeating the exasperated protests "against interpretation" of Susan Sontag in the 1960s and Jonathan Culler in the 1970s, I maintain that we do not now need yet more explications of Swift, Keats, and Henry James, whether New Critical or structuralist, deconstructive or New Historicist. I'm not at all sure we *need* any explications or interpretations. The question, that is, is not of need, though professional pride has long led us to suppose or dream of a public deficit that we as critics would address and fill. Instead of a lack in the addressed public, I propose that we think of exciting an interest, whetting an appetite. Such a (changed) perspective would shift emphasis from *their* lack or need to *our* responsibility to interest and engage, perhaps to create (rather than to fill).

That new and different perspective entails, indeed requires, the radical changes Fetterley says she underwent in the course of working on *Provisions*. In "A Personal Note on Process" included in her introduction to that volume, Fetterley explains: "In the process of working on women writers, I had changed my critical persona, style, function, and stance from 'masculine' to 'feminine.' I had exchanged the authoritative for the tentative, the impositional for the instrumental, and the antagonist for the lover."[34] She had, it seems, found the essayistic, if not the essay.

Despite the efforts of feminists, however, the pressures to depersonalize continue, often barely relieved, and these pressures weigh equally on the established, on academic stars and "super-stars," and on untenured faculty and graduate students. Insidiously, they become internalized and thus rationalized. A case in point is Jane Tompkins, whom I cited earlier, a well-known scholar of American literature, an author of widely respected articles and books, the editor of the enormously successful anthology *Reader-Response Criticism*, and a professor of English at Duke University. In "Me and My Shadow" (1987), Tompkins speaks up and out. Confessing to an increasingly uncomfortable and demoralizing self-division, a split between her heart and her mind, between competing sets of wants, needs, and allegiances, one prominent, the other silent and seething, Tompkins voices the (feminist) desire to combine the public and the private, the professional and the personal. Her words are strong, passionate, and moving—when I first read them, largely unfamiliar with feminist efforts, they struck with revolutionary force:

> The problem is that you can't talk about your private life in the course of doing your professional work. You have to pretend that epistemology, or whatever you're writing about, has nothing to do with your life, that it's more exalted, more important, because it (supposedly) *transcends* the merely personal. Well, I'm tired of the conventions that keep discussions of epistemology, or James Joyce, segregated from meditations on what is happening outside my window or inside my heart. The public-private dichotomy, which is to say the public-private *hierarchy,* is a founding condition of female oppression. I say to hell with it. The reason I feel embarrassed at my own attempts to speak personally in a professional context is that I have been conditioned to feel that way. That's all there is to it.[35]

Tompkins proceeds to elaborate on this second, if not quite secondary, other voice, perhaps the "other" of criticism: "The thing I want to say is that I've been hiding a part of myself for a long time. I've known it was there but I couldn't listen because there was no place for this person in literary criticism. The criticism I would like to write would always take off from personal experience, would always be in some way a chronicle of my hours and days, would speak in a voice which can talk about everything, would reach out to a reader like me and touch me where I want to be touched. . . . I want to speak in what Ursula Le Guin called the mother tongue."[36]

Tompkins then quotes Le Guin. The voice Le Guin describes as the mother tongue, the one that Tompkins wishes to empower, is that of the essay, though neither Tompkins nor Le Guin mentions the essay and its striking difference from that described and impoverished "father tongue," which sounds to my ears very much like the voice of the article (as well as of most classrooms). Here is Le Guin:

> The dialect of the father tongue that you and I learned best in college . . . only lectures. . . . Many believe this dialect—the expository and particularly scientific discourse—is the *highest* form of language, the true language, of which all other uses of words are primitive vestiges. . . . And it is indeed a High Language. . . . Newton's *Principia* was written in it in Latin, . . . and Kant wrote German in it, and Marx, Darwin, Freud, Boas, Foucault, all the great scientists and social thinkers wrote it. It is the language of thought that seeks objectivity.
>
> . . . The essential gesture of the father tongue is not reasoning, but distancing—making a gap, a space, between the subject or self and the object or other. . . . Everywhere now everybody speaks [this] language in laboratories and government buildings and headquarters and offices of business. . . . The father tongue is spoken from above. It goes one way. No answer is expected or heard.
>
> . . . The mother tongue, spoken or written, expects an answer. It is conversation, a word the root of which means "turning together." The mother tongue is language not as mere communication, but as relation, relationship. It connects. . . . Its power is not in dividing but in binding. . . . We all know it by heart. John have you got your umbrella I think it's going to rain. Can you come play with me? If I told you once I told you a hundred times. . . . O what am I going to do? . . . Pass the soy sauce please. Oh, shit. . . . You look like what the cat dragged in.[37]

In "Me and My Essay," Cheryl B. Torsney takes personal criticism a step beyond Tompkins. "How," she asks, "would I describe a literary criticism written in my own voice?" and proceeds to answer as follows: "It would sound, I suspect, more like an informal essay than like a tight, comfortless piece of academic prose."[38] Unlike Tompkins, then, Torsney links personal criticism to the essay, effectively drawing an analogy between that form and quilts, as I have done above: "A literary criticism written in my own voice might look more like a quilt, pieced together, than like what we recognize as an academic article." At its heart would beat the personal: "A literary criticism written in my own voice would begin with the personal, not with the history of received critical thought on the text at hand because I want people to know that my deep, real, personal response to a work of literature is a valid register of the strength of the writing. For me."[39]

Torsney proceeds to enact the personal criticism she has described. Hear her set the stage for that discussion:

> In other words, I want to make visible, hearable, tastable, touchable experiences that constitute my reading contexts. Reader-response theory tells us that a text can only mean insofar as the reader constructs a conversation between herself and her text, yet reader-response based theories rarely focus on the reader's side of the conversation, particularly on the intimate relationship among her many narratives of self, which insinuate themselves in the reading experience, thus creating a peculiar intertextual construct. But in the academy, where the distant, not the personal, is the privileged discourse, the personal, the self-disclosing embarrasses. When a critic gets personal, as Rachel Brownstein does in *Becoming a Heroine*, her writing is deemed eccentric or otherwise peripheral to "real" academic discourse. When Alice Walker writes of her private search for Zora Neale Hurston's grave in "Looking for Zora," Walker's work is relegated to the essayistic rather than elevated to the critical.

Torsney's aim in this essay is thence "to initiate a conversation with my reader, to tell her or him . . . about my context for reading and teaching Alice Walker's short story 'Everyday Use.' " [40] This she does by narrating the story of her encounter with Lucille Sojourner, a black inmate of the psychiatric hospital at the Mississippi State Penitentiary, who makes Torsney think of Sojourner Truth. A white, northern, Jewish intellectual, Torsney met this woman while teaching at Delta State University and working on quilting as a metaphor in women's writing; she had heard of Sojourner's quilt making from her husband, Jack, who at the time worked at the hospital. With such details, and those of her first meeting with Sojourner in the prison cafeteria, Torsney makes understandable and vivid, if not exactly "visible, hearable, tastable, touchable," this personal experience. Sojourner's story, as Torsney recounts it, is one of commitment to the art and craft of quilting: she "quilts all day every day, taking time out only for trips to the bathroom. . . . Constantly working—it makes the time pass—she can piece a top in a week and quilt it in three days." Why do it, Torsney asks her: " 'It gives me constellation,' she responds unhesitatingly. What a wonderful concept, I thought: quilting as consolation enlarged and exploded into cosmic fact. Her art not only allows Lucille to maintain her sanity—her word, not mine—it also gives her a star-like quality: fiery, sparkling, solitary, and distant. Those attributes shine as she tells me, disgustedly, of the guard who has asked her to quilt an already-pieced cover for free, since she is a convict with time on her hands. Lucille is clearly insulted, noting that she is studying for her Graduation Equivalency Diploma." Of course, the real answer Torsney comes to realize later, possibly in the course of writing her essay, at any rate presented her with a nice pun: in quilting, Lucille Sojourner "establishes her own parole from the general language of art and humanity."[41]

Torsney proceeds to explain how meeting Lucille Sojourner altered her "entire understanding" of Walker's "Everyday Use." But the relation of the one to the other, that meeting and the short story, does more; like all good criticism, "Me and My Essay" asks what the critic wants and endeavors to show the difference reading makes. In considering in a new light the emotions prompting Walker's character, with some direct experience of the fictional situation, Torsney realizes she

> must reevaluate my own desire to meet Lucille Sojourner, to commission her to make me a quilt. Am I trying to forge some feminist link between races and regions? If so, then I am as criminal as the flashy sister [in Walker's story] who is trying to "preserve" her past in the sterile, academic hanging out of the family linen as though it were a formal blazon. And who is the prisoner? Is it really Lucille, or am I a prisoner of some inadvertently racist dream of equality, of a liberal philosophy that is oh, so easy to maintain from my position as an educated white woman who can come and go at will? Am I hostage to trends in literary theory and feminist criticism that create the interest in quilting in the first place? Moreover, if I'm the real inmate, why don't I dare a prison break?

Whatever the answer to those hard questions, Torsney's "whole notion of 'everyday use' was transformed by [her] own sojourn to Parchman Farm."[42] In fact, she writes, the cover Lucille Sojourner quilted for her, "patched in primary colors and backed in the bright red of Isis, the goddess of creativity, is that narrative that now gives me parole, passing down to me, as it were, like Maggie's quilts [in Walker's story], her stories for everyday use." And Torsney, in turn, passes down her story, hoping, moreover, to encourage her readers, in their turn, "to respond with their own experiences of the text so that they will enrich my context, allow me to stitch the reading histories into my own critical text of the narrative."[43] Torsney has not only raised difficult and uncomfortable questions about herself and her motives in seeking out Lucille Sojourner, but she has also brought her understanding of life and literature into a position of reciprocity and mutual enlightenment.

AS THEY RESIST (masculinist) professional conventions, feminists, or at least many of them, adopt alternative modes, forms, and styles of discourse. Diane Freedman has rationalized this procedure in the following terms: she utters the lament of many women, but perhaps all too few men, when she writes of being "caught in the crossfire between cold, competitive, critical writing on the one hand, and personal, even confessional, creative responses to literature and life on the other"; she proceeds to enunciate a refusal any longer to be "co-opted by the usual critical conventions of impersonality coupled with one-upmanship and the linear 'logic' which keeps the poetic and personal from the professional and theoretical." Olivia Frey, similarly, disavows "discourse conventions" that include "the use of argument as the preferred mode of discussion, the importance of the objective and impersonal, and the importance of a finished product without direct reference to the process by which it is accomplished."[44] Though neither Frey nor Freedman says so, nor does anyone else I am aware of save Cheryl Torsney, what feminists are objecting to is the article, the exclusive style of academic discourse: linear, argumentative, competitive, and driven by the desire of mastery.

Open, collegial rather than competitive, nurturing, uninterested in winning—these and other related "maternal" values many feminists now seek to transfer to, represent, and embody in their writing. Laurel Smith thus reminds us that Adrienne Rich some time ago "imagined a world that celebrates affiliation over competition," and Brenda Daly now writes, "It was, and still is, kinship that I want to create through words. . . . And yet it seemed that, within the conventions of academic discourse, spoken or written, only the 'warrior' self, the armored and competitive self, were possible." Form thus assumes particular and great importance for this writing that is often, even largely, autobiographical. With some irony, as well as with quite deliberate defiance, women are taking up those forms that at least once and for a long time were branded as womanly and so devalued as serious literary performances, forms such as the journal and the diary, which indulge the private and the personal.

Violet Weingarten's *Intimations of Mortality*, posthumously published by Knopf in 1978 and prefaced by Robert Gottlieb, is one striking instance of artistic and enduring achievement in this personal form, response considerable to those who would relegate the journal or diary to secondary or tertiary status or worse. More recently, and daringly, Barbara Ryan has undertaken a dissertation in journal form, in which she recounts her desires, the opposition she encountered, and her own struggles with her two voices, having "internalized the pressure to depersonalize," which causes wrenching doubts and fear as she proceeds, seeking to return to the personal.[45]

"Intimate Criticism: Autobiographical Literary Criticism" spotlights some of the current feminist experimentation with form. That volume significantly includes a chapter of critical commentary on Virginia Woolf entitled "Saturdays, Kitchens, and Motorcycles: 'Life in the Usual Sense' " and presented as an informal and wide-ranging conversation among Michelle Johnson, Pam Marshall, and Linnea Stenson. It begins thus: "There are many women in a kitchen on a Saturday. Three of us are white lesbians, graduate students, workers—all from a middlebrow background. We position ourselves on stepstools. Gathered with us, the remaining women are present yet invisible—a combination of our inside and our outside selves participating with Virginia Woolf, 'thinking in common . . . thinking by the body.' "[46]

The *locus classicus* of feminist experimentation with literary form, at least in this country, is probably Rachel Blau DuPlessis's "For the Etruscans," first published in 1981. Exactly what lies behind such experimentation DuPlessis makes clear as she herself seeks to embody—and empower— a "female aesthetic," which would be, unlike prevailing forms, noncompetitive, nonaggressive, nonlinear, even contradictory, often lyrical, in short, different. She ascribes a "both/and vision" to this effort, explaining it in the following passage, itself redolent in style of the desired aesthetic:

> This is the end of the either-or, dichotomized universe, proposing monism (is this really the name for what we are proposing? or is it dialectics?) in opposition to dualism, a dualism pernicious because it valorizes one side above another, and makes a hierarchy where there were simply twain.
>   a " 'shapeless' shapeliness," said Dorothy Richardson, the "unique gift of the feminine psyche." "Its power to do what the shapely mentalities of men appear incapable of doing for themselves, to act as a focus for

divergent points of view. . . . The characteristic . . . of being all over the place and in all camps at once. . . ."
A both/and vision born of shifts, contraries, negations, contradictions; linked to personal vulnerability and need. Essay and sermon. (I don't mean: opportunistic, slidy.) Structurally, such a writing might say different things, not settle on one, which is final. This is not a condition of "not choosing," since choice exists always in what to represent and in the rhythms of pre-sentation. It is nonacademic; for in order to make a formal presentation, one must have chosen among theses: that is the rhetorical demand. Cannot, in formal argument, say both yes and no, if yes and no are given equal value under the same conditions. Either one or the other has to prevail. But say, in a family argument? where both, where all, are right? generates another mode of discourse.[47]

"For the Etruscans" has drawn praise both for its arguments and for its expressive form. One can certainly understand and sympathize with the desire for and the drive toward a "female aesthetic," present since at least Virginia Woolf's embrace in *A Room of One's Own* of a "woman's sentence." But the risks here, I think, are considerable—though worth taking. What I refer to, what worries me, is the temptation to bring it all down to this: to *express yourself*. That understandable, even laudable, wish for freedom too often translates as indulgence, giving free rein to the natural willfulness and wildness of prose. Form, style—they can easily come to be seen as repressive, as part of the male hegemony under which women have long suffered and against which the "female aesthetic" and personal and autobiographical criticism now bravely fight. Feeling, or content, is thought to matter most, above all else, it being mistakenly sup-posed that *that* can be separated from style, form, expression. You express yourself best, however, when you lavish attention on the writing, when the *how* joins with the *what* to effect something of more than momentary interest. Form and style allow so-called self-expression to transcend itself and become something more and other, something of value to someone besides the author. Successful writing need not, of course, very often it does not, conform to inherited or traditional styles and modes, but it does require that you know the forms that are available: *estranging the familiar* is the name of this game too.
I know of no one who has said it better than Annie Dillard. In *The Writing Life* she describes powerfully, and essentially, the judgment, courage,

pain, and travail needed to turn "notions," however worthy in and of themselves, into words, sentences, and paragraphs deserving of a reader's properly hard-won attention. The writing changes, she says, in skilled and attuned hands, "and in a twinkling, from an expression of your notions to an epistemological tool. The new place interests you because it is not clear. You attend. In your humility you lay down the words carefully, watching all angles. Now the earlier writing looks soft or careless. Process is nothing; erase your tracks. The path is not the work. I hope your tracks have grown over; I hope birds ate the crumbs; I hope you will toss it all and not look back." I'll quote one more paragraph of this strong writing about writing, for it too is essential, given the pride that accompanies the movement of the pen or the pressing of typewriter or computer keys, shadowing the work of every writer; the emphasis must be on *the work* (as Phyllis Theroux noted in the account I cited earlier): "Courage utterly opposes the bold hope that this is such fine stuff the work needs it, or the world. Courage, exhausted, stands on bare reality: this writing weakens the work. You must demolish the work and start over. You can save some of the sentences, like bricks. It will be a miracle if you can save some of the paragraphs, no matter how excellent in themselves or hard-won. You can waste a year worrying about it, or you can get it over with now. (Are you a woman, or a mouse?)" [48] Hard to take, this advice, unflattering to our vanity, chilling to the heart—because it's true, and we know it.

Thus it is that I worry some about the claims made on behalf of the "female aesthetic," autobiographical literary criticism, and, more simply, experimentation (by feminists and others alike). I worry when I read, in "For the Etruscans," the following devaluation of art and the judgment and control Annie Dillard extols: "The holistic sense of life without the exclusionary wholeness of art. These holistic forms: inclusion, apparent nonselection, because selection is censorship of the unknown, the between, the data, the germ, the interstitial, the bit of sighting that the writer cannot place. Holistic work: great tonal shifts, from polemic to essay to lyric. A self-questioning, the writer built into the center of the work, the questions at the center of the writer, the discourses doubling, retelling the same, differently. And not censored: love, politics, children, dreams, close talk. The first Tampax in world literature. A room where clippings paper the wall." [49] I prefer Annie Dillard. For writing that is uncensored by the writer's own sharpest blue pencil, that has not passed through the fires of revision and literary judgment, is more licentious than free verse, more indulgent and easier than playing tennis with the net down. It is freedom gone amuck, unanswerable, and irresponsible. It is certainly not literature.

THE RECEIPT, as I was writing this chapter, of Mary Ann Caws's *Women of Bloomsbury: Virginia, Vanessa, and Carrington* heartens and encourages. Caws entitles her opening chapter "Personal Criticism and a Matter of Choice," providing as epigraph from Virginia Woolf the words "to suggest, not to conclude." Caws's effort here recalls Carolyn G. Heilbrun's remark, in *Writing a Woman's Life*, that she has been inspired by "the danger we are in of refining . . . theory and scholarship at the expense of the lives of the women who need to experience the fruits of research." At any rate, Caws proceeds to describe her work this way, echoing at least some of Cheryl Torsney's desires: "Above all I intend this to be an example of personal criticism as I am trying to work that concept through. Personal criticism as I intend it has to do with a willing, knowledgeable, outspoken involvement on the part of the critic with the subject matter, and an invitation extended to the potential reader to participate in the interweaving and construction of the ongoing conversation this criticism can be, even as it remains a text. The experience is open and fluid, as in the transcription of the implicit conversation. 'We are the music, we are the thing itself,' says a character in Virginia Woolf's *The Waves*; readers, critic, and subject here can echo that belief, according to which they work." Caws adds that "what personal criticism aims most urgently at creating and recreating" is "that very participation in the subject seen and written about, soliciting, quietly or openly, the reader's own views." The point is a good one: "I see this," she writes, "as a three-way concern, and prefer to think of writing *along with*, rather than writing on, or about." [50]

Turning to the particulars of her study—Virginia Woolf, her sister Vanessa Bell, and Dora Carrington, one of them a great writer, another an acclaimed painter, two of them bisexuals, two of them artists living with gay men, two of them suicides—Caws writes, "I have wanted to present—from closer up than any brand of impersonal criticism would suggest or even allow—with love and warmth and respect toward their lives and works, these women of Bloomsbury, with whom, over the years, I have become so personally involved." About that involvement, and especially its relation to the kind of criticism she now practices, Caws explains:

> As the art of personal criticism requires a willingness—an eagerness, even— to be more than a simple observer of a subject, so the act of personal criticism requires a certain intensity in the lending of oneself, in the giving of a role to the past of the artist as to the textual present and the possible future, to the elements inside and outside the mind, unafraid as they are of mingling. It is around such an experimental generosity of community that characters in and out of the text may find themselves grouped, reading together, seeing together. Such criticism is the deliberate opposite of a cool science, but is not in disregard of fact; it is composed of an unshakeable belief in involvement and in coherence, in warmth and in relation.[51]

There is so much in this to admire, applaud, emulate, and envy that it may seem churlish to quarrel, but quarrel or at least qualify I must. As heartened as I am in general by this thoughtful embrace of personal criticism, especially its implicit acknowledgment of critics' "writing *along with*" and so striving toward art themselves, I am disappointed with Caws's self-representation. Unfortunately, that is, she promises more than she delivers. This is what she says about her own obviously deep and abiding engagement with and involvement in her subject: "As an advocate of this kind of personal criticism and life-telling, I feel deeply obliged, in my own relation to it and of it—bound both by my project and my most fundamental belief—to make an open statement about my involvement in the issues aroused. Towards our understanding of one well-known writer and two lesser-known figures, this personal advocacy of freedom and unjudgmental evaluation wants to contribute what it can, based on my own intensity of feeling." What follows, that announced "open statement," ultimately described as writing "still more drastically in my own name," is remarkably nonrevealing, not distanced to be sure, but restrained, still scholarly in tone, baring too little of the heart's stirrings that I at least have come to desire and solicit—and that, at least on occasion, the contributors to "Intimate Criticism," for example, are willing to reveal, whatever their inadequacies as sculptors of prose.[52] It is not easy, whether you are a woman or a man, a Mary Ann Caws or a Geoffrey Hartman or a Tzvetan Todorov, to write a truly personal criticism or to offer a book of experiences or confessions.

96

My own predilection, long ago apparent, I reckon, lies with a courageous criticism that records personal encounter, evincing an author's or a text's power and the reader's powerful, whole response: a responsive because personal criticism. If the text is not thereby illuminated for another reader, the resultant writing surely doesn't deserve to be called literary criticism. If, on the other hand, the experiencing, responding critic is not interestingly and effectively represented, I don't know why anyone else would want to read him or her or should be expected to do so. What I solicit, therefore, is "a brief, highly polished piece of prose that [may be] poetic, [sometimes] marked by an artful disorder in its composition, and that is both fragmentary and complete in itself, capable both of standing on its own and of forming a kind of 'higher organism' when assembled with other essays by its author. Like most poems or short stories it should be readable in a single sitting; readable but not entirely understandable the first or even the second time, and rereadable more or less forever."[53] That is, of course, the essay, enlisted in the service of literary commentary: for us professionals, accustomed to the article as our primary if not sole mode of discourse, *the familiar estranged.*

CHAPTER SIX

Toward an Answerable Style: Critical Experiments and Artful Criticism

A well-known writer got collared by a university student who asked, "Do you think I could be a writer?"

"Well," the writer said, "I don't know. . . . Do you like sentences?"

The writer could see the student's amazement. Sentences? Do I like sentences? I am twenty years old and do I like sentences? If he had liked sentences, of course, he could begin, like a joyful painter I knew. I asked him how he came to be a painter. He said, "I liked the smell of the paint."

Annie Dillard, The Writing Life

When we encourage experimental critical writing, we do not always know what we will get, but we stimulate the profession to grow and to change. We don't control the future of the profession only when we give grades or make hiring or tenure decisions; we control it at the level of the sentence.

Marianna Torgovnick, "Experimental Critical Writing"

ALTHOUGH he is by no means a feminist, and although he does not engage in personal criticism, despite some statements seemingly to the contrary, Geoffrey Hartman echoes many of the dissatisfactions with academic writing we encountered in the preceding chapter. Since at least 1975, as a matter of fact, Hartman has animadverted against the limitations and reductiveness of "plainstyle" criticism. Invoking the notion of "answerable style," he argues that critics are "scared to do anything except convert as quickly as possible the imaginative into a mode of the ordinary." Although he grants that he "may be overstating the case," Hartman contends that "the spectacle of the polite critic dealing with an extravagant literature, trying so hard to come to terms with it in his own tempered language, verges on the ludicrous." The problem is that criticism "does not show enough of itself while claiming to show all."[1] Not wanting to "appear," or "come out," the interpreter or critic may settle for being "a pedagogue, or what Blake calls a 'horse of instruction,' " or if not that, he or she may become one "who judges only in order not to be judged." In the latter event, the critic's unanswerable "relation to art is like that of Man, in Blake, to the Divine Vision from which he has shrunk into his present, Rumpelstiltskin form."[2]

In response to this psychoanalytically charged situation, Hartman proposes, and offers, "creative criticism," especially the critical essay as "intellectual poem." "Not extraliterary, not outside of literature or art looking in," criticism is, on the contrary, Hartman passionately argues, within it, "a genre with some constant and some changing features." It is now, he believes, writing in *Criticism in the Wilderness* in 1980, "changing its form and occupying more intellectual and creative space."[3] Like Theodor Adorno, whom he much admires and in much resembles, Hartman calls into question "the very boundary between criticism and creation, without, however, ever effacing it entirely" (he continues to believe in, he avers, "the separation of genres," as of "the distinctness of the sexes").[4] For Hartman, the relation of criticism to creation is symbiotic. There is no longer a "master-servant relation between criticism and creation," then, with the former merely subservient. But if a renewed "creative criticism" "liberates the critical activity from its positive or reviewing function, from its subordination to the thing commented on," it does not, in Hartman's view, absolve it of responsibility to the inspiring or calling text (I have labeled Hartman's a reader-responsibility criticism).[5] The question may thus be how to reconcile the idea of the essay "with the rigor that evaluative or historical criticism should ideally bring to its subject."[6]

This book constitutes my effort to address that question. In what follows in the present chapter, I look at the possibility of an "answerable style" for criticism, especially some experiments in criticism. My own suggestion perhaps represents a counterstatement to Hartman: I agree with him that responsible criticism will appear in and as an "answerable style," but I am also interested in restoring emphasis to the art in the embraced ideal of the critical essay as "intellectual poetry." Without, I hope, unduly minimizing or reducing the intellectual, conceptual, and theoretical, where Hartman's (different) emphasis lies, I have argued that the way to success runs through the personal—and only through it. Embrace of the personal will certainly enliven and may well empower critical writing, exciting interest hitherto unarousable, but by itself it lacks the strength to revitalize it. Something else is needed, and that is nothing else, or less, than art. To be a writer, and not merely a critic, means more than "writing as a person with feelings, histories, and desires," as important, indeed, necessary, as that be.[7] As they come to be figured in criticism, these must be expressed with the narrative skill and craft of expression, the nuanced sensitivity to detail, the metaphorical gymnastics, and the familiar employment and development of character that we associate with literature. And literature is, I am maintaining, exactly what criticism must strive to become.

In so saying, I go against the grain of some of our most cherished beliefs. Not only do I run counter to powerful professional assumptions, longstanding and seemingly impregnable, but I also affront the beloved views of nonacademic critics and "creative" writers (for example, Octavio Paz, recent recipient of the Nobel Prize for literature). But as novel and abhorrent as it may seem, the notion that criticism is art, or at least can and should be, is neither new, the product of poststructuralist dehierarchizing, nor alien to right-thinking folk. I cite three perhaps surprising instances of the latter. The essayist Samuel F. Pickering, Jr., no liberal he and certainly no friend of theory, wrote not at all begrudgingly not so long ago in the *Sewanee Review*, itself a stalwart of conservative critical opinion: "although some misanthropes have said that literary critics are just honey-dippers gone uptown and wearing fancy pants and perfume, most 'right-thinking' people recognize that literary criticism, though receiving its nourishment from other literary forms, can be an art." Richard McKeon echoes the point, appearing less tentative, in fact. McKeon was a distinguished scholar of literature and the history of rhetoric and a founding member of the "Chicago School," a neo-Aristotelian: "the discussion of art is itself an art, and is, in many analyses, possessed of the same characteristics and directed to the same end as the artist treats." And then there is the curmudgeonly H. L. Mencken, writing in no uncertain terms in the *New Republic* in 1921:

> Nearly all the discussions of criticism that I am acquainted with start off with
> a false assumption, to wit, that the primary motive of the critic, the impulse

which makes a critic of him instead of, say, a politician or a stockbroker, is pedagogical. . . . This is true, it seems to me, only of bad critics. . . . The motive of the critic who is really worth reading . . . is not the motive of the pedagogue, but the motive of the artist. It is no more and no less than the simple desire to function freely and beautifully, to give outward and objective form to ideas that bubble inwardly and have a fascinating lure in them, to get rid of them dramatically, and make an articulate noise in the world. . . . Everything else is after-thought, mock-modesty, messianic delusion.[8]

The *locus classicus* of the argument Mencken and I and others advance is probably Oscar Wilde's "The Critic as Artist," fictively presented as a dialogue involving "Gilbert" and "Ernest," who are not so much characters—they are distinguished only by their arguments—as names. They represent strikingly different positions, Gilbert arguing for the critic as artist, Ernest arguing (rather meekly) against. Gilbert apparently carries the day, although in light of Wilde's penchant for irony it may be a *literary* question as to which argument the author himself endorses or how far he subscribes to either. Gilbert's main contention, and probably Wilde's too, is that, tradition and perhaps common sense notwithstanding, criticism is not just equal but superior to creation.

"Criticism is itself an art," Gilbert proclaims. "And just as artistic creation implies the working of the critical faculty, and, indeed, without it cannot be said to exist at all, so Criticism is really creative in the highest sense of the word."[9] Gilbert professes to be "amused by the silly vanity of those writers and artists of our day who seem to imagine that the primary function of the critic is to chatter about their second-rate work."[10] In fact, he announces, criticism is independent as well as creative and so "no more to be judged by any low standard of imitation or resemblance than is the work of the poet or sculptor. The critic occupies the same relation to the work of art he criticises as the artist does to the visible world of form and color, or the unseen world of passion and of thought."[11] Like poetry, explains Gilbert, criticism "works with materials, and puts them into a form that is at once new and delightful"; it is thus "a creation within a creation." Moreover, because it is "the purest form of personal impression," criticism "is in its way more creative than creation, as it has least reference to any standard external to itself, and is, in fact, its own reason for existing, and, as the Greeks would put it, in itself, and to itself, an end." For Gilbert, criticism derives from the soul; "that is what the highest criticism really is, the record of one's soul," not unlike the way in literature we encounter "soul speaking to soul." He recalls Sir Philip Sidney's defense of poetry in claiming that criticism "is more fascinating than history as it is concerned simply with oneself. It is more delightful than philosophy as its subject is concrete and not abstract, real and not vague. It is," he goes on, connecting criticism and the critic's life but in a way different from recent feminists, "the only civilised form of auto-biography, as it deals not with the events, but with the thoughts of one's life; not with life's physical accidents of deed and circumstance, but with the spiritual moods and imaginative passions of the mind." [12]

To Ernest's mild objection, Gilbert acknowledges another theory of criticism, by now familiar enough, which contends that its "proper aim" is "to see the object as in itself it really is." But this, retorts Gilbert, is "a very serious error": it "takes no cognisance of Criticism's most perfect form, which is in its essence purely subjective, and seeks to reveal its own secret and not the secret of another. For the highest Criticism deals with art not as expressive but as impressive purely." Nor, importantly, does criticism "confine itself . . . to discovering the real intention of the artist and accepting that as final." After a while, Ernest reconfigures the argument Gilbert is developing in these pointed terms: "The highest Criticism, then, is more creative than creation, and the primary aim of the critic is to see the object as in itself it really is not." Here I part company with Wilde, or at least Gilbert, much preferring Hartman's "responsible" position on "creative criticism": "the situation of the discourse we name *criticism* is . . . no different from that of any other. If this recognition implies a reversal, then it is the master-servant relation between criticism and creation that is being overturned in favor of what Wordsworth, describing the interaction of nature and mind, called 'mutual domination' or 'interchangeable supremacy.'" [13] Unfortunately, Gilbert accepts Ernest's extremist description of his theory and proceeds apace to his central declaration: "To the critic the work of art is simply a suggestion for a new work of his own, that need not necessarily bear any obvious resemblance to the thing it criticises. The one characteristic of a beautiful form is that one can put into it whatever one wishes, and see in it whatever one chooses to see; and the Beauty, that gives to creation its universal and aesthetic element, makes the critic a creator in his turn."[14] Later Gilbert grudgingly concedes that "some resemblance, no doubt, the creative work of the critic will have to the work that stirred him to creation, but that resemblance," he carefully explains, "will be such resemblance as exists, not between Nature and the mirror that the painter of landscape or figure may be supposed to hold up to her, but between Nature and the work of the decorative artist." Gilbert then concludes as follows: "so the critic reproduces the work that he criticises in a mode that is never imitative, and part of whose charm may really consist in the rejection of resemblance, and shows us in this way not merely the meaning but also the mystery of Beauty, and, by transforming each art into literature, solves once and for all the problem of Art's unity."[15]

It is one thing to *argue* that criticism is creation, quite another to be able, as Wilde was, to *write* criticism worthy of the term "art," a point that should give us pause. Hartman has suggested that "the creative spirit" has shown itself in "Hegel's *Lectures on Aesthetics*, Ruskin's *Queen of the Air*, Pater's *Renaissance*, Erich Auerbach's *Mimesis*, [and] certain essays of Barfield, Lukács, Benjamin, and Derrida." But the indwelling of some perhaps romantic "creative spirit" does not guarantee artistic accomplishment nor equate with literary achievement. Accomplishment may appear easier if we slide from the designation "artful" to that of "literary." Can we agree with Hartman that the essays of Friedrich Schlegel, Valéry, and Ortega (if not quite of Freud or Heidegger) constitute "intellectual poetry" deserving of both honorific terms? Can we also accept as "literary texts in their own right," thus belonging to the realm of letters, such "experiments as Norman O. Brown's *Closing Time*, Harold Bloom's *The Anxiety of Influence*, Maurice Blanchot's *Le pas au-delà*, Derrida's *Glas*, and Barthes's *A Lover's Discourse*"? The problem is, according to Hartman, that we "have narrowed the concept of literature."[16] That I grant, but I would not want us, in haste to redress an imbalance, to designate as literary what is merely severe, experimental, or strains to the breaking point the notion of the critical. For a critical text to deserve the epithet "literary," it should not lack those qualities of form, style, substance, appeal, and significance that we associate with art and always have.

If there are, in the history of criticism, many texts with various literary features, precious few, unfortunately, deserve to be called art. Pope's *Essay on Criticism* is one that does. This magnificent poem combines the wit of poetry with the judgment required of criticism. In fact, in this instance wit serves judgment neither more nor less than judgment serves wit—and that happy reciprocity confirms me in the belief that the highest criticism (I take Wilde's term) is that that combines the artful and the judgmental, the literary and the critical. It is in, through, and by means of *An Essay on Criticism* itself that Pope earns the right to speak as a critic— at least that is the poem's argument—for as he puts it: "Let such teach others who themselves excell,/ And *censure freely* who have *written well*." This advice or dictum is as stern, necessary, and worthy of heed now as three hundred years ago. Delivering critical commentary in poetic form, significantly called an essay, Pope thus literalizes the artfulness of criticism and so the literary and artful nature of the essay. If he thereby set a standard nigh on impossible to attain, *An Essay on Criticism* nevertheless points the way and inspires us, at least it does me, to hanker after a genuinely *literary* criticism.

WHETHER OR NOT they have aspired to art in their critical writing (some no doubt have), let alone attained that distinction (fewer have succeeded), many critics have experimented with form. What we might call, from the hegemonic vantage point of the scholarly, or definite, article, experimental critical writing has a long, distinguished, and indeed venerable history, by no means limited to the feminist-inspired embrace of such "alternative" forms as autobiography, diary, and journal. That history traces an arc that runs from Plato through Dryden to Virginia Woolf and on to a clearly increasing dissatisfaction with professionally sanctioned forms.

Some explanation of, and a rationale for, such experimentation was given by Marianna Torgovnick in the fall 1990 *ADE Bulletin*, which carries the imprimatur of the Modern Language Association, of which the Association of Departments of English is a "subsidiary." Although Torgovnick does not specifically mention Jane Tompkins, clear echoes of "Me and My Shadow" may be heard in "Experimental Critical Writing" (which is not surprising, if for no other reason than that both teach at Duke University). Like Tompkins's, Torgovnick's essay—or so I will denominate it—recounts her growing disenchantment with a long-favored style that "censored my own experiences and visceral responses and that hid my writing's source of energy." Here, of course, she echoes those feminist critics we heard in the previous chapter. It was a considerable struggle,

but assisted by what she calls her "newly formed writing group," Torgovnick eventually arrived at "a place where I was not afraid to write in
a voice that had passion as well as information—a voice that wanted to
be heard." This new, stronger, more personal, passionate style, she now
writes, "meant letting myself out of the protective cage of the style I had
mastered—a style I now call the thus-and-therefore style because it naturally tends to include distancing words like those. Before I could change
my thus-and-therefore style, I had to defamiliarize it; I had to know my
cage so that I could open it at will"—in other words, *estranging the familiar*.
To break out of that reductive, confining style not only was difficult but
also took time and effort. Hard-won (Torgovnick confesses to writing
"excruciatingly bad" prose "roughly eighteen months" after vowing to
leave her old style behind), her new style is fluid, easy, and attractive, if
we can judge by "Experimental Critical Writing." [17]

Crucial to more successful, livelier, and more interesting writing than
at present marks literary commentary, argues Torgovnick, is not just the
personal but an adjustment in our self-conception: the critic must start
thinking of him- or herself as "a writer, not just a critic." That difference
entails the earlier-mentioned desire "to be heard," to reach that larger,
perhaps "general" audience that I have maintained we should seek to
interest. What Torgovnick says, elaborating, gives cause for hope: "When
critics want to be read, and especially when they want to be read by a
large audience, they have to court their readers. And the courtship begins
when the critic begins to think of himself or herself as a writer, a process
that for me, as for some other critics of my generation, means writing as
a person with feelings, histories, and desires—as well as information and
knowledge. When writers want to be read they have to be more flexible
and take more chances than the standard scholarly style allows: often,
they have to be more direct and more personal." About this last point,
Torgovnick adds, again connecting with the voices and desires we heard
in the last chapter, "In a very real way (although my writing includes
precious few autobiographical revelations), I could not think of myself
as a writer until I risked exposing myself in my writing." Not exactly a
feminist, despite sharing certain desires and insights, she proceeds to indicate some qualified difference from the "autobiographical literary critics"
we earlier encountered. "I am not talking here, necessarily," she writes,
"about full-scale autobiographical writing—though I am not ruling it out

either. But I am saying that writerly writing is personal writing, whether or not it is autobiographical. Even if it offers no facts from the writer's life, or offers just a hint of them here or there, it makes the reader know some things about the writer—a fundamental condition, it seems to me, of any real act of communication. And real communication is exciting. For me, at any rate, the experience of this new kind of writing—which not only recognizes the pitfalls of the standard academic style but goes out of its way to avoid them—has been exhilarating." [18]

Those are Torgovnick's concluding remarks, but I want to go back and pick up her sage advice concerning experimental critical writing, necessary, she maintains, for professional health and vigor. She is well aware, as all too few unfortunately seem, of the importance of style. "When we pass on the academic style to our graduate students or newest colleagues, we train them to stay within the boundaries, both stylistically and conceptually. When we encourage experimental critical writing, we do not always know what we will get, but we stimulate the profession to grow and to change. We don't control the future of the profession only when we give grades or make hiring or tenure decisions; we control it at the level of the sentence." [19] I would add, by way of elaboration or perhaps qualification, that what matters is both the kind of sentence encouraged and honored (the essayistic or that of the article) and its quality (whether it aspires toward, even if it does not achieve, the artistic level). It is, in any case, the sentence with which we must start. I also think, contrary to Torgovnick, that a revitalized critical writing will bear considerable traces of the writer's life; otherwise, it makes little sense to talk of a recovery of the personal or to suppose that a large readership will be successfully courted.

THE CRITIC perhaps most readily identified with experimental writing is Ihab Hassan, a pioneering student of postmodern fiction and one who in his own writing has assimilated that style. The most experimental of Hassan's many books is no doubt *Paracriticisms: Seven Speculations of the Times* (1975). The term "paracriticism" may or may not owe something to Dryden's distinction among metaphrase, paraphrase, and imitation, paraphrase being defined in part as "translation with latitude," representing "the liberty, not only to vary from the words and sense, but to forsake them both as [the translator] sees fit." Hassan himself defines "paracriticism," not in altogether dissimilar fashion, as "an attempt to recover the art of multi-vocation. Not the text and its letters but metaphors thereof. Not a form strictly imposed but the tentativeness between one form and another."[20]

In what he calls a "Personal Preface" (as variously evidenced he too, like Torgovnick, participates in "the return of/to the personal"), Hassan elaborates on the idea of paracriticism as something that exists *alongside* commentary, and indeed he expresses a desire "to break out of criticism." Clearly, Hassan's desire is to find a voice—and to be a literary artist. Referring to the "speculations" comprising *Paracriticisms*, he writes: "I am not certain what genre these seven pieces make. I call them paracriticism: essays in language, traces of the times, fictions of the heart. Literature is part of their substance, but their critical edge is only one of many edges in the mind. I would not protest if they were denied the name of criticism. Perhaps I should simply say: in these essays I write neither as critic nor scholar—nor yet impersonate poet, novelist, or playwright—but try to find my voice in the singular forms that speculation sometimes requires. Yet what, finally, is singular? Every voice is cursed by its echo, blessed by an answer this side of mortality."[21]

The issue is not one, insists Hassan, of "criticism imitating art; it is rather one of writers using the resonances of their voices, the values of their lives."[22] Thus conceiving of himself as a writer, and not (merely) a critic, Hassan offers in *Paracriticisms* writing that is indeed experimental. Specifically, in line with postmodern fiction, it engages in "playful discontinuity," frequently having the feel of such collage as some feminists admire. Instead of straightforward argumentation there is speculation; instead of linear advance, juxtaposition. Hassan seeks in *Paracriticisms* to body forth the postmodern view that criticism "should . . . become itself less than the sum of its parts. It should offer the reader empty spaces, silences, in which he can meet himself in the presence of literature."[23] The book thus exploits "typographic variation and thematic repetition, serialism and its parody, allusion and analogy, query and collage, quotation and juxtaposition."[24]

As an example of Hassan's play or experimentation I cite the following passage, reproducing its typographical play, from the chapter "The New Gnosticism: Speculations on an Aspect of the Postmodern Mind," evidently offered as a prose poem:

The theme of this
       paracritical essay
              is   the growing
              insistence of Mind
to apprehend reality im-mediately;
to gather more and more mind
              in itself;
              thus to become
              its own
              reality.
Consciousness becomes all.
And as in gnostic
        dream,
             matter dissolves
                  before the
    Light.[25]

But, of course, consciousness is not all, nor is unmediated access to things possible, a point demonstrated by, among others, Geoffrey Hartman, as early as 1954.[26] For Hassan, modern-day Gnostic, language exists as hardly more than a transparent pane, a pain that might, or so he dreams, sometime, somehow, be removed. And as to such experimentation with form: I find myself thinking of Hartman's disparaging reference to "certain, let us call them unisex, experiments in critical writing"; they "weaken," he argues, "the task of interpretation by spicing it up with parafictional devices."[27]

But if he may be said to employ a style answerable in its highjinks to postmodern iconoclasm, Hassan seems hardly more interested in Hartman-like rigor than in the notion of the essay. Responding in kind— that's what Hassan is doing, as he parallels postmodern novels, his commentary existing *alongside* them as a postmodern text. Hassan's experiments alert us that the idea in and of itself of an "answerable style" is not enough—unless we find those experiments more appealing than I expect. There remains the matter of the sentence and, encompassing it, the question of art. What is needed is something more meaningful and substantial than a text jazzed up with various so-called literary devices. We need a critical essay crafted with care, invested with the "suggestive power" Virginia Woolf extols, and capable not merely of withstanding a second reading but of soliciting one return after another, so interesting is it as prose.

THE MOST COMMON and, arguably, the most important experimental literary criticism is one of several versions of "fictive commentary." That term I borrow from Cynthia Ozick, who means something rather specific by it, namely "a literature of *midrash*": "Jewish writing, . . . whether or not developed by Jews," claims this artist in prose, this lover of sentences, equally gifted as maker of essays and of fiction, "was that literature which dared to introduce into the purely imaginative the elements of judgment and interpretation."[28] Which is, of course, what Matthew Arnold, he who recognized the value in combining Hebraism and Hellenism, sought in calling for a literature of "imaginative reason." It is also what Pope wrought in and as *An Essay on Criticism*, bringing together wit and judgment, poetry and criticism, indeed one as the other.

By "fictive commentary," I mean something less specific than Ozick, though it might include that combination of the imaginative, the judgmental, and the interpretive that she has in mind (her own redaction of the Ruth story from the Old Testament stands as a powerful instance of this, framed by a beautifully rendered autobiographical account, sensitive to rabbinical exegesis of the eighty-five verses, and empowered by the critic-novelist's ability to get inside Ruth, her mind and heart, and so to elaborate on her story, so much can imagination effect).[29] By "fictive commentary" I refer to the increasingly popular effort, marked by considerable variety, to render criticism in a fictional context or setting. Wilde's "The Critic as Artist" belongs here, even though setting is not there specified and even though the characters Gilbert and Ernest are, I have claimed, largely ciphers. Belonging here too, and representing a fuller discharge of fictional opportunities, are Plato's dialogues, imaginative as well as analytical and rigorous, consisting of a realized setting, plot (including discovery and climax and perhaps peripateia), and the dramatic encounter of developed characters, the most fully drawn of whom, of course, is Socrates himself. A later and well-known example of this kind of "fictive commentary" is Dryden's *Essay of Dramatick Poesy*. This "essay" consists of witty, gentlemanly conversation among four speakers, who debate the relative merits of such topics as the Ancients and the Moderns;

the British and the French; the "last age" and the present; the rules; just-ness and variety in drama; and the value of rhyme in serious plays. The setting is at once concrete and symbolic: 3 June 1665, and Crites, Euge-nius, Lisideius, and Neander, all of whom stand for historical persons, the last for Dryden himself (Neander = new man), are on a barge, drift-ing down the Thames, past Greenwich, as shots ring out from the naval battle being fought in the Channel between the British and the Dutch invaders. The war present as background contextualizes and accentuates the literary discussion, framing it and emphasizing its significance within the large arena of Britain's claims to political, economic, and literary as-cendancy. Criticism and politics here are interimplicated, as morality and criticism are in Pope's *Essay*.

"Fictive commentary" must be judged, I would think, not just on how well it does what it sets out to do but also according to what the ex-perimental form accomplishes that conventional procedure could not, that was perhaps unavailable to it or even precluded by it. In the case of Dryden's *Essay*, criticism transcends itself to become art. We read the *Essay of Dramatick Poesy*, as we do *An Essay on Criticism*—at least I do—fully as much as a piece of compelling imaginative writing as a critical docu-ment, whose arguments may now be dated and seem of little more than historical interest. But what of other, somewhat similar experiments?

In *Swinburne: An Experiment in Criticism* (1972), the critic-editor-theorist Jerome J. McGann directly addresses this issue. His experiment involves the dialogue form and for specific, necessary reasons, or so he argues. "For Swinburne, as for a number of other literary figures," McGann writes, "it has become increasingly difficult to practice any of the varieties of pure formal analysis or polemical New Criticism and to remain, at the same time, critical of one's own judgments." This last point being cru-cial, McGann turns to the familiar tradition of the dialogue, in order, as he puts it, "to reopen the discussion of Swinburne from a slightly altered perspective." His discussions "proceed from a variety of approaches, some historical, some psychological, some textual. Within these various ap-proaches, alternative attitudes toward each general method are always present, while the several analytic methods are themselves subjected to a continuous critique from different quarters." McGann's described pro-cedure, or critical form, differs from that of the Socratic dialogues in that "a master's voice has been dispensed with," all the characters' positions being "subjected to the implicit or, in many cases, explicit criticism of the others engaged in conversation" (the six dramatis personae, by the way, are earlier scholars of Swinburne, all now deceased, McGann making relatively free with the representation of their ideas).[30] Deliberately, *Swinburne: An Experiment in Criticism* "lacks the appearance, if not the premeditation and design, at least of a singleness of purpose"; there is, then, nothing "definitive" here, McGann avers about this essayistic effort, neither the "developed argument" nor the "structured presentation characteristic of most works of literary scholarship." Any conclusiveness *Swinburne* attains, continues McGann, is "related, somehow, to the emphatic and, as it were, fatal lack of any single generalizing conception," and such an idea, moreover, "is neither expressed philosophically nor embodied in a single character nor implied in any set of notions reasonably deducible from the whole."[31] Rather than to the Socratic dialogues, then, McGann's experiment in criticism relates to Friedrich Schlegel's *Dialogue on Poetry*, which is quite essayistic in temperament, neither master nor pupil long residing in a position of authority but, instead, engaging in such "mutual domination" or "interchangeable supremacy" as that that Wordsworth describes in *The Prelude* and that Hartman regards as constitutive of the literature–criticism relation. McGann concludes his apologia for this experiment in dialogue with strong words directed at what we might call, although he does not, the assumptions, procedures, and style of the professional article, co-dependent with analytical knowledge: "this work has been written in a spirit of earnest self-parody—not because the subject does not seem to deserve the most serious sort of attention, but because the critical act is of all things the most dangerous necessity of art. The dialogue form has been adopted because it illustrates, in a dramatic and recreative fashion, the absurd limits of analytical knowledge."[32]

SOME VARIETIES of fictive commentary much more fully engage the fictional than do such experiments with dialogue as we have noticed, though few more directly or closely justify their efforts than does McGann in *Swinburne*. An entire spectrum exists, ranging from texts that enlist fiction in the service of criticism to those that, in different ways, enlist criticism in the service of storytelling. The line between fiction and criticism toward the middle of the spectrum blurs, and it becomes difficult if not impossible to distinguish an essay from a short story or to decide

III

whether, in a particular text, the emphasis lies with the criticism or the fiction. We classify Gordon Lish's "How to Write a Poem" and "How to Write a Novel" as short stories, as we do Lorrie Moore's "How to Become a Writer." Lish and Moore are, after all, celebrated as imaginative writers, as writers of fiction. But so is Amy Hempel, and so is Tim O'Brien, and yet when the *Alaska Quarterly Review* published the former's "The Day I Had Everything," it was represented as a story plus commentary, and O'Brien's "How to Tell a True War Story" is included in *The Bread Loaf Anthology of Contemporary American Essays*, whose editors describe it in fact as "a short story . . . written in the guise of an essay" and as "an intriguing use of the essay voice."[33] Yet instinct, or perhaps it's literary judgment, leads us to denominate as fiction such texts, along with the complex discussions of writing fiction by Cees Nooteboom and by Peter Handke in *The Afternoon of a Writer*. Despite the deliberate blurring of boundaries, and the often-intriguing mixture of commentary and fiction in such work, we feel, with various degrees of assurance, that the imaginative weighs more heavily than the critical.

In the remaining pages of this chapter I want to look, rather briefly, at some other, generally more complex and problematical fusions of fiction and commentary. Again, I pretend to no exhaustiveness of treatment. These texts occupy widely different places on the spectrum that encompasses commentary and fiction, some perhaps better being labeled "interpretive fiction" than "fictive commentary," not exactly a nitpicking distinction, as I hope you will agree.

I begin with Austin M. Wright's *Recalcitrance, Faulkner, and the Professors*, which might be considered a variation on experimentation with the dialogue form. A novelist, critic, and professor, Wright calls this work "a critical fiction," although the fiction seems finally in the service of the criticism. Set up as a debate at an imaginary university involving various characters, who are by no means crudely drawn, the book centers on current theory, related issues, and the kinds of response generated. Not surprisingly, the personal gets involved, and not just in the power struggles and turf battles between the tenured and the untenured, those sympathetic and those hostile to theory, but also in the love interest that develops and energizes the hero, Charlie Mercer, smitten with wealthy graduate student Eve Birdsong, whose curiosity concerning theory prompts the discussions constituting Wright's uneasily titled book. *Recalcitrance, Faulk-*

ner, and the Professors consists not just of conversations but also of written exchanges, including position papers, with *As I Lay Dying* serving as focus and test case.[34]

A different kind of experimentation, another variation of fictive commentary, is represented by Herbert Lindenberger's *Saul's Fall,* which purports to center on the work of one Orlando Hennessey-Garcia, a drama "in seventeen episodes," said to be edited by Milton J. Wolfson, who provides "an authoritative text with relevant background materials and essays in criticism," this amounting to more than 250 printed pages. A respected scholar, comparatist, and professor at Stanford University, Lindenberger pretends to have written only the foreword. At least for those interested in academic criticism and scholarly procedures, *Saul's Fall* is a veritable *tour de force,* an elaborate and extensive play on an imagined text and its supposed problems and opportunities, covering the range of professional involvement and response, from the biographical to the textual and on to the interpretive and critical. It is part of a well-established fictive and often-parodic tradition that runs through Borges's fiction to Carlyle's *Sartor Resartus* and Pope's *Dunciad* and Swift's *Tale of a Tub,* texts that are, differently, both commentary and fiction. Another close example is Nabokov's *Pale Fire,* published in 1962, ten years before *Saul's Fall.* Termed a novel, *Pale Fire* consists of similar, if not so extensive, critical and technical apparatus: a foreword, signed by Charles Kinbote, to a poem in four cantos said to be the work of John Francis Shade, which is followed by more than two hundred pages of commentary and an elaborate index.

If *Pale Fire* is a novel, and *Saul's Fall* a critical parody, Virginia Woolf's *A Room of One's Own,* first published in 1929, is criticism that borrows from fiction, uses it to make points as exciting as they are telling, to achieve powerful effects unavailable to purely discursive prose, and thereby—at least it is my judgment—to become art. Seminal for women's studies as it remains important for criticism, this slender volume of six chapters— Woolf calls it an "essay"—ponders, in the context of women writing, why men have always had money, power, and influence while women have had none, lacking even a room of their own in which to work. Occasioned by an invitation to Woolf to speak about women and fiction, this deeply felt and carefully pondered book describes what has "no existence": it tells the story, that is, and explores the implications, meaning, and effects of a visit to "Oxbridge" by a narrator about whom Woolf says that "'I' is only a convenient term for somebody who has no real being. . . . Call me Mary Beton, Mary Seton, Mary Carmichael or . . . any name you please—it is not a matter of any importance." [35] What *is* important is the exactness, subtlety, and power with which Woolf renders that visit to the fictional Oxbridge, where the "I" is shamefully denied access to the library—because she is a woman. This event, which cuts to the heart and sears the soul, activates the mind and generates a series of deep and passionate reflections on women and "the writing life."

In *A Room of One's Own*, wisdom and humanity combine with emotion not so much to control it as to keep it from becoming bitterness, resentment, and hatred—and to direct it instead toward art, producing writing resonant and successful because of both the fire burning within and the form given it, the way Woolf shapes experience and sentences alike, never indulgent or careless of her readers, in fact as sensitive to and respectful of them as of language and the shape it assumes in her sentences ("a book," she writes, "is not made of sentences laid end to end, but of sentences built, if an image helps, into arcades or domes"). [36] All the while, Woolf remembers what women (and essayists of both sexes) continue to hear—"the perpetual admonitions of the eternal pedagogue," who speaks now for professional conventions: "write this, think that"— and of course, write this in this particular way, with this tone, this kind of sentence, a sentence impersonal and abstract, the virtual opposite of Woolf's. [37] It is, precisely, "the power of suggestion" that Woolf brings to commentary: not discursive logic, nor really the rigor of analysis, though her reflections are close and careful, but imagination. She evokes, rather than argues: "when a book lacks suggestive power," writes Woolf, "however hard it hits the surface of the mind it cannot penetrate within"— a powerful evocation of writing at once feminine and essayistic. [38] For her, the aim is always "to use writing as an art, not as a method of self-expression" (though the therapeutic value of writing should not be discounted). [39] Woolf's may be as close as we have come to the last word in "fictive commentary."

Far more fictive is the commentary that figures prominently in the work of the late Argentinian writer Jorge Luis Borges. Intent on erasing "the old distinctions among fiction, poetry, and essay," he produced dozens of short stories built around issues of reading and writing, some of which masquerade as critical commentary, and numerous essays that approach, involve, or, a few of them, become virtually indistinguishable from fiction—what we might call estranging the familiar from both directions.[40] Into the former category fall some of Borges's best-known works, including "Tlon, Uqbar, Orbis Tertius" and "Pierre Menard, Author of *Don Quixote*," as well as "The Approach to Al-Mu'tasim," all published in *Ficciones*. An account of "Menard's" work, the second of these, more complicated than "The Approach to Al-Mu'tasim," could well be taken for straight literary criticism—except that it too is all made up. The story represents a plausible enough, if extreme, literary-critical endeavor. What Menard wanted, devoting his life to the endeavor, was not to write "another *Don Quixote*—which would be easy—but *the Don Quixote*," not "to produce a mechanical transcription" of Cervantes's novel (1605) but, instead, "to produce pages which would coincide—word for word and line for line—with those of Miguel de Cervantes." This effort would acknowledge and respect historical, cultural, and biographical differences—they, indeed, lie at its very heart, fueling desire. Suppositious erasure of such differences, moreover, seemed to Menard "less arduous—and less interesting—than to continue being Pierre Menard and to arrive at *Don Quixote* through the experiences of Pierre Menard."[41] Borges concludes this intriguing story with the following critical remarks, directing attention, as so often in his work, stories and essays alike, to the question of reading: "Menard (perhaps without wishing to) has enriched, by means of a new technique, the hesitant and rudimentary art of reading: the technique is one of deliberate anachronism and erroneous attributions. This technique, with its infinite applications, urges us to run through the *Odyssey* as if it were written after the *Aeneid*, and to read *Le Jardin du Centaure* by Madame Henri Bachelier as if it were by Madame Henri Bachelier. This technique would fill the dullest books with adventure. Would not the attributing of *The Imitation of Christ* to Ferdinand Celine or James Joyce be a sufficient renovation of its tenuous spiritual counsels?"[42]

If such stories are woven of literary commentary and indeed masquerade as one or another kind of criticism, some of Borges's essays—many of the best of them available in the English translation *Other Inquisitions, 1937–1952*—"are closer to fiction than to conventional criticism."[43] Among these essays blurring the distinction between commentary and fiction, as "The Approach to Al-Mu'tasim" does from the other direction, is "The

Enigma of Edward FitzGerald." This brief essay consists of two virtually equal parts; the first treats Omar Khayyám, the eleventh-century Persian poet, and the second, his translator of *The Rubáiyát* seven hundred years later. The point again concerns sameness and difference and especially the "metaphysical" conjecture that "perhaps the soul of Omar lodged in FitzGerald's around 1857. . . . Speculation (its technical name is pantheism) would permit us to think that the Englishman could have re-created the Persian, because both were, essentially, God—or momentary faces of God." At any rate, "The Enigma of Edward FitzGerald" concludes with the following critical assessment, more speculative and daring no doubt than most commentary but perhaps even more estranging of the short story: "All collaboration is mysterious. That by the Englishman and the Persian was more mysterious than any because the two were very different and perhaps in life they would not have become friends; death and vicissitudes and time caused one to know the other and made them into a single poet."[44]

In the Borgesian mode belongs Carlos Fuentes's tribute to the late master, the wonderfully titled "Borges in Action." By no means a simple imitation, this—what to call it? fictive commentary? interpretive fiction?—blends commentary and fiction at greater length, more elaborately, and in even more complex fashion. The result is the most sophisticated example I know of the fusion of these two genres.

A novelist of power and fame, Fuentes opens with a detailed description of a chance meeting, in Mexico City, between his narrator and an enigmatic blind man, mesmerizing in the way that "he seemed to be literally looking inside himself, as if this were the only thing that counted in matters of sight—seeing outside himself being a totally frivolous affair."[45] For some reason, I think of Alice Walker's "Looking for Zora," itself an unfamiliar, perhaps defamiliarizing approach to literary commentary, although Fuentes's is a much more complex and difficult attempt to "find" an author, an author complex and difficult. At any rate, what follows in "Borges in Action" is a story that takes us into the very heart of Borges's world, into what he saw, blind. In certain ways, it goes beyond Borges, taking him a step further, for he and his fiction become the focus of this fiction: they constitute the story Fuentes tells.

That story continues as the narrator follows the blind man home, where they encounter Erasmus, importantly for this story the author of *The*

Praise of Folly (the street *is,* after all, Amsterdam Avenue, so related are things in this world, though the nature of the relation is the question). They encounter him just in time, for, believing that "all the wisdom of the world is contained in thirty-two volumes," he is about to cast into the fire a book entitled *The Aleph* (one of Borges's, of course). His book saved, the blind man himself tells a story of his "rival" in literature and love, one Carlos Argentino Daneri, significantly "not a poet but a land surveyor," handicapped because his only eyes are physical, or so "Borges" claims.[46] According to "the blind man who called the narrator of his story Borges," this Daneri, "for all his stupidity, was a writer who had to face the seasons of discontent, trying to wrest language out of the order of succession and into the order of simultaneity, where he might contemplate his own action as if it were a painting."[47] The blind man, Borges, having announced, "We have left the world behind," we are soon transported to the worlds of Borges's fiction, including the famous, or infamous, Tlon, Uqbar, and Orbis Tertius. About that created—or seen—world, "Erasmus" makes this analysis: "We are being offered by our fleeing blind friend two, and why not three, six, nine, infinite readings of the same text. Do you understand now?" he asks. "Not just your single, fateful past, or your single radiant utopian future; oh, no—but the infinitely shapable, re-creatable, prefigurable, but also retroactively diversifiable times of freedom."[48] Other revelations follow, what on another level would be called literary analyses or interpretations; for example, about Cervantes's and Menard's *Don Quixote*: "the text is the same, but the intention is different"; and this interpretation of the recurring Borgesian theme I noted above, offered by "Erasmus," who shows himself thoroughly conversant with the blind man's works even if they don't figure among the thirty-two volumes containing all the wisdom worth having: "The sum of all spaces can only be read by one man who is many men, but it could only be written by one writer who sees all writers, and his work, in consonance with this principle, could only be one work: one vast narrative in which space has been seen and defeated in and by the Aleph of Literature, an endless, multifarious, multi-cultural time taking over its space: space is only memorable when time occurs in it."[49]

In the end, Erasmus is "shrouded in the darkness of the cave," while Borges balances himself "above the cave on a tight wire, dressed in rags and with a colorful umbrella in his upraised arm," and the narrator is back on Amsterdam Avenue, where he "encounters" again one of those count-less "infinitely sad little boys . . . destined to grow up swallowing fire at selected intersections during a perpetual rush hour, in exchange for a few copper coins."[50] Should he wake him, the narrator wonders, hand him a few pesos, perhaps invite him to have "cake" with him—but then maybe he is "being dreamed": "What if that boy," after all, "is the child of the man who has dreamed him—a ghost that does not know its name? . . . the projection of another man's dream?" Wake him the narrator does, though he immediately regrets doing so, wishes that he "had left well enough alone. I swear to you," he says, "I never intended to wake myself up and see what I am now seeing."[51] Seeing is all, then, although seeing is in-separable from dreaming. Thus closes—"concludes" hardly seems right, nor does "ends"—a text in which creation and commentary, fiction and criticism, exist in almost perfect balance and play equal parts. Who can say that in "Borges in Action" the fiction exists for the service of the commentary rather than the commentary for the fiction? What we can say is that fiction (along with insight and skill, of course) allows Fuentes to accomplish in twenty pages what would require ten times or more of discursive prose.

Turning to Fay Weldon's *Letters to Alice on First Reading Jane Austen*, we find ourselves back on solid ground and in much more familiar terri-tory. Unlike Fuentes's story, Weldon's epistolary novel comforts rather than estranges. But it too manages to balance, albeit in distinct fashion, the claims of creation and commentary, offering at once a spirited and fresh defense of Austen and her enduring "relevance," a subtle and shrewd argument for the unparalleled pleasures and value of reading, and a deeply felt and sensitive insider's view of "the writing life." There is little doubt, however, that this is a novel. The plot consists, simply enough, of Aunt Fay writing mainly from Australia to her "niece," age eighteen and with hair black and green, trying to convince her of Austen's importance as she slogs through a university course in English literature. The situation is therefore pedagogical, for us as well as Alice, though it is particularly pleasurable instruction Weldon offers (here instruction has found "a way to become art, a pleasurable and responsive activity, 'the breath and finer spirit of all knowledge' [Wordsworth]").[52] So effective is Weldon that, even though we never hear directly from Alice, we feel we know her, as we do Aunt Fay—and thanks to her, Jane Austen and her novels.

Weldon says so much that is good and fine and necessary to hear: for example, describing "the kind of swooning, almost erotic pleasure that a good passage in a good book gives"; asserting that as a result of her "English literature course" at university Alice "will know more, but understand less," having "more information and less wisdom"; wisely speculating about readers needing happy endings and reading so as "to be told how to live" and about writing as *amateur's* work and, even more finely, as "the gathering in of connotations, the harvesting of them, like blackberries in a good season, ripe and heavy, snatched from among the thorns of logic." But the center of attention is always Austen and her novels, which Weldon treats one after another in their biographical, historical, and cultural contexts. She largely succeeds, I think, in establishing Austen's relevance and significance in a world grown increasingly impatient with the written word and too little familiar with the nuances of feelings and the centrality of personal relations. In Weldon's words, Austen "struggled to perceive and describe the flow of beliefs that typified her time, and more, to suggest for the first time that the personal, the emotional, is in fact the *moral*—nowadays, of course, for good or bad, we argue that it is political." [53] We thus need Austen lest we forget the moral force of the heart's stirrings.

Few have done a better job of confronting the world's skepticism about fiction's importance, especially its social function, and none that I know of has done a better job of answering the familiar complaint about Austen, infamous for treating a world of manners, isolated from history and politics, what Austen herself described as merely "a crowd in a little room." [54] To her credit, Weldon tackles the problem head-on: "Millions starving, then and now, I hear you protesting," she writes to Alice, who has decided to become an English major and is at work on a novel. "And Jane Austen! What *are* you going on about? All I can know is, plaintively, man, and especially woman, does not live by bread alone: he has to have books." To say as much goes only a short way, and Weldon immediately recognizes that she must do better. So she repeats the imagined question, only more pointedly: "what *are* you going on about? I hear you repeat. Why this reverence for Jane Austen, who was blind (in our terms) to so much?" Her answer, which is fresh if not exactly surprising, runs as follows: "The gentry, then as now, *has* to read in order to comprehend both the wretchedness and the ire of the multitude. It is not only ignorance in the illiterate we need to combat, it is insensitivity in the well-to-do. Fiction stretches our sensibilities and our understanding, as mere information never can." The "art of empathy" is what Weldon finds so wonderfully executed in Austen's novels—and what she herself effectively teaches both about and via that fiction. "I am not offering," she writes, "quite so severe a doctrine as Auden's—'we must love one another or die'—rather that we must learn to stand in other people's shoes and look at the world with their eyes, or die." [55] A romantic, an idealist, a dreamer, Weldon believes that if you know how it *feels* to fail, you will show mercy to those who do. That is often so; maybe it always is, though I have doubts, as I do about some other of Weldon's idealistic teachings. Their improbabilities make them all the more needful, however. Who can quarrel, who can but applaud and cheer, when she pens—the right word, for, praise God, she is no friend of either the typewriter or the word processor—such a sentence as the following: "You must learn to respect anything, even if only furniture, in which human care, effort and affection has been invested." [56] It may not top the list, but writing surely occupies a secure place among respect-ful human efforts.

A RANGE of experiments in literary criticism, a spectrum of opportunities—that's what we have observed in this chapter. We still have to ask what we have *really* learned, how far we have got. What form, in short, should a revitalized critical writing take? The possibilities, clearly, are several, if not infinite, and each seems to carry advantages and disadvantages. In my judgment, Fuentes's "Borges in Action" is the most complex, sophisticated, and technically brilliant of these attempted fusions of commentary and fiction. It may not, however, be the most satisfying, or the most successful. Dependent on the complex, sophisticated, and difficult texts of its subject, it is tough sledding, posing problems and mind games that intrigue and fascinate. But I'm not sure they engage the heart and soul, quicken the blood, excite even the muscles, or induce "the kind of swooning, almost erotic pleasure" that comes (for some of us) from reading Virginia Woolf or Cynthia Ozick.

This much seems unexceptionable: there appears no one quick cure, no single prescribed way for revitalizing critical writing. Some requirements are clear, nonetheless. If we think of writing that will be read, that will enlist the interest and care of an audience beyond the merely professional, we have to consider, as Marianna Torgovnick suggests, the sentence, its nature and shape. We have to do more, have to go beyond the sentence, as crucial as attention to that neglected level is. We have to think of tone, voice, and character, as well as "the power of suggestiveness" (Woolf), the very ingredients of literature. It's hard, very hard, to get away in this regard from the notion of the essay, which belongs with imaginative literature, experiments in literary criticism not necessarily and only occasionally. Given "the return of/to the essay," and its command of considerable interest, it seems at least reasonable for critical commentary again to give that protean form a chance, to consider anew the opportunities it makes available. Interpretive fiction is one thing, fictive commentary another. The essay remains capacious, artful, and increasingly attractive to a large audience. Might we (re)turn to it?

PART THREE

CHAPTER SEVEN

Some Adventures of the Soul:
A Journey around Essay

For those who have dwelt in depression's dark wood, and known its inexplicable agony, their return from the abyss is not unlike the ascent of the poet [Dante], trudging upward and upward out of hell's black depths and at last emerging into what he saw as "the shining world." There, whoever has been restored to health has almost always been restored to the capacity for serenity and joy, and this may be indemnity enough for having endured the despair beyond despair.

> *E quindi uscimmo a riveder le stelle.*
> *And so we came forth, and once again beheld the stars.*

WILLIAM STYRON, *Darkness Visible*

THE ESSAY may seem the most indulgent, the most self-centered of literary forms. Certainly more so than the novel or short story or drama, which mediate self-expression, objectifying feelings, thoughts, needs, and desires; but more so even than the lyric, where form—at least—works against self-indulgence, and the memoir, journal, or auto-biography, where both narrative and claims to truth ensure restraint. In the essay, instead of restraining the self, form, the slippery, slithery, protean nature of the thing, encourages waywardness and willfulness and actually gives the self seemingly full rein. The personal essay *is,* as Montaigne famously announced, about nothing else: "It is myself that I portray. . . . I am myself the matter of my book."[1]

The self on display in—better: created by—the essay is always on the move, frequently walking (think not just of Hazlitt's "On Going a Journey" but also of Edward Hoagland's "City Walking" and the work of Colin Fletcher), traveling, having adventures, be they with red wolves and black bears (Hoagland) or the texts literary and graphic, familiar and esoteric, that Guy Davenport visits. According to William Howarth, itinerancy constitutes an essential feature of the essay. As texts, writes Howarth, no mean essayist in his own right, essays "open doors, take to the road, launch a stream of discourse. Their authors begin and move out, heading for uncertain destinations, carrying readers through a succession of events that pass like the flow of experience. Essays provide us with safe passage to ideas, arguments, stories with characters and dialogue— always unfolded as an ongoing process."[2] Essays thus share something, whatever their ostensible subject, with travel literature, the picaresque romance, even the epic.

What happens to the self (or soul) in the course of—and as a result of—its adventures with "the stars, the snow, the fire" in the Northern Wilderness that is Alaska (John Haines), to Salman Rushdie in Nicaragua or V. S. Naipaul in the American South, searching for "our mothers' gardens" (Alice Walker), writing about writing (Annie Dillard)—this commands attention. I refer not merely to the plot of such different, but related, adventures, the narrative of people, places, texts, flora, and fauna encountered but, more important, to the effect of such encounters on the experiencing, *reading* self. Though none of those writers I have mentioned do, that self may begin as indulgent and egoistic, but in the end it emerges transformed, newly sensitized to otherness and capable of strong love. Travel, after all, not unlike critical commentary, brings you into contact with the Other.

But what about the essay?

IN ONE RESPECT, at least, a product of the sixties, I began teaching at the tail end of that Age of Relevance. In college I came to literature, and after wandering around, and occasionally skirmishing with, history and religion decided to major in English, because I encountered a teacher— Vincent E. Miller is his name—who *looks through* great novels and poems and for whom literature exists to give us eyes to see with and ears to hear with. I did not agree with Dr. Miller's conservative politics (he was enamored of Pound and, like his friend Hugh Kenner, wrote for the *National Review*, for which he once tried to recruit me), and I never have been able to grasp quite what he meant by the particular understanding a certain literary (and political) tradition makes available. But my God, what worlds he opened up! *What* Vince Miller taught now seems less important, though, than *that* he taught me to regard literature as a path to understanding. That the goal of reading novels, poems, plays, great nonfiction is enlightenment, insight into the heart and soul, awareness of meaning and significance, possibly—as he thought—understanding of an order built into the nature of things, objectively *there,* and apparent to eyes properly trained—this, or at least much of it, has remained with me, despite the best efforts of my very different graduate school teachers to turn me into an "old-style scholar." Lord knows, I have often enough forgotten, and even flouted, the commitments I piously announced in my Danforth and Woodrow Wilson applications for graduate fellowships. I have thus written as Vince Miller never would: as a "competitive scholar" (a term I picked up in graduate school), less interested in the understanding a great book bequeaths than in "the truth" concerning its provenance, historical context, or its author's intentions (an obvious positivist residue). I was afraid to challenge professional convention and write about what interests me and always has, which is the relevance—that word!— of what I read to my own life, the relation of a book or poem to "what is happening inside my heart or outside my window"—a personal criticism.[3] But, thank God, my teaching has remained more in touch with the ideals I took in at Wofford College, precious milk from that kindly mother's ample teats. I remember one student, at the height of my scholarly period fifteen years ago, writing on the course/instructor evaluation form: "unlike other teachers I've had, what matters to him is how literature relates to life." If not so well expressed, that compliment has served more than once to recall me to neglected possibilities, has helped bring me back around, reminding me of "home."

Even though I have failed to act on the desire, from lack of courage no doubt, I have always *wanted* to write directly about what we (can) learn from literature, how its particular and striking ways of teaching, by no means reducible to didactic content, open up fresh and unparalleled paths, bring into view new vistas, produce shocks of recognition that course through the blood and resound through the heart, making the skin tingle and the soul quicken. Approaching fifty, after twenty-plus years of teaching, I find myself more willing now to take risks. Job security, and some little professional stature, as well as age, no doubt contribute to this newfound penchant for assertiveness, or maybe it's just cantankerousness. For whatever reasons, I now find myself heading out on new journeys, trying on new garb, engaging in relationships, experimenting with forms I would not have dared only a few years ago. The essay, of course, encourages such adventures and, with its definitional focus on the personal, provides the opportunity for me (and others) to write about what interests (us) most. It may be surprising, but theory has played no small part in creating these opportunities, this freedom, feminism and deconstruction, especially, encouraging in their respective ways the establishment of relation, notably including that—often considered a simple opposition—between the personal and the professional.

If it is not the greatest story ever told, *The Odyssey* comes close. I first encountered it in 1962 in Vince Miller's class in practical criticism. The story of Odysseus's return home is also a journey toward understanding, an account of the adventures of a soul, and the dramatization of the changes in an egoistic, indulgent, and reckless individual. *The Odyssey* pulls no punches, never verges on the sentimental or engages in cheap psychologizing or romanticizing; it is, instead, the hard-bitten story of pain and suffering, toughness and commitment, a story that can celebrate tenderness because it never minimizes travail; it suggests, in fact, that tenderness may not be genuine or even possible apart from such knowledge and experience. The heart must be prepared for the joys of home and love, and preparation may necessitate passing through the flames of suffering, which burn off the dross of egoism and egotism alike.

I encountered *The Odyssey*, beginning the adventures of my soul with this masterpiece, the second semester of my sophomore year at Wofford. I was the youngest member of that senior-level class, pitted against stereotypical English majors, the editor of the literary magazine (James Kilgo, who went on to write *Deep Enough for Ivorybills*), future professors and clergymen, all of whom appeared to have already read everything. I, on the other hand, had read practically nothing. Just as important, or more so, I lacked experience in "the world." I had no idea what was going on in *The Magic Mountain* or in Allen Tate's *The Fathers*, could barely grasp the issues radiant in *The Immoralist*, and was at a loss to fathom Emma Bovary's craving. Shortly after mid-semester, overwhelmed with the workload amid my shortcomings, I teetered on the brink of, first, physical exhaustion and, then, a nervous breakdown. My pride had led me, headstrong as I was, to attempt a course for which I was by no means ready. That painful experience began a continuing education.

I entered college a sheltered adolescent, an only child, proud and pampered—"spoiled" is really the word. Wofford was barely twenty miles from the small, parochial community in which I had lived all my life and to which, though a resident student, I returned each weekend. Like the rest of the week, the days at home were spent studying, reading for Dr. Miller, struggling with the Old and New Testaments, trying desperately to memorize the two hundred–plus French words W. R. ("Peg") Bourne assigned per class. I did not have time to indulge the loneliness that, nevertheless, on occasion managed to penetrate the defenses I erected. I did not socialize much, beyond a nightly walk to McDonald's, did not go out drinking, did not play pool or touch football, dated only three times my entire four years at Wofford. I was shy, timid, afraid, inept, knew little of girls and both wanted to and was afraid to. Getting involved would turn my head, take me away from my studies, ruin me, or so my mother insisted (that Wofford was then all-male made it a logical choice for me, at least in her view). As a result, in addition to being horribly lonely and stunted, I was intolerably self-centered. I cared for no one, really, though I certainly professed love of my parents, a favorite aunt and uncle, my maternal grandmother (it was she, buxom and wonderfully earthy, who explained "this boy-girl bizness").

I was not only sheltered and inexperienced, but I was also sanctimonious and quick to judge and condemn (they seem to go together). I did not taste alcohol until the summer of college graduation (when I sipped champagne at Fred Robbins's wedding), did not smoke, did not cuss (indeed, I then thought profanity childish, obscenities abhorrent, taught by my mother to do as she said rather than as she did), did not *know* a woman until I married at twenty-four. A prime candidate for sainthood, or so I must have acted—and, Jesus Christ, probably thought! No wonder at mixers girls removed their numbers when they matched mine, for I fairly exuded piety, with close-cropped hair, shiny forehead (I once actually thought of becoming a Southern Baptist minister), protruding ears, and severe expression: a Cromwellian Roundhead among Cavaliers, whose earthy, sensual, simply human behavior I dreamed of sharing even as I outwardly condemned it. I was no more a saint, of course, than were Cromwell's legions.

I had little notion of human feelings, either my own or others', because I had had no schooling in the heart, only in things of the mind, and as Keats knew, souls are made only by "the medium of a world like this": "Do you not see how necessary a World of Pains and troubles is to school an Intelligence and make it a soul? A Place where the heart must feel and suffer in a thousand diverse ways!"[4] Exactly, but I had been kept from "the world," protected from suffering, driven to elementary school only a few blocks away, kept home when the thermometer dropped much below freezing—I was never more embarrassed than when, at a gathering of us new Wofford students and their parents, my mother, having heard of "wild parties" and panty raids, asked the dean of students for assurance that I would come out of college "as good a boy" as when she brought me there. No piker in pride and ego, I had no heart. All the love I knew had been directed toward me, with precious little returned. Small wonder that I could not understand Emma Bovary, whose world consists, as far as she is able to discern, of unromantic, insensitive clods, like her husband, the inept and incompetent, though studious, "Charbovari."

SUCH IS a broad, major reading context of my first adventures with *The Odyssey*. The extent to which the reading I will now offer is my own rather than Vince Miller's I can no longer determine, if indeed I ever could. But as Wordsworth observed in *The Prelude*, "Who that shall point as with a wand and say/ 'This portion of the river of my mind/ Came from yon fountain?' " What I know is that I have always read this magnificent story as a "journey toward understanding" (I don't even know whether the phrase is mine). And I have always read it in the prose translation of W. H. D. Rouse, first published in 1937, whose modern diction and realistic renderings scholars scoff at. I go beyond the translator's considerable liberties with Homer, or whoever it was, or they were, that finally transcribed—created, really—one version of the story from the many that had circulated orally, taking additional liberties of my own. I read Odysseus, in fact, as a novelistic character possessing the psychological depth we know—from Erich Auerbach's *Mimesis* and other studies—ancient Greek writing had no knowledge of. My justification, or excuse perhaps, is that *The Odyssey* I cherish *is* Rouse's translation. When I refer to *The Odyssey*, therefore, I mean this modern, realistic, novelistic version. *In it,* the hero changes from a reckless, irresponsible egoist to a man patient, respectful, and sympathetic, taught by experience, and able to govern others because he can control himself. "Give, sympathize, control"—the English translation of the Hindu words that resound at the end of *The Waste Land*—comes close to the lesson Homer had in mind for Odysseus and us.

Framed by the (related) narratives of his Hamlet-like son Telemachos's search for his father and of the collapse of Ithacan social order in the absence of his strong leadership (Robert Con Davis has well described the Lacanian implications of this tale of "the absent father"), Odysseus's is the story of a return home, to family, love, and what matters most in life.[5] Following the Trojan War, Odysseus spends twenty difficult years in the essay, seven of them with the beautiful Calypso, who finally tires of his pining for Penelopeia, the mother of his son, his faithful wife. We first encounter Odysseus there, in fact, lamenting his thralldom, no longer responsive to Calypso's passionate embrace, long since weary of the delights of their pleasure palace, and determined to return home. The story of his strength, cunning, and craft precedes this, our first glimpse of Odysseus, in accounts rendered by, among others, his former companions Nestor and Menelaos and the latter's boozy, bloated wife, Helen, *cause célèbre* of the strife that took Odysseus from his happy home. Before we actually meet our hero, we thus have before us ways of living with which to compare and contrast his: the "old cavalier" Nestor, living only in the past, constantly reminiscing; Menelaos, interested mainly in acquiring more and more wealth, an early example of conspicuous consumption; the reckless and unscrupulous suitors, bidding against each other for the hand (and body, though never mind the heart) of the faithful Penelopeia as they blithely eat Odysseus out of house and home, all the while mouthing platitudes of public responsibility in the same breath as they plot his death, should (as they doubt) he ever again show up in Ithaca.

In order to get back, Odysseus has not merely to undergo and survive a series of incredible adventures, but he must also earn the love of Penelopeia and the respect of his people. And for that he must be educated into the ways and truths of the human heart, purged of a reckless ego, and made newly aware of the value of breath itself. What Odysseus was before his education appears with particular vividness in his encounter with the Cyclops. Proud, headstrong, and reckless, he selects "twelve of the best men [he] had" to accompany him, against his companions' advice, on a trip to see the one-eyed monster up close and "claim the stranger's gift."[6] As a result of his willfulness, six of his (best) men are lost, made horrible meals for the giant, the rest put at grave risk. Ever a master of "schemes and machinations" (106), Odysseus devises an escape plan, which begins with driving a fiery stake into the eye of the besotted giant. Once he and his men manage to escape from the monster's cave, clinging to the far side of rams so that the now-blind Cyclops cannot detect them, Odysseus taunts his victim, calling out "in mockery" to him, which all the more infuriates the giant, who tosses at the Achaians a huge rock that barely misses their ship (109). Intent on credit for his feat, Odysseus proudly, and stupidly, identifies himself: "I say, Cyclops! if ever any one asks you who put out your ugly eye, tell him your blinder was Odysseus, the conqueror of Troy, the son of Laërtes, whose address is in Ithaca" (110). Odysseus's recklessness spells more trouble for him and his men, for now Poseidon Earthshaker, father of the Cyclops, will be able to avenge his son's injuries, knowing who inflicted them.

Odysseus's ineffectualness and irresponsibility are again highlighted in the following episodes with the Winds and, later, Circê. Aiolos gives the visiting Achaians a bag of air to secure their passage home, and with this gift they get "so close that [they] could see [their countrymen] tending their fires." At this point, literally within hailing distance of home, their long travails at an apparent end, Odysseus relaxes: "when I saw the island I fell into a deep sleep, for I was tired out" (112)! Curious and greedy, left without a leader, and perfectly human, the men seize the opportunity to look inside the bag Odysseus had up to now "let no one else touch" (112); the winds escape, of course; and the ship is blown back out to sea, and thus they are sent on more disastrous adventures. A pathetic figure, "the conqueror of Troy" is at a loss: "This waked me up; I did not know what to do, whether to throw myself overboard and be drowned, or grin and bear it in the land of the living. Well, I just bore it and stayed where I was. I covered my head and lay down" (113).

With Circê, Odysseus appears hardly more heroic, though, to be sure, he is shrewd enough to resist her initial charms and so is not turned into a pig. Yet with her he and his men "remained for a whole year, with plenty to eat and drink" (121). *Almost* pigs, in other words. Not for the first time, his men display the leadership he has apparently relinquished, showing the judgment he lacks: "Good heavens, have you forgotten home altogether? Do remember it, if it is really fated that you shall have a safe return to your great house and your native land!" (121). Headstrong, conceited, reckless, irresponsible—and now Odysseus has forgotten home, dallying with Circê a whole year, in thrall to her many charms. Finally urged on by his men, he reminds Circê of her promise to help them on their "homeward way," a promise that she, true to her word, keeps. But first, declares she, they must go to the Kingdom of the Dead and ask directions of Teiresias, the "blind Theban seer." Reluctantly, Odysseus agrees and heads out again—on a fortunate detour.

In Hadês, populated by "the empty shells of the dead" (124), Odysseus sees straightaway his ill-fated comrade Elpenor, whose body he had left at Circê's, "unmourned and unburied, since," he lamely asserts, "other tasks were pressing" (125). Given what we know of Odysseus, that neglect is hardly surprising. What *is* surprising is his response here and now: "I was moved with pity for him" (125). Pity we have not seen, nor had any reason to expect, in Odysseus, even as his men were being eaten alive by the Cyclops. But it reappears as he soon thereafter catches sight of his mother, alive when he left Ithaca: "My tears fell when I saw her, and I was moved with pity" (125).

The effects of being alive among the dead, of encountering nothingness, are thus immediate and dramatic. Odysseus is learning, and that education advances significantly when he meets Teiresias, the reason for his visit to Hadês. The Theban seer offers valuable prophecy, certainly, but more important is his advice, which has a pertinence even he may not fully realize: "You seek to return home, mighty Odysseus, and home is sweet as honey. But God will make your voyage hard and dangerous; for I do not think the Earthshaker will fail to see you, and he is furious against you because you blinded his son. Nevertheless, you may all get safe home still, although not without suffering much, *if you can control yourself and your companions*" (126; my italics).

As important as this lecture on control is, even more so is the lesson being taught concerning the heart, resumed as Odysseus talks with his mother and discovers how, and why, she died. Anticleia is piercing: "The Archeress did not shoot me in my own house with those gentle shafts that never miss; it was no disease that made me pine away: but I missed you so much, and your clever wit and your gay merry ways, and life was sweet no longer, so I died" (128). How that must have hurt even Odysseus, who surely felt rebuked, whether or not responsible for his mother's death.

In any case, the lesson Odysseus is being taught revolves around the fact, the brutal, hard fact, of death and, its flip side, the value of life, as well as what is important in life, a point driven home in his encounter with a "crowd of women" and then Agamemnon and Achillês. The women are "wives and daughters of great men" (128), and what they talk about, the questions they ask, the concern they give voice to is family, husbands, children—this is what matters to them. When, shortly thereafter, Odysseus meets up with Agamemnon, the point is reiterated, for it is about his son Orestês that the great hero talks. To his question about his son's present situation, Odysseus responds callously: "Why do you ask that, Atreïdês? I know nothing, whether he is alive or dead; and it is a bad thing to babble like the blowing wind" (133). The lesson has obviously not taken. Himself babbling on to Achillês about *that* great hero's accomplishments, the honor his name carries, the pride of place he enjoys in Hadês ("now you are a potentate in this world of the dead. Then do not deplore your death, Achillês" [134]), he has to be set straight, and in no uncertain terms: "Don't bepraise death to me, Odysseus. I would rather be plowman to a yeoman farmer on a small holding than lord Paramount in the kingdom of the dead" (134). Achillês, too, wants to know about *his* son; this time Odysseus responds sensitively. Afterward, Achillês "marched away with long steps over the meadow of asphodel, proud to hear how his son had made his mark" (135).

That something is happening to Odysseus, something significant, appears most clearly in his tender and respectful response to Aias, who, according to Menelaos's account earlier in the story, "could have escaped death, although Athena was his enemy, if he had not uttered a boastful speech in his blindness—for he declared that he had escaped the devouring gulf 'God willing or not!'" (54). The resemblance here to Odysseus I find interesting; it may help to account for the nature of his response to Aias, in whom he may recognize much of his own (former) self. At any rate, here is what he says, elegant in its reflection of a responsive heart, concerned for and respectful of an-other:

> The other ghosts of the dead halted in turn, and each asked what was near to his heart; but alone of them all the soul of Aias Telamoniadês kept apart, still resentful for my victory over him when there was question about the arms of Achillês. The goddess his mother set them up as a prize for the best man. How I wish I had never won such a prize! What a life was lost for that! Aias, first of all the Danaäns in noble looks and noble deeds, except Achillês the incomparable. And so I addressed him in gentle words:

"Aias, great son of a great father! were you never to forget your anger against me for those accursed arms, not even in death? That prize was a disaster, seeing that we lost a tower of strength like you. Our whole nation mourns your loss continually, no less than we mourn Achillês Peleïadês. Zeus alone is to blame and no one else, because he hated the Danaän host so vehemently, and brought fate upon you. Nay, come this way, my lord, and listen to my pleading: *master your passion and your proud temper.*" (135; my italics)

Exactly what Odysseus must do.

Shortly thereafter, the lessons of Hadês concluded, Odysseus follows his mother's advice to "make haste back to the light" (128). Now respectful and caring, knowing what is right and proper and quick to act upon such recognition, he makes as his first project burial of Elpenor. But as much as Odysseus has learned and obviously changed, so psychologically realistic is (this version of) Homer's presentation that on occasion he reverts to his former reckless and egoistic ways. Thus he must be rebuked by Circê for wanting to take on Scylla: "You hot-head! fighting and asking for trouble is all you care about!" (140). Lamentably, Odysseus forgets her "injunction, when she told me not to arm myself" (141). As a result, the monster makes off with six of his men. The situation here parallels that earlier with the Cyclops, but this time Odysseus is deeply affected by the sight of his men being devoured, "shrieking and stretching out their hands to me in the death-struggle. That was the most pitiable sight my eyes ever beheld in all my toils and troubles in the weary ways of the sea" (143).

The Phaiacians prove to be a formidable test of the lessons Odysseus has learned—as well, they represent a way of life in vivid contrast to that Homer has in mind for us. The Phaiacians are the last group Odysseus meets before reaching home, and it is to them that he narrates the series of adventures beginning with Circê and culminating in that with Scylla and Charybdis. They are an unfriendly people, uptight, and inhospitable to strangers, regarding the *other* as a threat, more, as an enemy. And indeed, Odysseus proves to be exactly that, a threat and an enemy to Phaiacian existence, a point figured in Homer's description of him as he emerges, naked, from the bush to confront the king's comely daughter Nausicaä and her maidens: "he strode like a lion of the mountains, proud of his power, who goes on through wind and rain with eyes blazing, as he pounces on cattle and sheep, or chases the wild deer; indeed he is ready to follow belly's bidding, and to invade even a walled close in search of the bleaters" (75–76). How apt the description we shall soon see. A nation of sheep, the Phaiacians live walled-off from the rest of the world: having fled ages ago from the savage Cyclopians, unable to compete, they settled, Homer tells us, "far from the world of men who earn their bread in the sweat of their brows," and to provide extra protection "their great king Nausithoös . . . ran a wall round the city" (73). What they now "delight" in, perhaps understandably, is womblike: "Feasting, . . . music, and dancing, plenty of clean linen, a warm bath, and bed" (92).

Though apparent in several ways, the Phaiacians' weakness is best fig- ured in the games to which they challenge the stranger Odysseus, dis- guised as a man old and decrepit. "Game is the best way to fame," they announce, "what you can do with your arms and legs" (90–91). Inept, insecure, and fearful of the other, the Phaiacians compensate by boasting and bragging; they expect Odysseus to "report to his friends when he gets back home how we beat the world at boxing and wrestling and jumping and running" (90). Believing him no threat to their vaunted claims, the young men taunt the stranger, who now exercises the self-control he had earlier lacked. When, to their surprise and chagrin, he beats them badly, they quickly and shamelessly change their tune, disavowing those earlier boasts: "The truth is we are not first-rate boxers or wrestlers, but we are fine oarsmen and the best of seamen" (92). As always, it seems, the Phaia- cians adjust, adapt; when unable to compete successfully in one area, they move to another in which they again lay claim to be the best, so in need of aggrandizement is their collective ego: "Let our friend have something to tell his friends when he gets home—how we beat the whole world at shipwork and footwork, dancing and song!" (92–93).

If Phaiacia proves a significant test of Odysseus's self-control, much more so is his return to his homeland, disguised as a beggar and thus subject to verbal abuse, ridicule, and on several occasions physical vio- lence. The taunts he suffered in Phaiacia pale in comparison to those he must endure at home, himself a test of respect. At one point, having been kicked by a goatherd, Odysseus "thought for a moment that he would kill the man with a blow of his staff, or lift him by the waist and dash his head on the ground"—as he might well do—and no doubt would have done earlier. But instead, "he controlled himself and bore it" (195): "His heart came to heel like a hound, patient now until the end" (226).

If for Odysseus the encounter with the suitors and their minions is a severe test of his newly learned control, for us as readers it represents an education in the art of living, for Odysseus acts as a test of the Ithacans, frequently offers mini-lectures, providing opportunities for suitors and others to save themselves. The education spotlights giving as opposed to taking. Whereas the suitors—it is a good image—"helped themselves to the good things that were before them" (167), reckless, careless of others, and prizing consumption, Odysseus's faithful servant Eumaios, the lowly swineherd, is a steward, "careful of his master's property when the master was not there" (168). Why does he remain faithful to his master after twenty years of absence—and treat the beggar with welcome and respect? Unlike the suitors, "I do it because I fear the god of strangers and I am sorry for thisen" (166). The swineherd adds, with the wisdom lacking in the suitors and their entourage, "The Lord gives and the Lord takes away, as it pleases him, for he can do all things" (167)—a point worth remembering and taking to heart.

Fear and respect—along with control, that is much of what this richly layered tale is all about. And they are, all three, closely related to the necessity, indeed the primacy, of giving. Give, sympathize, control—we are back to *The Waste Land* and an awareness crucial to a responsible life. Odysseus himself teaches the lesson, most effectively in a set-to with Antinoös, ringleader of the suitors and (so) the first to die in the savage battle soon to follow. Giving presupposes respect and should follow from acknowledgment of otherness, especially the recognition that things could change and that you too, no matter how well off now, might one day be a beggar. What goes around, comes around: "Give, my friend; you seem to me no common man, but the highest in the nation, for you look like a prince. Then you ought to give even more than others, and I will sing your praises over the wide world. I once had estates myself in the world; I lived happy in a rich house, and often gave to a homeless man, whoever he was and whatever he needed" (199). What Antinoös gives, though, is a footstool to the back. Undaunted, Odysseus continues the lesson in his confrontation with Iros, "the sturdy Beggar." Things can be *otherwise,* he insists: "nothing is bred that is weaker than man. He thinks no evil thing can ever come upon him, so long as the gods give him power and his knees are nimble; but when the blessed gods bring sorrow, he has to bear this also, unwillingly yet with patient heart" (206). Ever the fabulist, Odysseus concocts a story of how it was with him; an acknowledgment of his own mistakes perhaps shines through this fictional account: "I myself was once like to be happy amongst men, but I gave way to violent passions and did reckless deeds. . . . Therefore no man should ever disregard justice, but let him enjoy in silence the gifts which the gods may give him" (207). Giving versus taking; the good things in life, even breath itself, understood as a gift, rather than merely the fruit of our own labors, the result of our own efforts.

At the end of the great battle, Odysseus thus insists that the slain suitors and their hangers-on "have been brought low by God's decree and their own wicked deeds. They respected none of those who walk on the earth, neither good men nor bad; therefore their recklessness has brought them to a dreadful end" (251). So attuned, at-one, are they that Penelopeia echoes her husband: "they respected no man on earth that ever met them, good or bad, and therefore they have been punished for their recklessness" (254).

ODYSSEUS'S is a story of the adventures of a soul and of the education, the change of heart, necessary for a triumphant return home—and for the love of a woman whose loyalty, wisdom, and respect deserve no less than a heart prepared, atoned, at-oned. Understanding *The Odyssey* as the story of interior life, of suffering and change wrought by that suffering, makes it difficult to keep it at arm's length, safely distanced from your own life. I am suggesting how the story has provided a structure for shaping events in one person's life, helping me to understand myself better. My own experience, in turn, helps me better to understand *The Odyssey*. In this light, I want to return to the turning point in Odysseus's story, his remarkable "detour" in the Kingdom of the Dead. I've barely scratched the surface, I feel, of what happens there, its meaning and significance.

If Odysseus's return home requires this detour, what is Homer suggesting? What does he understand about the schooling of the human heart? For some of us, less proud and egoistic, an encounter with death and nothingness may be unnecessary. But others of us, less fortunate, like Odysseus and me, seem unable to respect and love before and apart from some such transformative encounter. I think of G. K. Chesterton: you know nothing until you know *nothing*. Odysseus emerges from his encounter with nothingness a changed man. So did I.

IT WAS the week before Christmas 1982, a snowy Friday evening. The tree was up, and the house smelled of pine and gave off a once-a-year warmth. I was in my study, the door shut against my wife and my children, alone with my problems. This was four years before the divorce, but my marriage, such as it was, was over really, the divorce itself merely the legalization of what had long ago happened, or not happened. My septuagenarian parents, back in South Carolina, themselves teetered on the brink of an abyss: my mother had recently broken first one then the other hip and now suffered from paranoid schizophrenia, accusing my father, in fact, of causing her falls, and he, in the meantime, had contracted her disease, victims of what is labeled *folie à deux*. I had just spoken with them the day before, or rather I had listened, disbelieving still, to their mad ravings, wild accusations, threats, and counterthreats. So far away, I felt helpless—and guilty. Closeted among my beloved books, I was as far away from my wife and my children.

Weighing even heavier that night than my marital and parental problems, inching me toward my own abyss terrible and seemingly inevitable, was the charge first brought against me eleven months before of improper attribution of sources used in my first book—*read* plagiarism— I who taught graduate students methods of research and who had been so painstaking in that book that it took me nearly eight years to complete. Life had been hell ever since I came across the accusation. It was a cold, gray Saturday afternoon in January that the jaws of this hell opened, hard upon my return from one of several recent trips to South Carolina. At the office, sorting the accumulated mail, I eagerly seized upon a review, in a major journal in the field of eighteenth-century studies, but my excitement immediately turned to anxiety and dread when I saw the name of the reviewer: it was the very scholar whose arguments concerning Dryden's religious positions I had sought to overturn—and who had pointedly snubbed me a few weeks before at the Modern Language Association convention. The beginning of the review was unfriendly, the ending devastating, designed to convict me of plagiarism, even though that term was never used. My ears fairly burned as I skimmed, finding it hard to take in the whole thing. But curiously, as my heart sank, my mind raced, and I began to chart a reply, so sure was I that a response would not only be expected but welcome. That thought diverted my attention, and comfort came from the expectation, naive assurance from somewhere, that even without a response from me, fair-minded people would recognize the truth.

I said nothing about the review to anyone, not a word over the weekend to my wife, until Monday when I took it to my department chair, who read it and then solicited my response, which appeared to satisfy him. I asked him to inform the departmental Advisory Committee at its meeting later that day and to convey my willingness, indeed my eagerness, to respond to any of their concerns, to answer any of their questions.

Two days later I was disinvited to a campus interview in Texas for a departmental chairpersonship.

At the end of the week a senior colleague, a person I had always thought a good friend, stopped by to offer advice. "You must be considering suicide," he said.

For a while thereafter the fires merely smoldered; the Advisory Committee did not seem especially concerned, but glances grew furtive as I entered the humanities building, or so I imagined.

If you're not an academic, you may have trouble understanding just how highly charged and electric an issue plagiarism is or quite the energy and excitement that surrounds its suspicion. I do not mean to excuse those who take as theirs the words of others—they are at once cheating, lying, and stealing—nor do I seek to extenuate any complicity of my own. We do, however, literature professors especially, become quite exercised, defensive, and self-righteous about alleged misappropriation of words. Maybe inordinately so. As Neil Hertz has written, "You don't have to be over thirty or a bourgeois humanist, for example, to find yourself beside yourself about a paper you suspect was plagiarized."[7] Like Hertz, I wonder about "the vehemence" of our response. We seem positively eager to find evidence of plagiarism, to sniff out offenses, ever alert, it seems, and ready to pounce, suspecting the worst. (This very day, the day I am drafting this paragraph, a colleague stopped by, gleeful and triumphant, to announce that he had "just nailed another damned plagiarist.") Plagiarism must surely represent a threat to some cherished ideas with favored-notion status, notions on which poststructuralism has cast new and disturbing light: I mean that we are all caught, and write, in a tangled web of intertextuality and that we have reason, accordingly, to doubt the possibility of originality and the various versions of the proper (i.e., property, one's own). Our ability to detect the crime, to collect evidence, and to cinch the case against the offenders, may represent some needed confirmation: perhaps of our scholarly and rhetorical skills, our own integrity, good judgment, and moral worth, thus our difference from *them*—but also the trustworthiness of the word, its monogamous nature, words' fidelity to us, licensed interpreters and sometime caretakers, husbands in the most basic sense. *We* feel cheated when a student short-changes or short-circuits an assignment by offering someone else's words as her or his own, and we take positive pleasure in gaining some manner of revenge, perhaps enjoying the opportunity to judge, forgetting or ignoring the biblical injunction that, given what we know of intertextuality, plagiarism spotters would do well to consider. But that's conjecture. All I know is what it feels like to be—falsely—accused of the crime.

Months passed. I sensed a lull before a storm. The days were of dread and fear, the nights of emptiness and apprehension, barely relieved by the larger and larger amounts of Scotch I consumed—constant, abiding anxiety, bordering on terror, never worse than in the early hours of the morning. I can now recall little more of that semester of "wine" without roses than, via an attorney, seeking to bring pressure upon both the reviewer and the journal that published the accusing review, in the vain hope of securing a retraction, or, if not that, at least the opportunity to give my side of the story. I had not yet considered suicide.

May brought an invitation to a campus interview in Florida, and shortly thereafter an offer of a departmental chairpersonship, much-needed assurance that, in spite of all, I still had a career, even the possibility of the professional advancement my soul craved.

The offer was attractive, I had long dreamed of living in Florida, away at last from the cold and snow I'll probably never grow accustomed to. I wanted to go. My ex-wife did not, would not.

We went into counseling. First she, then I, retained a divorce lawyer. But rather than go alone, I stayed, afraid of the unknown, dependent on the familiar and comfortable, not yet able to see that life without love is little more than vegetable existence.

More months passed, less agonizing, but burdened still by anxiety, if no longer terror. Then, in mid-November, following my return from yet another trip to South Carolina, my chair came in to announce that the Advisory Committee would consider "the scandal" that afternoon. "What happened?" I asked, my voice cracking. He said something about professional jealousy stemming from the job offer in Florida. "Besides, it's being talked about around the country. The department's at risk."

For nearly two hours I sat, or rather slumped, in surroundings no longer familiar but surreal, my ears flaming, my heart pounding, in mortal fear and sweating profusely, among colleagues turned accusers, judges, and jury. The debate was intense, but for the most part academically civil. I was not without supporters nor without detractors. I recall mainly feeling hollowed out—and on trial, like the yellow owl that Tarrou in Camus's *The Plague* remembers his father judging, convicting, and sentencing. And I too wondered—how can they be so sure?

Finally the committee voted, five to three, against any further action.

Unsatisfied, some in the department sought redress outside. I hit bottom, or almost, the afternoon that, hands trembling, I took from my mailbox a copy of a petition signed by seven influential colleagues, asking the dean of the Graduate School to conduct an "immediate and thorough" investigation. The petition was framed in such a manner that I had to wonder how impartial such an inquiry was to be.

Even if others did, I never doubted my innocence. But like Camus's "yellow owl," I feared "the system." Clinging to the unrealistic hope the whole bloody mess would somehow just blow over, I tried to avoid the confrontation without which I could never find peace and from which I would emerge cleared of all charges. I was afraid.

And though I bravely tried to look my colleagues straight in the eye, I *felt* dirty, certainly pinned to the wall, wriggling, available for examination. Whether or not it was so, I imagined everyone talking about me, poking around, some feeling sorry for me. With agony fueled by imagination as well as fear and dread, my professional life no longer buoyed me, provided nothing unavailable in my personal or private life. The acceptance of a second book by the publisher of the first, desired sign of confidence and support, was lost amid the terror that was again my constant companion. The worst thing was not knowing: where lightning would strike next or how, what further missives would suddenly appear in my mailbox, what plan would be hatched, what announcement of effort I would next hear about. Not knowing, but imagining, even coming to expect, daily . . . God only knew what. And I had lost the respect of others, or so I imagined.

Anyone so accused would feel vulnerable and afraid, so much was at stake, plagiarism being the heinous offense it is. My fear was exacerbated by weakness and limitations peculiar to me. You see, I stood to lose—I don't think I exaggerate—all those professional aspirations, and respect, that had long before come to vibrate as the very heart of my existence, and without which I would have little reason for being. It was my career that I lived for, not my family, not my children. I had no hobbies and few friends. Work was my consuming passion, career the false idol I worshiped. I thought first of work, not as commitment or responsibility, which is healthy, but as both avenue to some imagined success and escape from a sadly unsatisfying personal life. To work I thus gave priority, lavishing on it time, energy, and spirit, as well as hope, courting its favors, in pursuit of position, stature, money, prizes, grants, and publications, above all, publications. Career was the comely figure I lusted after; she was the elusive female, the only one, I then sought and with whom I imagined fulfillment. Alone in my study, the door shut to keep out wife and children—that pretty well figured my existence.

That wintry night, alone with the books I cherished but now found of little comfort, with hope difficult to rouse, something happened. I am still not sure quite what or how, though of its occurrence I have no doubt. I felt it immediately. Proof of its happening lies in its effects. I remain convinced of a certain parallel with Odysseus's education in the Kingdom of the Dead.

Beset with anxiety and fear, not yet besotted with drink, I began to experience an intense feeling of hopelessness bordering on despair, such as I had never felt before or—praise God—have since, and accompanied by a sense of being utterly alone. My study, cramped and dark, I now felt as squeezing the very life out of me. I struggled to breathe, began to sob, softly, and leaning my head back against a bookshelf, I gazed—first at nothing and then at nothingness.

The thought came with surprising quickness. A way out appeared with a diabolical clarity: suicide. A possibility, an escape where mere seconds before none had seemed imaginable. I had never before seriously thought about it, despite my colleague's suggestion, though I remember with what force an influential religion professor in college, himself a minister, averred that "every serious person" considers it sooner or later.

I grabbed at the possibility, trying to embrace it. But it vanished almost as quickly as it had appeared, an empty shell. Face to face with nothingness, I drew back, wet with sweat, terrified, aware as never before of both vulnerability and emptiness. And at that moment, I *let go,* releasing my death grip on the idol I had worshiped. I faced, and fully admitted, the possibility of failure. I think I was then born as a person, no longer first and foremost a scholar, critic, professor.

A strong affirmation in the form of a fierce will to live replaced the despair that had been slowly tightening its grip about me. And I knew that I could and would survive, could and would be able to take care of my family, could, if I had to, live and function without the precious career to which I had given all (and for what?). I might be selling insurance or working for a newspaper, and it might be in Evanston, or Boise, or Anniston, but I would make it.

I have never before or since felt such a strong sense of self-worth, accompanied by humility, a combination almost mystical in formula. I felt most keenly that no matter what some tribunal concluded, no matter what my colleagues believed, no matter how censorious the profession might become, I had—gained—respect for myself and so knew I was worthy of others' respect. The worth I realized lying deep and permanent within has not merely to do with me as an individual but also to do with human being itself. As a person, I am no better or worse than others with whom I share the gift of breath, a body endowed with passion and reason, a creature given the gift of life and response, a soul entrusted with freedom and responsibility. There is, I now understood as I never had before, something strong, good, quite possibly imperishable about human life, something that can survive "the slings and arrows of outrageous fortune," perhaps survive all—but suicide. Quickening my soul as it excited my senses, life's preciousness burned with a flame whose source lies no doubt with the eternal.

I made haste to the light, determined to fight, knowing I would not merely endure but prevail, realizing—maybe for the first time—a kinship with struggling humanity.

My journey toward understanding had (just) begun.

(As hard to believe as it may seem—I cannot say it without questioning it—what happened in the matter of the charges brought against me was, in any event, anticlimactic. I still harbored doubts about the outcome of the investigation but none about survival or my own self-worth. Confidence thus marked my steps, and I began to smile again. As the investigation proceeded, expressions of support increased. In early May, following a two-month-long inquiry, conducted by a blue-ribbon panel of distinguished scholars, I was cleared of all charges. I remember embraces from colleagues, warm, genuine, sometimes unexpected.)

I HAVE by no means completed my adventure with Odysseus, my journey around him and me—and essay (I play a little on the subtitle of Wole Soyinka's *Ìsarà*). If I have something in common with Odysseus, I now find myself feeling quite a bit like an essay and less and less like the proud, defensive, uptight, definite article: attentive to nuances, sensitive to feelings (or trying to be), exploring, looking for the meaning of events. It is a loving kind of thing, the essay, tentative, yes, skeptical and exploratory but unwavering in its commitment to certain implied values, and aware of its own strengths and weaknesses, vices, and a few virtues, unlikely to overestimate, or underestimate, its worth. It knows itself pretty well and is pretty sure of itself, without being arrogant. Experienced, with considerable maturity, though certainly susceptible to error, it has been schooled in the truths of the human heart.

The essay is a rambling, adventurous, as well as protean thing. Peripatetic and unhurried, curious, often easily charmed, and occasionally charming in return, it sets out on its adventures, sauntering (says Sam Pickering), looks first this way and then that, opts for one direction, usually the road less traveled, and proceeds down it for a while, more than willing to stop and chat (where is it going, after all?), to enjoy the sights and smells, to take in the beauty of a sunset or the glory of an opening rose (in the hands of a male writer), to admire a woman's fine-turned leg, the curve of her breasts, and unashamed to admit such interests. Though it welcomes and embraces a detour and is, in a very real sense, constituted as a detour, the essay eventually gets somewhere, usually somewhere important, and as often as not it's home, understood as what lies closest to the heart.

THERE IS no straight way home, this I know now, no way to avoid the travail of experience, no escaping the peril of deciding between Scylla and Charybdis, little chance of immunity to the seductive call of the Sirens. Detour is fortuitous, though; at least it was for Odysseus, whose time in Hadês prepared his heart for the joys of home. Understanding requires the mediation of experience, the necessary otherness. "Do you not see how necessary a World of Pains and troubles is to school an Intelligence and make it a Soul? A Place where the heart must feel and suffer in a thousand diverse ways!" One difference between the meaning of Odysseus's story and that of the essay lies in this: his odyssey prepares him for a homecoming, whereas for the essay, the adventure, the process remains as important as any point reached, any destination achieved. Because meaning lies *there,* home gets redefined in the essay, the journey itself both quickening the heart and constituting its lasting abode.

The essay has, nevertheless, a good deal in common with Odysseus himself, whose "heart came to heel like a hound, patient now until the end." You can think of him as a figure for the essay: controlled and caring, rather than reckless and indulgent, schooled in the ways of the heart— and respectful of the other.

And me? I'm essaying—to be.

CHAPTER EIGHT

Bringing Theory to Life:
Crossing the Line

> . . . In criticism, we deal not with language as such, nor with the philosophy of language, but with how books or habits of reading *penetrate* our lives.
>
> GEOFFREY HARTMAN, *Criticism in the Wilderness*

"THEORY" and "ethereal": they sound enough alike that you think them somehow connected, deriving perhaps, way back, from a common root. Of course, that isn't so. Still, people persist in thinking of theory as ethereal: airy and tenuous, having to do with the nether regions of cerebration and little or nothing at all with the lower regions of emotion and passion, with the real world and things everyday and practical and human. In many minds the word "theory" conjures up images of something precious, abstruse, inevitably philosophical, and therefore noisomely intellectual. It best be avoided, then, maybe dismissed rather than inveighed against, for its power to infect is almost legendary, capable as it is said to be of ruining minds and turning hearts to stone—more: of denying the very existence of heart, soul, reality, value, and truth. Heady stuff, indeed—dangerous. For God's sake, don't let your sons or daughters grow up to be theorists.

I don't think I exaggerate. Though it has made impressive headway in colleges and universities in the past few years, theory remains a perceived threat outside the academy. Inside, it is now increasingly tolerated, often co-opted, grudgingly absorbed, sometimes embraced, on many campuses still an issue of hot debate. What all the fuss is about often seems hard to figure. Personal ambitions certainly get involved, along with politics obviously, as well as defensiveness and fear. I have no wish to engage in the debate here. Nor do I wish overtly to defend theory or to argue its function and significance. Instead, I want, simply, to talk about what theory has meant to my life. Whether, not so simply, I thereby bring theory to life I leave up to you to say.

First of all, I will say that theory has, for the past ten or twelve years, massively affected my *professional* life; it has, in fact, throbbed as the very heart of my teaching and writing. The autobiographical arc marking that has been one, at least as I perceive it, of growth and expansion of consciousness and concern. I began my career as a professional student of English literature, that is, as a professor, by identifying myself as a scholar of Restoration and early-eighteenth-century literature. As such, I was hired as a university teacher; as such, I taught and wrote for roughly ten years; and as such, I was given tenure and twice promoted. Afterward, more secure, I could afford to grow restive of the lines defining me, weary of the narrow questions I treated, and admittedly ambitious of wider appeal and recognition. Aware of exciting and heady developments under way in the late seventies and early eighties, I turned to theory, returned really, for I had long had an interest in it and had studied it at the University of Virginia with E. D. Hirsch, then known as author of *Validity in Interpretation* and proponent of authorial intention (a position I was soon to reject). A whole new world of opportunities suddenly opened up: courses, workshops, fellowships, speaking engagements, friendships, possibilities for publication. First articles, then monographs, and finally editions and collections sprang forth, and they found publishers and eventually a few readers; they were, therefore, suspiciously regarded by my colleagues, who considered the work not merely trendy but easy (whether or not it was the former, it certainly was not the latter). More than one reviewer of my new endeavors considered me a quisling, a traitor to the ideals of scholarship, a sycophant yielding to the pressures of time and opportunity. What matters most, to me, is that I was actually enjoying, for the first time, what I was doing, both my teaching and my writing. I began to treat, for the first time, large and significant issues, questions of meaning and social, rather than narrowly textual or professional, significance, those issues that my soul had fairly craved. From theory I have, over the past couple or three years, gravitated—"modulated" may be better, truer—toward the essay as the center of my attention. That, I contend, is not so much a turn-around as a logical development—as I hope this book makes clear.

It is not, in any case, my professional life on which I wish to dwell but the "interior life," which in my case has been deeply affected and shaped by theory. Here the professional and the personal come together, as feminists insist they always should. To a large degree, theory deserves credit for significant changes in the person I am. It has altered the way I perceive and respond to people and events, the way I comport myself, the values I hold, the truths I give myself to, my very reasons for living. Theory has, in short, taught me what it is often thought to deny, threaten, and even to destroy: what it means to be human.

In the preceding essay, I wrote about a central, formative, transformative experience in my life, my version of encounter with nothingness and death, a variation of Odysseus's visit to Hadês. If *The Odyssey* helped me understand, interpret, and give shape and significance to that event, theory showed me how to build on it, what to do with it. Whereas my flirtation with death taught me, as it did Odysseus, to "make haste back to the light," theory has taught me how to live with the lessons learned.[1] By "theory," I should say, I mean especially the work of Jacques Derrida, René Girard, and Geoffrey Hartman, as well as that of their epigones.

I will begin with a key passage in Derrida's *Of Grammatology*, a major text in the movement known as deconstruction: "Without a retention in the minimal unit of temporal experience, without a trace retaining the other as other in the same, no difference would do its work and no meaning would appear. It is not the question of an instituted difference here, but rather, before all determination of the content, of the *pure* movement which produces difference. *The (pure) trace is différance.*" The terms remain difficult, even today, the neologism unsettling, the ideas complex and foreign. Look again at that first sentence I quoted, which, I am tempted to say, says it all. Keep it in mind, as you glide, slide, over to Barbara Johnson's lucid exposition of another, analogous Derridean notion, that of *supplement,* a term that harbors the two quite different meanings of "a substitute for" and "an addition to":

> The logic of the supplement wrenches apart the neatness of the metaphysical binary oppositions. Instead of "A is opposed to B" we have "B is both added to A and replaces A." A and B are no longer opposed, nor are they equivalent. Indeed, they are no longer even equivalent to themselves. They are their own differance from themselves. "Writing," for example, no longer means simply "words on a page," but rather any differentiated trace structure, a structure that *also* inhabits speech. "Writing" and "speech" can therefore no

longer be simply opposed [nor can theory and practice, I add], but neither have they become identical. Rather, the very notion of their "identities" is put in question.

This effects, concludes she, "nothing less than a revolution in the very logic of meaning."[2]

More is at stake here than perhaps linguistics or a narrow conception of philosophy has dreamt of. The linguistic situation Derrida describes, and that Barbara Johnson has elaborated, carries an important lesson concerning relations of whatever kind, including those between and among persons. Consider: a "trace" of the "one" resides in the "other" (the reason for the troublesome quotation marks should soon become clear, if it isn't already) and therefore vice versa. Not only, then, do entities—human as well as linguistic—differ from themselves, but, thanks to the work, the ceaseless movement, of the "trace," neither absolute difference from nor simple identity with is possible. Instead of being identities, individuals distinct, autonomous, and absolutely separated from one another, enti-ties—again, human as well as linguistic—are *related*. As in linguistics, so in life: meaning is a negative matter; it does not reside (positively) in a distinct unit or individual but instead derives from the play of differ-ence between—that is, from the relation of—one to the other. Relation, then, rather than difference: meaning lies in the way you play out your relatedness, how you get along with other people.

Easy to advocate, wonderful in the achievement, is the necessary libera-tion from our almost-insatiable quests of difference. Those are, according to René Girard, linked to "mimetic rivalry," essentially the desire of an object desired by a model who then necessarily becomes an antagonist or opponent. The upshot of this "dangerous craving for differences" is vio-lence, of one kind or another; often it is literal. For Girard and those he has influenced, Jesus, the paradigmatic scapegoat, points the way to rela-tion rather than difference. Listen first to Andrew J. McKenna, who, in a review of John Dominic Crossan's *Raid on the Articulate: Comic Eschatology in Jesus and Borges*, draws Nietzsche in for support, citing *The Will to Power* among other texts:

> "Utter indifference to dogmas, cults, priests, church, theology is Chris-tian." . . . Jesus' indifference to dogma, etc., partakes for Nietzsche of his active indifference to difference: "The 'glad tidings' are precisely that there

are no more opposites." . . . It is just this "faith in opposite values," which Nietzsche reproaches to metaphysicians, . . . that is lacking in Crossan's Jesus, whom he portrays as jousting, joycing and joking with his audience's notions of good and bad, wealth and poverty, prodigal and dutiful, friends and strangers—indeed the whole conceptual and moral economy by which a culture defines, structures and regulates its existence.

Now listen to the Swiss counseler-writer Paul Tournier in a recent book, *The Violence Within*, also deeply indebted to Girard:

> The religion of the sacred was founded on the distinction between the sacred and the profane, between the clean and the unclean. The casuistical morality of the Pharisees, which Jesus challenged, was based upon a distinction between the righteous and the unrighteous. The righteous were those who scrupulously respected the sacred, and the arguments of the doctors of the law were all aimed at fixing its boundaries precisely. To these arguments Jesus brought a "loss of distinctions": no distinction between righteous and unrighteous; all are sinners if one takes into account not the subtle quibblings of legalism, but the unlimited demands of God.

And remember Paul's conclusion: in Jesus is neither Greek nor Jew, male nor female. The question always seems to come down to this: where to draw the line? According to Samuel Weber, deconstruction, which Girard and his followers both sometimes parallel and often repudiate, concerns itself with "the very dividing-line that enables differences to be determined—and arrested—as oppositions." It demonstrates, Weber continues, "the dynamic and unstable process of demarcation itself."[3]

Jesus' indifference to difference, not an opposition to it, is what links up with Derridean *differance*. Difference there is—we hardly need Girard or, before and in back of him, the structuralists to tell us that—but it is not absolute, as we may be inclined to think. Each of us is, simply(!), "always already" related to the "other," a "trace" of that "other" being in us as we are in that "other." In every sense, we are born in relation.

Differance thus deconstructs—the term seems unavoidable—that sense of an isolated, separate, and autonomous ("fixed") self, to the possibility of which we piously and defensively cling. *Differance* is nothing if not risk, involving a questioning of all treasured distinctions, the problematizing of those privileged dividing lines that allow us to pigeonhole and gain apparent control over the flux of experience. It shakes the very foundations of what we hold most dear. Instilling us with what Herbert N.

Schneidau calls "sacred discontent," *differance* constantly, incessantly, un-relentingly disillusions us about the idols we erect in our vain quests of mastery, control, stability—and difference.[4]

I conclude from theory's lesson regarding relation that what ultimately matters in life is how we get along with one another. This, it seems to me, constitutes the heart of our existence and the center of what religion—and especially Christ—teaches (recall that *religio* means "to bind," that is, to bring people together). All the glib, easy talk about God, the Ten Commandments, the observance of rites and rituals and dogmas, the pious pronouncements concerning faith, the smug, sanguine discourse about the soul, heaven, and salvation is just that: talk, not worth a tin-ker's damn, apart from concern, care, and love of the "other." Talk of being "born again," no more or less than the intellectual posturings of theology, runs the great risk of evading the issue—worse, of diverting attention, like the tub tossed out to Leviathan, from what really mat-ters. It bears repeating: as in language, so with the texts that are persons, meaning emerges only from, in, and by means of relationship.

At one point in a remarkably sophisticated book that happens also to be immensely popular (*When Bad Things Happen to Good People*), Rabbi Harold S. Kushner writes that "one of the most important things that any religion can teach us is what it means to be human."[5] And at the heart of what it means to be human is how to get along with other people. We still don't, after countless eons, understand and practice that lesson. Abstractions rush in and usurp our attention, and we think in terms of -isms, -ologies, and theories, finding differences, making differ-ences, craving them—drawing the line, fiddling while Rome burns and individuals suffer. Scanted is the science and art of human relationships.

We have often enough been urged, by one preacher or another, to act, like Eumaios serving Odysseus, as stewards of the absent master's estate. What if by "estate" we understood, not property, but human being? What if, that is, we understood human relations, human feelings, the fragile heart itself as that with which we have been entrusted?

THE LINE. . . . The line of thought that has brought me to that indif-ference to difference practiced by Jesus and essential for life truly, fully human—how straight is it (and why do I care)? How do I now, having reached this point, get back to the line, the line I first laid out?

From Marshall McLuhan to Martin Heidegger the line is very much in question. As it is in Derrida, who deconstructs all versions of linearity ("All the revolutions in [philosophy, science, and literature] can be interpreted as shocks that are gradually destroying the linear model. . . . What is thought today cannot be written according to the line and the book"). Likewise in Geoffrey Hartman's prophetic wandering in the wilderness, the Wandering Jew, recording "the adventures of his soul among masterpieces": not only are "all boundaries in dispute (between nation and nation, outside and inside, text and commentary, . . . literature and philosophy)," but "the subject matter of exegesis" is often nothing else than "the line of the text."[6] The very existence of the line can now be doubted. Linear thinking gives way to something mazy and wondrous.

One name for that something is the essayistic. Linear thinking takes the article as form, nonlinear the essay (which I am trying to write, even as I continue to worry about straying, so ingrained is the professional predilection for the line and the article). The essay and theory thus come together, their difference hardly being absolute, our suppositions notwithstanding. They head in the same direction, in fact, all the while questioning that direction, even the notion of direction itself, wary alike of attempts to move too quickly, to reach a conclusion, to draw the line, to expect that the way will be straight. Each in its own fashion, theory and the essay broaden the path, embrace the "outside," well aware of the complicity of inside and outside, aware too of the exclusions involved in adhering to the straight and narrow. They take their time, are about time, the essay and theory.

BEFORE coming to theory I walked the straight and narrow, toeing the line. If, to my children, American Beauty roses, and Kansas sunsets I was shamefully indifferent, from others I was different, or at least liked to think and even claimed so. I remember once, not so many years ago as to remove the sting of the memory, refusing to invite to a party a graduate student couple reputed to be "living in sin." I was different.

The path then appeared straight and direction clear. Wandering could not be tolerated. I was a good person, clean-mouthed, hardworking, God-fearing, a good provider for my family. I was (also) different—and goddamned proud of it.

For the follies and vices, for the failings of those around me I had little sympathy and no feeling. How could I? I was different from them, after all. I had little knowledge of human being, had little experience, really, of temptation, had no involvement or very little with the muck and mire, the blood and guts, of life. I had never really suffered the pains or tasted the glories possible to the human heart. And so if you strayed, you deserved judgment, condemnation, and punishment. Things were really quite simple.

Things seem much less simple now, grayer, now that I have become more involved in life, having gotten my hands soiled, my "reputation" sullied, my heart bruised and once or twice broken. At least, I know that I have a heart. I know now what it means to love and to hurt, to awake in the arms of someone you care for more than yourself, to long so hard for another human being that nothing much matters besides that absent lover. I no longer feel so different, because I *feel* when I pick up the telephone and it's my daughter Leslie, now decided to major in English and drama at the University of Virginia, calling to tell me of the criticism of her sentences as too long and complicated (we are so much alike, says my ex-mother-in-law). Tears well up too, hot, embarrassingly, when I wave good-bye to my son Christopher, living with his mother in Salina, two and a half hours away that might as well be twelve or twenty. I see tears in his fifteen-year-old eyes, and I know love. The way I feel a part of my children while being apart from them helps me to internalize, to make human, Derrida's point concerning the relation effected by the "trace" of the "one" in the "other."

Having wandered, having erred, straying from the straight and narrow, I no longer find it easy to judge and condemn others' failures. I've grown a little more tolerant, lost some of the inflexibility and hardness I've described. I know how it feels to be judged and condemned. Suffering is a powerful teacher, and the lesson concerns fellow-feeling, as Adam Bede comes to understand: "I used to be hard sometimes. I'll never be hard again." His agonizing recent experiences, the death of his father, the discovery that the woman he loves had given birth to, and then taken the life of, the child begot upon her by the young squire, these now "made Adam look back on all the previous years as if they had been a dim sleepy existence, and he had only now awaked to full consciousness. It seemed to him as if he had always before thought it a light thing that men should suffer, as if all that he had himself endured and called sorrow before was only a moment's stroke that had never left a bruise. Doubtless a great anguish may do the work of years, and we may come out from that baptism of fire with a soul full of new awe and new pity."[7]

I work on my failures, vowing to overcome them. My children, friends, colleagues, the people I love seem all too willing to extenuate these persistent failures of spirit and flesh. They say I've changed—and markedly. I *have* changed—and, despite my erring ways, for the better. Others' failures I at least try to understand and sympathize with. Better to expect much of yourself than of others; better to err—and erring is inevitable—on the side of sympathy than of judgment. I feel different now from the way I used to because I no longer consider myself essentially different from other people.

Nor am I now so much interested in *winning* as I used to be, another lesson taught by theory and life working toward the same end—and leading me, not coincidentally, to the essay. The lesson here relates to the one Girard teaches concerning difference. As I claimed some years ago in a rather heated exchange with the Dryden biographer James A. Winn, a debate fomented by the editors of the journal *The Scriblerian*, we play to win—precisely as my "opponent" was doing, engaging in a rigorous, even ruthless police action against the barbarian, terroristic theorists poised at the gates of the academy.[8] Human psychology is such, the drive to win so ingrained and powerful, that I wanted to respond in kind—violence begets violence, after all, as Girard teaches. In fact, it took a careful, sensitive, but unsparing critique of my response by students in my graduate seminar to show me that Winn and I had become—to use the Girardian term—"doubles," identical to each other in our desire for difference. I was, then, despite my desire, no different. I wanted to win—as I always have, whether locked in combat (at croquet or volleyball) with my imagined competitor for my ex-wife's affections, or with her concerning our children's education; thus I worked for grades in college and honors in graduate school and erected compelling arguments as a "competitive scholar" engaged in the business of overturning previous interpretations of Dryden's or Pope's religious positions.

The point—pointedness is itself a form of violence—has recently been elaborated by the critic-theorist Jane Tompkins. In "Fighting Words: Unlearning to Write the Critical Essay," she shrewdly notes, and I shall quote her at some length:

The showdown on main street isn't the prerogative of the western; it's not the special province of men (as opposed to women); or of popular culture as opposed to literary criticism. TV cop shows, Rambo and Dirty Harry, and their fans do not occupy a different moral universe from the one populated by academicians. Violence takes place in the conference rooms at scholarly meetings and in the pages of professional journals; and although it's not the same thing to savage a person's book as it is to kill them with a machine gun, I suspect that the nature of the feelings that motivate both acts is qualitatively the same. This bloodless kind of violence that takes place in our profession is not committed by other people; it's practiced at some time or other by virtually everyone. *Have gun, will travel* is just as fitting a theme for academic achievers as it was for Paladin.

I'm tempted by Tompkins's conclusion no less than by the preceding remarks to stand and cheer. She does not hide her own complicity as she dramatizes a theoretically inspired self-consciousness:

It's difficult to unlearn the habits of a lifetime, and this very essay has been fueled by a good deal of the righteousness it is in the business of questioning. So instead of offering you a moral, I call your attention to a moment: the moment of righteous ecstasy, the moment when you have the moral advantage of your adversary, the moment of murderousness. It's a moment when there's still time to stop, there's still time to reflect, there's still time to recall what happened in *High Noon*, there's still time to say: "I don't care who's right or who's wrong. There has to be some better way to live."[9]

This is powerful stuff, capable of shaking the very foundations of individual lives, erected on professional conventions, and of the academic profession itself.

What Tompkins does not do, despite her title, is to note the involvement of the form critical and scholarly writing takes in the violence she so well describes. Hers is an *essay*, but the "fighting words" of her title apply to the article, the darling of the academic profession. Years ago, Keith Fort exposed the militaristic nature and strategies, and the implied violence, of critical writing.[10] Because that writing is argumentative, it engenders hostility rather than encourages agreement: it concentrates on winning. Not so the essay, which seems (whether or not it actually is) more mature, too knowledgeable and experienced perhaps merely to argue, uninterested now (if it ever was) in winning, having long since tried to give up the playthings of the mind for the deeper, more lasting joys of the heart.

(Do I go too far here, seeking for the essay to win out over the article, which I seem to want to squash, forgetting—yet again—the lesson of theory, life, and the essay itself?)

THERE'S RISK involved in flouting linearity, of whatever kind: whether you are writing an essay and following its wandering, wavy, mazy track, or negotiating life's many temptations. You can easily flounder. There's always the possibility of indulgence, a menacing Siren, when you opt for the essay rather than the article, when you no longer walk the straight and narrow. The essay certainly risks waywardness, and among scholars, and in tenure decisions, its behavior is not infrequently judged as inappropriate, not quite proper, even promiscuous. The risk is worth taking, however. Not to risk is death. The result need not be waywardness, recklessness, indulgence. That the choice is no simple either/or is a lesson of theory. Theory and life: they are involved, one with the other.

CHAPTER NINE

Finding a Voice

IN WRITING, especially in essays, you respond to the sound, feel, and semblance of voice. Not least in sentences, including their rhythm. Consider if you will this sentence, the opening of my second chapter above: "Essayists, teachers, or both, we typically, indeed unavoidably, use various metaphors in attempting to describe this baggy, perhaps unwieldy, seemingly (but only seemingly) shapeless, in any case lovable, thing, the essay." You may not like the periodic sentence in general or this one in particular: mine is full of commas, reflecting what one of my favorite students calls my accommodating style. But maybe you can be persuaded to consider it reflective of my argument there, for like the essay it maunders, divides, takes first this turn then that, and only after so long a time reaches its apparent point, the rhythm indicative of a voice (I like to think) controlled, supple, and warm. When I wrote the sentence, I certainly was not aware that I might be engaged in anything so artsy. It was only in self-defense, after being challenged by another favorite student, who hated my sentence, that I began to consider what I had wrought, finding it at least defensible, at best expressive. Perhaps I am, at last, on the way to being a writer. Perhaps I am only deceiving myself.

What I have been, for nearly twenty-five years, is a professional student of writing, a teacher first and foremost, but also a scholar, critic, and sometime theorist. When, daringly, I allow myself to think of myself as a writer and not merely a critic, I feel as if I have at last grown up, have left behind the pastoral or merely preparatory activities of commenting on someone else's work and set out to create my own. Emboldened, empowered, I think I can write about what lies nearest my imagination and closest to my heart, giving vent to my own voice. I grant that scholarship, criticism, and theory are all forms of writing, and that their practitioners, commentators on literature all of them, are writers. But we don't ordinarily honor them as such, nor do they, I suspect, ordinarily think of themselves as such. Even though, when pressed, we may admit that all writing is to some degree creative, we nevertheless persist in thinking only of novels, short stories, poems, and plays, really, as creative writing. We regard the critic as one who merely explicates, evaluates, or writes *about* literature. Since a critic doesn't "do" literature (the way a student of philosophy *does* philosophy, *is* a philosopher), a critic is not a writer; his or her work is subordinate to the creative effort that called his or hers into being. A writer, on the other hand, is someone for whom the writing comes first, for whom—in Cynthia Ozick's beautiful phrasing—nothing matters "so much as a comely and muscular sentence."[1]

Writers traffic in words and sentences; scholars, critics, and theorists deal with ideas. Ideas count for writers, naturally; otherwise, their writing would be vacuous. But scholars and critics, for all their interest in the language of the texts they study, tend to give far too little attention to the language of the texts they create. Ideas and expression, thought and language, content and form—they cannot be separated, except for purposes of academic argument. A sensitivity to and a feel for the materiality of language, its warp and woof, constitute writing. The shape and sound of the sentences, their rhythm, mark the writer and distinguish that artisan from his or her fellow toiler in the vineyard of words. It's time, I am arguing, along with Marianna Torgovnick, for critics to graduate to become writers, or at least to try to.

I want to be a writer. It is a desire, perhaps a need, shared by a significant number, maybe even a majority, of English professors. But wishing doesn't make it so. Besides, as John Boy Walton learned early on, locking his door so as to be alone with the Big Chief tablets his Pa had given him one memorable Christmas Eve, wanting to be a writer doesn't translate into being one; nor is it the same as wanting to write. He, of course, John Boy, harbored the latter, and more difficult, ambition, but what about us would-be, perhaps failed, or merely fearful word-slingers who traffic in ideas, obeisant before the words of others even as we contravene our desires in committing sentences to paper, too often careless of the craft it is ours to honor and preserve? Can we endure the pain, withstand the pressure, exercise the patience to carve "comely and muscular" sentences out of the granite of words, ideas, and feelings? Can we find "the right distance" from what we cavalierly call our material, our subject? Do we have a distinctive voice, articulate and attractive? Craft won't tolerate indulgence or suffer impatience. If writing well brings unspeakable joy and satisfaction, writing poorly is intolerable once you have allowed the desire to write to infiltrate your blood. Admiring the achievements of others, you can be only too aware of your own limitations.

I have long wanted to write. I don't know why, exactly. God knows, my early "compositions" in school were not met with either enthusiasm or encouragement. Wherever the desire came from, I "wrote" my first "book" the summer following seventh grade. For whatever reason or reasons, now lost to memory, I wanted to write a book—stories or poems, which I occasionally essayed, were not enough. The topic, genre, or mode (distinctions then unknown to me, of course) hardly mattered. It may have been the idea of *book* that attracted: single, freestanding, an object to be touched, caressed, enjoyed, and kept. I barely knew books, though. We had precious few at home, and I would not for another year come to know the joys available through the county lending library; my reading was confined mainly to the newspaper and sports magazines, especially *Ring* and *Boxing and Wrestling*. (I fantasized about being a professional wrestler, like Nature Boy Buddy Rogers, a villain with long blond hair, who was quoted as saying what would have been music to my ears, "women stand for me.") By then I had a pretty good toy typewriter, a metal one that actually worked, albeit with considerable effort; a slate gray metal typing table, on coasters and with extendable leaves; and, most important, a set of *Compton's Pictured Encyclopedia*, which my parents had, to my great delight, recently bought for me, as dearly as it had cost them on my father's meager mechanic's wages. Thus equipped, I set to work, my mother proud and encouraging. (She says I always wanted to be a writer—my hated beard now a sign marking a writer's scruffy appearance.) I had no room of my own, but that hardly mattered. I chose the "hall" in our five-room house on Pennsylvania Avenue: not at all a corridor but a square, largely wasted space in the center of the house where, below floor level, resided the smoking oil furnace, topped by a grate on which rested two legs of the straightbacked kitchen chair in which I sat as I typed, sweating freely but happy, pretending. My "book" was a biography of an eighteenth-century fur trader in the Hudson Bay Company, whose name is also now lost to memory. The material I lifted directly from *Compton's*, adding few words I could call my own. At least I had the good sense to augment the biography with historical, political, and geographical background, equally cribbed, unfortunately, from a single source. At the end of two weeks I had produced ("written" hardly seems right) twenty-three single-spaced pages. The manuscript resides today, as it has for thirty-five years, in a desk in my parents' house in Greer, along with an unfinished "novel" I attempted the following year, evidence perhaps of determination, indication perhaps of an unmoved center in my life. Am I still pretending, I wonder.

My copy of his poems *Akiba's Children* Geoffrey Hartman inscribed as follows: "For Doug, a poetic soul. Poet-to-be?" Fuel for hope, inspiration to essay.

THE GOAL, I reckon, is a voice of your own. What you hear and feel in the words and the sentences, their shape and rhythm, must be distinctive. Though the voice should be one you would recognize anywhere, who can vouchsafe what its qualities are, in the abstract?

Achieving such distinctiveness, let alone distinction, is tough, more so for critics, for criticism is defined by reliance on the words of others. Though criticism is secondary, at least in the sense that it comes after, it may be impossible, finally, to separate the one who comments from the one commented on. So argues Geoffrey Hartman: "the critic is 'of' the writer he is discussing, a creation 'of' the Book he is writing or writing about."[2] In *Erring: A Postmodern A/theology*, Mark C. Taylor elegantly exploits this intertextuality: his book is stitched, quilted, and taylor-ed as a text(ile) of quotations and commentary, apparently seamless and lacking marks of difference except for the quotation marks.

I rely heavily on quotations, as has been apparent no doubt throughout this book, preferring—at least such is my claim—to let "my" authors have their own say. I admire the voices of those I have written about: Dryden, Pope, Keats, Derrida, Hartman, and others. Whenever I indulge in the luxury of quotation, I see the admonishing finger and sense the wrath of my Bibliography and Methods of Research teacher at Virginia, Lester Beaurline, who did his best to get us to adduce eleven lines of commentary for every line quoted (why eleven exactly, I have never understood). I can rationalize, if not quite justify, my waywardness by recalling William H. Gass's claim that "the apt quotation is one of the essayist's greatest gifts," and by appealing to poststructuralist theory, particularly the notion of intertextuality.[3] Moreover, I have been praised for my apt quotations. But let's be honest here. No matter the (small) talent represented in adducing quotations, quoting quickly becomes a habit, a crutch. My own voice is frequently hard to find through the maze of quotation, citation, and attribution.

Geoffrey Hartman points to the problem, rebuking those of us who quote closely rather than analyze. In allowing us to fill blank pages quickly, quotations deceive about accomplishment. Ultimately, however, a habit deriving for many of us from grade school, relying on the (authoritative) words of others can signal a tendency to bite one's tongue and, more sinisterly, to deny its existence.

The voice of criticism is what I have been discussing throughout this book, wondering about the proper distance between responsive and responsible criticism and the text commented on, wondering too whether there is a correct voice for that commentary. The question of voice links the professional and the personal, being both metaphorical and literal.

I HAVE never liked the sound of my own voice. For one thing, my voice remains annoyingly nasal, despite a childhood operation to remove the adenoids. Moreover, even after twenty-plus years in the Midwest, it still sounds bothersomely southern. It isn't the pronunciation of words— over time and with effort I've managed to improve that. Instead, it's the quality of voice I'm talking about. Mine is, I'm afraid, irremediably of the discount, "food for less" variety. To my ears, I certainly don't sound the way (I think) a professor should. I sound, rather, like a small-town southern boy who has acquired some book learning and, thanks to years in the Midwest, a way of pronouncing most words that almost transcends regionalism.

THERE IS a meeting of the Davenport Junior High Student Council, held in the dark, cramped, basement library. I represent Dewey Huggins's eighth-grade homeroom, a position I craved, primarily for its symbolic value: my first electoral victory. I prevailed this time because, violating an unspoken rule, I voted for myself.

At the first meeting of the year, Grace Medlock presides. She is Student Council sponsor, the new school librarian, and my sixth-grade teacher—the best teacher I had had, in fact. Grace-ful she always seemed, a lady of impeccable manners and remarkable energy, with a mellifluous voice, definitely southern, but Piedmont rather than coastal. She began the meeting with an issue that she obviously found painful, indeed, repugnant. A number of books had recently disappeared from the school library, stolen, it appeared. She sought our advice. Books, precious words lovingly crafted and with the power to quicken the mind and excite the passions, even as objects talismans with proud power—books had been taken. Mrs. Medlock was shaken—this was, you must understand, the mid-1950s, in a small, isolated, rather homogeneous southern town. The theft of books represented for her a kind of barbarism.

Mrs. Medlock immediately turned to me and asked what I thought of someone who would—or could—steal books. I wriggled, began to blush, my ears flamed, and sweat suddenly rose on my neck. I imagined all thirty-some sets of eyes trained on me, and I felt at once exposed and vulnerable. After what seemed an eternity, I managed to emit a few banal words. Then my voice quavered and cracked. Mrs. Medlock thanked me, even praised what I had said. She had not intended, I am sure, to imply that I might have some knowledge concerning the theft of the books, but I nevertheless felt on the spot; called to speak out, I had not my own say, but rather I stole a voice, aping some moralistic, pietistic sentiments I felt expected of me—unreal.

I STILL get stage fright, even after more than twenty years of teaching. Anytime I'm called upon to speak before a group, sometimes even in my classroom, I suffer from performance anxiety. The more I think about being "on stage," fearing the embarrassing quaver and expected break of the voice, the more self-conscious I become. Sometimes I fight to control my voice when merely identifying myself at small-group meetings. The occasion doesn't seem to matter much; it's all the same, whether the audience is ten or two hundred, whether a job is on the line or I'm "merely" doing an introduction in our graduate student colloquium series. It's as if I'm stealing a spot or attention of which I am undeserving. Who am I that I should speak up?

EARLY in my marriage I became fearful of speaking up, lest I express an opinion contrary to my wife's. Not that I feared physical violence. Rather, I feared most the results of disagreement, including the stony silence that could drag on for days. There was, too, the latent fear that saying the wrong thing would set off a chain reaction of charge and countercharge, the end result of which might well be the collapse of a materially comfortable if unloving way of life. A few words might easily do it, so firm in her opinions was my wife, and in fact right about so many things. Her voice was so firm and strong, disguising (I now realize) a self desperate to dominate life and to preserve a bubble of control. Who is more to blame is now moot and was always an academic question: she for dominating, I for allowing it, so weak was my voice.

One bright, warm May morning I found a voice, sadly late. It was during the divorce proceedings, with our implacable attorneys present and bored. How bizarre, almost surreal, a deposition is: before strangers, your words preserved for any and all to read, you tell your story, recount the most intimate and the most embarrassing details of your married life, divulge your secret passions and desires, hear yourself derided, rebuked, reviled, embarrassed—and reduced one last time. Before strangers and to each other, you give voice to pent-up feelings that you've been unable to express but that, having been expressed, just might have made this moment unnecessary. The bitterness, frustration, and anger of nearly twenty years spewed forth in a torrent of words that my attorney later termed dramatic and artful. I don't know about that; I am inclined to dismiss as contrived almost anything lawyers say. But there's no denying the catharsis that depositions can produce.

WHEN I THINK of writing and no longer merely of criticism, of writers rather than of critics, I think immediately of the quite different and distinctive voices you hear in prose that bears the names of Flaubert and Joyce, Henry James and M. F. K. Fisher, Hemingway and Faulkner, Cynthia Ozick and William Gaddis. In criticism, too, you sense voice: Hartman's is different from Stanley Fish's, Gayatri Spivak's much more so from Frank Kermode's, and both of those, different as they are, from Leslie Fiedler's. Difference there is, then, but importance I'm not sure about. With *writing* there is no doubt; it's part of the appeal, of the significance and meaning. Voice matters. It emerges from and through, if not entirely by means of, sentences such as those I quoted earlier from Cynthia Ozick, as it does in Barry Hannah's *Boomerang*, Gordon Lish's *My Romance*, John Edgar Wideman's *Fever*, Harold Brodkey's *Stories in an*

Almost Classical Mode, and Michael Rothschild's *Wondermonger*. The essay-istic voice is perhaps more of a kind, maybe more easily recognizable to ears attuned and attentive, but it is hardly less important. For all their similarities there is significant difference among E. B. White, Edward Hoagland, and Nancy Mairs.

The voice we hear in Barry Hannah and Amy Hempel, in the essay-ists Sam Pickering and Albert Goldbarth, is not to be *identified* with the persons who ate, slept, put pen to paper, shat, and fucked. The voices we hear in essays and fiction alike are carefully crafted creations. There's a relation, and never merely a negative one, between the person and the adopted persona—just as there is between the personal and the profes-sional. My marriage ended at about the same time as my enthrallment to the (definite) article. I then turned to both a form and (the idea of) a woman open and accommodating, warm and responsive.

I RECENTLY READ an essay by Pat C. Hoy II entitled "Mosaics of Southern Masculinity: Small-Scale Mythologies." Largely autobiographical, but spiced with critical commentary, and less stuffy and pretentious than its title portends, this essay insightfully explores the southern male writer's struggle with tradition, community, and the competing pressures of "the higher values of law and order" and "the deeper values of life and nature." [4] Hoy's epigraph from Reynolds Price nicely figures the central issue: "No-body under forty can believe how nearly everything's inherited." As he probes his own cultural and moral inheritance, including his resemblance to his philandering biological father, Hoy considers the work of contem-porary southern male writers, many of them essayists, and examines the way his imagination "has led [him] back into community with the South, into community with Southern men." [5] The men Hoy treats include Sam Pickering and Roy Reed. Like him, and like me, they are southern-bred and "exiled," though Reed has now returned to Hogeye, Arkansas, fol-lowing a successful career with the *New York Times* that included a stint in London. Reared in Tennessee, educated at Sewanee, Princeton, and Cam-bridge, Pickering has taught at Dartmouth and is now at the University of Connecticut; he also served as the inspiration for *Dead Poets Society*. Hoy has taught at the U.S. Military Academy at West Point and now teaches at Harvard. Born in South Carolina, educated at Wofford College and the University of Virginia, I have taught at the University of Kansas since receiving my Ph.D. in 1969. Though some southern writers manage to stay home—I think, for instance, of the earlier-mentioned James Kilgo, another Wofford alumnus and the author of *Deep Enough for Ivorybills*—many do not, and an interesting pattern emerges. If we do not (or cannot) stay home, we never really leave the South behind or purge its particular ways and virtues from our hearts, minds, and perhaps bones. I think of David Huddle, who grew up in Virginia, now teaches at the University of Vermont, and writes often about growing up in Virginia, including in *Only the Little Bone*, and of Maine resident and Colby College professor Franklin Burroughs, who poignantly recalls his native South Carolina in *Billy Watson's Croker Sack*.

Hoy locates in the writers he treats a distinctive set of values. In recalling those of the late exiled rhetorician Richard M. Weaver, the author of such books as *Ideas Have Consequences*, they sound very much "old South," agrarian, if not actually antebellum, what Marshall McLuhan a half-century ago identified as Ancient, in contrast to the Modern values of the industrialized, "nonrhetorical" North. The values celebrated include honor, respect, manners, and commitment to communal life. Sam Pickering says it well: "Ours is an age more indulgent than stoic, an age that stresses cultivation of the self rather than loyalty to the communal. Instead of shaping stewards of the past, people who value institution and custom, our age turns out narrow people, seemingly Seneca-like propagandists of independence, but in truth only devotees of the indulgently personal." The goal should be, he says, "to move beyond self-indulgence and become an actor in a community, one who benefits himself and his fellows, thereby achieving the happy life."[6]

In many ways this picture is attractive. I for one am certainly drawn to the idea of civilization that Pickering represents, have myself courted it at various times. But listen carefully to Pickering's words: elegant, eloquent, and allusive, they recall the glories of Rome and the Ancient ideals of cultivation, but they wear their learning lightly as befits a gentleman, the ever-so-slight and delicate religious terminology employed in the service of secular and social ends. The language is also nostalgic, masculinist (if not sexist), and patrician. It expresses the classical ideal of leisured existence—and leisure depends on money. Sam Pickering (I suspect) has never wanted. Whether or not they were "the right schools," those he attended are certainly prestigious. He tells us he now summers in Nova

Scotia, and he leads, if not "the happy life" that embodies the Senecan ideal he mentions, at least a comfortable and enviable one.

I like Sam Pickering, man and writer. I like his writing in part because of that very whimsicalness, quaintness, and reversion to old-fashioned values, some of them universal and eternal. Time has passed him by, but Sam Pickering doesn't give a damn. He knows what he likes—and if that is not always something I want to share or can share, reading him reminds me of another world whose impossibility for most of us is not for mourning but for knowing.[7] We have much to learn from Sam Pickering.

The voice we hear in his essays, an important part of his charm and of the knowledge we can use, is a conscious creation deriving, at least in part, from Pickering's close knowledge of the history of essay writing. Over the years he has developed a distinctive voice, an essayist's voice: warm, personable, self-deprecating, unpretentious; set in determined opposition to systems, abstractions, and jargon; caring, craft-y, respectful; not so much committed to the concrete, particular, and quotidian as having lived sufficiently to know that that's where value and meaning lie. If you dismiss this voice as lightweight, and irrelevant, you're a fool. Its wisdom derives as much from experience as from books. You won't find it, though, if you don't listen patiently, attentively, and respectfully. That's something the essayist Pickering has learned, and it's something he teaches, as much through how he writes as what he says.

The voice of the *man* is sharper than you might expect from his essays, more pointed, less middle-aged than collegiate, casual in its profanity. Even after many years north of the Mason-Dixon line, that voice remains opulently southern. Hearing it, I recall the young men I knew at Wofford from the low country of South Carolina; they came from well-to-do families that had long formed the pillars of their communities. Bearing the first names Reeves, Cantey, and Fleming, they wore new Weejuns, chinos, and madras shirts, and they belonged to fraternities. Their girlfriends at Converse, Sweet Briar, and Agnes Scott also had money and came from families with equally distinguished histories. Well bred, that's what these young men were. They formed a closed circle and were none too supportive when Wofford admitted its first lone and lonely black student. They were none too kind, either, to those different in other ways— boys from the upstate like me, whose father was a mechanic and whose mother was a mill hand. I was not badly treated, not overtly anyway.

Eventually I became editor of the literary magazine and later was elected president of the Student Christian Association, at the time one of the top three campus-wide offices. Still, I never belonged to the inner circle. That wouldn't have mattered so much had I not wanted it so badly.

When I recall my well-to-do classmates, I inevitably think of their easy profanity (by which I mean their attitude of mind as well as their language), symptomatic at once of male bonding, as it is now called, of intellectual distance from sacred values that are acknowledged in the very acts that flout them, and of continuity with the father, figured as something of a cavalier, a rake, an unholy combination of Restoration English and Confederate values. The men I am attempting to describe, fathers and sons alike, would cuss a blue streak, drink hard, chase—discreetly, of course—after women, bedding quite a few and maybe getting some of them pregnant. Without blinking an eye, these men would defend to the death the ideals of womanhood, motherhood, alma mater, church, community, and region.

I AM DIFFERENT. I don't belong with the southern writers Pat Hoy discusses, and not just because I lack their talent and accomplishments. They speak one language, I another. Their voice is agrarian and inherited, mine bookish and acquired; theirs patrician and aristocratic, mine plebeian and populist. Twenty-plus years in the Midwest have strengthened my wariness of many of the longings voiced by so many southern writers.

I'm drawn at once to—though not torn between, I hope—the postures and perspectives of essayists like E. B. White and Edward Hoagland (significantly enough in this context, both northerners) and the intellectual and cultural values of Geoffrey Hartman (European, Jewish, speculative and brooding, deeply romantic, vastly informed by and sympathetic to poststructuralist critical and theoretical developments, a virtual embodiment of what Sam Pickering excoriates). I must find or create a voice different from Pickering's. Yet I embrace his description of what has happened to criticism, grown increasingly impersonal and irrelevant to "general" readers. It is not without interest, given my foregoing remarks, that his brief account occurs in an essay entitled "Son and Father," nor that that essay is included in a book bearing the title *The Right Distance*. These are his words: "At Vanderbilt during the 1920s literary criticism was shifting from the personal and anecdotal to the intellectual and the abstract.

Instead of explaining ordinary life, it began to create an extraordinary world of thought far from piles and bobbed hair. For Father such a shift led to boredom and the conviction that although literary criticism might entertain some people, it was ultimately insignificant. In the sixty years that have passed since Father entered Vanderbilt, criticism has become more rarefied, and the result is, as a friend and critic wrote me, 'we write books that even our mothers won't read.' "[8]

I am interested in responding to this situation and ultimately correcting it; such is the purpose of *Estranging the Familiar*. The answer does not, cannot, lie in a simple return to the simplicity and glories of the past, no matter how strong the tug of nostalgia. Pretheoretical, impressionistic criticism, such as "Father" evidently found interesting and significant, won't do—although I understand the wish and sometimes indulge it myself. Is compromise such an unholy solution? I don't mean to be melodramatic, but surely we've had enough of either/or thinking, which can too easily lead to ultimate solutions.

It's not necessarily a virtue, and it certainly entails risks and losses, but I'm neither completely one thing nor wholly another: a scholar-critic instead of a teacher, a Christian rather than (temperamentally) a Jew, a liberal instead of a conservative, a poststructuralist rather than a New Critic. Maybe that's one reason why deconstruction so appeals to me, at least as I understand it. I embody the indeterminacy deconstruction tirelessly proclaims and proudly reveals. Some such deep-seated proclivity, nourished by theory, fuels my hope for an essay mode at once more personal than Geoffrey Hartman sanctions and more philosophical than Sam Pickering can stomach.

THERE IS no getting away from voice, style, and character. The essayist, not quite like the novelist or short-story writer, must find, create, or assume a voice that fits. It's a little like selecting an article of clothing: a pinpoint Oxford from Abercrombie and Fitch or a silk shirt by Joseph Abboud would no more suit Edward Abbey (though it would Tom Wolfe) than a leather miniskirt would be right for Virginia Woolf (though it might be for Susan Sontag). E. B. White has written—I've quoted it before—that the essayist "selects his garb from an unusually extensive wardrobe." It's also true, as White goes on to say, that there is "one thing the essayist cannot do": he or she cannot "indulge himself [or herself] in deceit or in concealment"; "the basic ingredient" remains *natural candor*.[9] Even if the essayist needn't tell the whole truth and nothing but the truth, there cannot be a glaring rift between the person and the persona. What matters is that you must be willing to accept the voice you hear; if it doesn't appear real, or true, it will crack and break. But "real" means truthful within the created context, and the sense of natural candor derives as much from artistic design as from the vaunted notion of authorial sincerity. Thanks to poststructuralist revelations, we may someday appreciate that the person is no more a simple identity than the persona, each of us the product of "self-fashioning."

Sam Pickering's writing voice fits the man, whatever signs of strain appear between the benevolent casualness and cantankerous wholesomeness honored and displayed in the essays and the vestiges of collegial hell-raising that may linger in the man. I cannot, without deceit or concealment, put on such a voice. Nor can I wear the melancholy that Pickering has poignantly (but not, I think, accurately) identified with the essayistic voice ("essayists are pessimistic and melancholy. Often they are sad people"). If sadness there is, it would seem of the kind that "lies too deep for tears," the product of pain not completely overcome or forgotten but understood. I am more inclined to agree with Joseph Epstein that a certain affirmativeness, growing out of "love of life," marks the essayist—Hazlitt, for instance, "who, for all the obstacles life set before him, never ceased to love life." [10] I see the essayist as smiling, even though the smile be neither quick nor easy. It betokens neither ignorance of pain nor denial of suffering. On the contrary, the smile is earned by having come through trials of the flesh and of the heart, having arrived on the other side of loss, where shines "the light of common day." The essayist broods on experience, finds it more good than sad, and says so.

It's all a matter of distance. Finding the right distance is another name for finding a voice.

WHENEVER I return "home," which long ago ceased being home, I immediately become morose, not merely taciturn but sullen, unhappy to be there and impatient to be gone. When I speak, in response to a direct question, no strength appears in my voice.

It's difficult going back. The reason is not alone that I have outgrown the sleepy, wizened, and sad town that holds little interest for me and contains few people I care about. It's a largely unfamiliar world: different from what was mine for twenty-some years, different from what is now mine, what I call home. Part of it is that I see myself in my parents. I am embarrassed by their lapses, annoyed by their infirmities, angered by their failures, saddened that they are old, shamed by the way they live. I fear the future, mine as well as theirs.

There is more, much more, as I came to understand in the dog days of another depressing August. It—*might have*—happened this way, as I was polishing this very essay, assuming that it would end just before the last section break, treatment sufficient, I thought, of my struggle to find a voice, inseparable from "the right distance," the title of Sam Pickering's essay collection that I had been rereading.

Though I've never been exactly garrulous, I'm reasonably outgoing, but as soon as I set foot in the house I once loved, I clam up. I used to think my voicelessness in Greer was attributable to fear that I would unwittingly utter here too the wrong word, precipitating one of the violent and now daily fights that have marked my parents' existence for the past decade. Their world, through which, virtually an alien, I orbit twice a year, essentially consists of each other, an ever-blaring TV set, and their fertile and overactive imaginations, productive of fantasies succored and growing wild and unfettered in the two and a half rooms that for all practical purposes constitute their home. I mentioned in an earlier chapter that my mother, so long a pillar of strength, with eyes sharp and clear and mind firm and in control, is now afflicted with paranoid schizophrenia, a condition of alternating and deteriorating periods of lucidity and madness that has led to what a psychiatrist I persuaded her to see (only three times, unfortunately) labeled *folie à deux*. My father has caught and now shares her madness, adding fuel to the fire that consumes any hope for a happy end to their days.

It all started, at least the overt manifestations of their problems did— God only knows the true origin—ten years ago with my mother charging my father, then in his mid-seventies, with infidelity. It straightaway became apparent to me, summoned to Greer by frantic calls from both of them, that, despite the conviction with which my mother spoke and the many particulars she was able to adduce, my father was innocent (he remains one of the most honorable, if not always one of the most agreeable, men I have ever known). No man, let alone one his age, could perform

171

all the sexual acts with which my mother charged him. As she told and retold her story, details shifted, the accusations grew wilder and more and more ridiculous, and she seemed less and less familiar, so different from the embodiment of truth and judgment I had idolized.

Some years ago, my father began responding in kind, innocence cruelly generative of a different guilt. He began to accuse my mother of just the sort of sexual liaisons of which she had accused him. (I've never known her to be the least bit interested in sex.) Misreading people, situations, and occurrences as perversely as she, he became convinced, and remains so, that my favorite aunt and uncle, my mother's sister and her husband, along with my childhood buddy Leon, are out to filch the money he and my mother have worked so hard and sacrificed so much to save. Those three were determined, with my mother's knowledge and contrivance, not only to make off with what is now a considerable estate and so to deprive me of an inheritance but also to dissolve my marriage. (To this day, despite my most vehement protestations, he persists in blaming my divorce on the four of them, whose support and love are, I believe, unqualified.) My father squirrels away his financial statements under the front seat of their 1967 Impala, which is always locked; he holds the only key. My mother, equally convinced of *his* designs on *her* money, secures her papers and not a little cash (she has always liked to hold onto crisp, new bills) in the tattered chair in which she passes her life and that has served as her bed for over six years now.

The late autumn of their lives (I don't want to think "winter"), Thursey Mae's and George's, thus passes in fierce, unrelenting harangues, the intensity of which you can hardly imagine (I certainly wouldn't believe the horror, had I not experienced it firsthand, each renewal as shocking as the first, each renewal extending the crack in my heart). My father is, as used to be said, "hard of hearing," a lifelong and apparently uncorrectable affliction barely relieved by the powerful aids he wears in both ears. For him this unfortunate condition now functions as both a blessing and a curse, for he can, and does to my mother's everlasting chagrin and resentment, turn his hearing aids down and tune her out. Thus he misses out on most of what she screams, the mud she slings, as well as the incessant swipes, jabs, and floutings in which she engages when they're not actually fighting. As he says, she never has a kind word for him—though once the fighting begins, he is no piker, giving fully as much as she does, his ability to control what is heard adding insult to injury, infuriatingly: once the aids are off, there is no communicating with him, no way to reach him. Even with the Beltones functioning, my father understands less than half of what is said in his presence—a marriage-long source of friction, my mother never having shown much sympathy or support, or so he claims and I have to believe.

The daily outbursts now, which I have known to last from early morning to well past midnight, relieved only by the necessity of surcease in the form of a nap, constitute a kind of love-hate. The content of the mutual ravings, now so familiar as to be repeated almost word for word, like the oral performances of illiterate poets in Appalachia, no longer matters; structural relation constitutes the meaning. In other words, these horrible outbursts are now about the function each participant serves in a relationship sustained by and dependent upon the vicious verbal assaults. To anyone not party to that relation, these fierce and piercing battles appear less complicated. In any case, the most farfetched accusations and the most absurd threats are bandied about, the charges smacking of just enough truth to take in the unwary and untutored. My mother receives my father's belligerent and vengeful ravings and returns them, with the force and direction of a Navratilova forehand. His tall frame now bent nearly double, my father curses his "enemies," charging them with the most outrageous crimes, dredging up petty details from the distant past, twisted wildly to suit his argument, all this shouted in a voice nasal and shrill, provoked and provoking, setting already raw nerves on edge, generating a reciprocal response. On occasion, a bony, spotted fist slams down on a countertop, resounding on the stove top, figuring a fierceness matched only by the voice's explosive rage. Sometimes a pan is thrown, a broom taken up and poised menacingly, the walker, heavy and dangerous, suddenly appreciated as a threat lethal and final. Both claim to be victims of (physical) violence, my mother holding my father responsible for her broken hips and claiming—it is an image that a student of language can appreciate—that he frequently stuffs her mouth with dishrags, he that she has beaten him with that menacing broom and with that heavy and dangerous walker broken his glasses. I doubt most of this, though their stamina amazes. On several occasions my mother has apparently called "the law," summoning sheriff's deputies out of Greenville. At least twice (or so restive neighbors have confided to my friend Leon), my mother has fled the house, barely clothed even in the dead of winter, and been seen, well past midnight, lumbering up and down the street, evidently unaware and jabbering.

Into this surreal but all-too-familiar situation I come twice a year, anxious and, I admit, not a little resentful. I try not to blame my parents. Being ill, both of them, they cannot be held responsible for their actions. They can no more quit their fighting than I can stop remembering a happier past.

I grant that my voicelessness is not altogether their fault. I am a free individual and accountable in my own right. Yet for all their love, undeniable sacrifices, and gifts material and otherwise, my parents have never shown much interest in what I think, feel, want, and need. Part of the problem is that they don't listen well—neither of them (and least of all to each other). They talk, and talk, for long stretches of time—about what interests them, careless of whether you are interested or even listening, so familiar are their stories. Concrete and particular, and thus different from abstract academic discourse, my parents' talk now centers more and more on the unrecoverable past, inevitably viewed as a better, happier time. There is almost no dialogue, no exchange of ideas. They talk *at* me rather than *with* me.

I WAS, for a very long time, largely an extension of their personalities. Even as I near the half-century mark, I feel like a child when I'm with them (I'll always be her baby, my mother says).

Both of my parents insist on always being right. They are stubborn, hardheaded people, my mother both a Taurus and a Baptist, my father no less set in his ways, convinced of the validity of his interpretations, never mind that he hears very little of what is said around him. Knowing what was right for me, they controlled my life well into college. That control early appeared in the guise of overprotectiveness: from the elements, from the possibility of infection, from injury—not only did they demand (and still do when they can) that on cold or rainy days I "have something on my head," a mortification shaming my adolescence, but neither would allow me, even past teen age, to operate our power mower, a neighbor's child having once lost two fingertips to the rotary action.

Dating was also discouraged. *Girls are no good; they'll ruin you. You don't need them; you're not interested in that. You have your schoolwork. Get involved with some slip of a girl, and your grades will suffer. Think about college. You're a*

good boy. You have a reputation. Make something of yourself. Take advantage of op-
portunities we never had. We're so proud of you. You're what I live for. Nothing I
saw at home suggested I was missing out on anything important. My parents did not touch, kiss, exchange glances, or use terms of endearment.
I do not recall that they ever acknowledged, let alone celebrated, their
wedding anniversary, the date of which I'm not sure I ever knew. If they
ever made love, I'm not aware of it. Until I was six, I slept with them.

I remember how first dumbstruck and then angry my mother was
when, during my senior year in high school, I suddenly and proudly announced I had a date with "Linda Duncan," an object of long-standing
interest until then unexpressed. "You've throwed me over," she shouted
(I remember, it was in the parking lot of Community Cash grocery
store). "Tied to her apron strings" pretty well describes me then, as does
"mama's boy," an epithet whose sting I felt not a few times, even as I enjoyed the benefits of being an only child and having a mother who doted
on me. She indulged almost my every whim, whether for oyster stew,
pineapple upside-down cake, a toy typewriter, or boxing and wrestling
magazines. My memories of home life are thus, most of them, happy; it's
the retrospective analysis that reveals a story driven by motives I'm still
laboring to understand, an analysis I'm afraid estranging in its distancing and difference. What I prefer to remember, and to believe, about my
mother especially, is not always what I am slowly and reluctantly coming
to accept as truth.

My departure for college posed little challenge to her control, at least
initially. Wofford is less than twenty miles from Greer, and though I was a
boarding student I returned home every weekend, laden with dirty laun-
dry that my parents washed as I stole away to do homework, ravenous for
my mother's cooking, all the while hiding the secret of sexuality wither-
ing on the vine, sad when Sunday night came and I had to return to
Spartanburg and another week of little other than intense study. Graduate
school at the University of Virginia offered a more serious challenge to
my mother's power and influence over me, of course, but she did not lose
control until I married, halfway through my four years in Charlottes-
ville. The marriage was against her better judgment; my wife she thought
not "our type." On the whole, however, her protests now seem few and
mild. Less politic was her involvement in the first years of my marriage,
subtle and not-so-subtle intrusions that I did too little to parry.

Once I was in Kansas, and soon a parent myself, my mother's influence ebbed dramatically. It was gradual, almost imperceptible, the change that came. However egotistical it may be for me to say so, I believe that losing me (for that is surely how she must have felt) represented for my mother a defeat, one that cut her to the very quick, so close had we been—too close, no doubt. To her credit, she never let on, to me, how much I had hurt her. My wife knew, or at least suspected. About our decision for me to accept a teaching position in Kansas, she remarked, more aware than I that without some such distance our marriage was already doomed (because of *her* mother's influence as well as mine), "I don't know how you could do this to your mother."

My mother's world now consists of barely half their house, which she leaves only (and with increasing reluctance) twice a year, when I persuade her to get out for an hour or two's ride to Greenville, Spartanburg, or the mountains. My mother's control of even the little world surrounding her tattered chair has slipped from her bony, anxious grasp. Sad, desperate in the defeat she refuses to acknowledge, she is at once a pathetic and a heroic figure. The pain she endures I hope never to know—would that I could somehow relieve it, though.

Even over my father she now has little control, he who was allowed little say in my upbringing and little contact with his "side" even as my mother's next of kin were regular if not daily visitants, certainly fixtures of my childhood memories. At some point, after I moved to Kansas, my father evidently found a voice. Certainly he began to do things of which I had long supposed him uninterested, even incapable. He took charge of bill payments as well as of purchases and eventually assumed responsibility for virtually all cooking and cleaning. Necessitated by my mother's deteriorating mental and physical condition, this newfound assertiveness joined with my mother's losses to rend irreparably the fabric of her carefully tailored world. However she now really feels about me—she regularly insists that her grandchildren and I are "all [I've] got"—my mother does not suffer my father's contributions gladly, sometimes feeble and frequently misdirected as they are, often well-meaning, though sometimes designed as power plays. She retains at least this much power: she can claim that she, far better than he, knows how things *should* be done. Not being put to the test, she preserves some power inviolate.

Set in his ways as far back as I can remember, "an Atkins through and through," as my mother used to declare, increasingly bossy and dictatorial, my father cherishes the power he has wrested from her. He would like her approval, but control, new to him, he likes even more. He has apparently forbidden my mother the use of their telephone, an interdiction I suppose I can understand, in light of her former abuses (she indiscriminately spread the word of his imagined affairs). My father's domination, stifling, tyrannical, I have experienced via his vehement remonstrations concerning the alleged greed and almost murderous intent of Sammie, Lullean, and Leon. Although he has never actually forbidden me to see or call them, I can hardly mistake the pressure he applies. Even to speak with them would undermine his efforts to resist their unrelieved determination to ruin "us." Any interest I express in his enemies suggests to my father doubts about his story and, worse, that I'm siding—it's always a matter of sides—with my mother against him, history repeating itself. Of course, my mother interprets my neglect of Leon, Sammie, and Lullean as proof that I've swung to my father's side. I do not question his love, recently instanced in his gift outright, and as quick as generous, of $15,000, which made it possible for me to buy a house that he will probably never get to see. Can I now ignore or go against his wishes?

To THIS SITUATION I return twice a year—of course, I'm never really out of it. Long ago I abandoned hope for a miracle that would set things right. Instead, I dread the pressures that will immediately be applied in ways subtle and direct, caught between Scylla and Charybdis, hardly less under my parents' control than when I was a child. Though I have long harbored such thoughts as I have expressed here, not until my most recent visit did they break into full consciousness, radiant with the quickness and assurance that accompanies the irruption of truth. I understood, and I knew I had to act, at last.

The moment of understanding came on a Friday night, following a day of barely relieved raving by both my parents, the charges and countercharges no less horrible for being familiar and well rehearsed. As usual, once the sniping degenerated into fighting, I took to my bedroom, as far from my mother's seat of power and my father's piercing, thunderous dramatizations as I could get, closed the door, lay back on the bed, at once listened, attempted to read, and tried to think of a way out for me and for them. Somehow the day passed. With darkness came light. It struck me at once: what I was suffering was connected with what I had been writing about, the earlier portion of this essay. *I had no voice.*

Much followed from this recognition. Contrary to the overwhelming helplessness I had so intensely felt earlier in the day, there was hope, and the solution, it now appeared, was up to me. I would have to speak up to my parents, throwing off the noose of his strangling tyranny and of hers. I *should* be able to call and to see Sammie, Lullean, and Leon, and I *should* give voice to the truth that I had long known lay elsewhere than in their wild and irrational stories. That night I slept with hope.

The next morning rose hazy and threatening, early full of the languor of a South Carolina August. By eight my mother's sniping was already showing signs of erupting into the familiar harangue, horrible with obscenities. She could not, she announced, afford to leave the house for our planned trip to the mountains. She had to protect her watch and rings, linen, photographs of my house, and so on, lest they be stolen by those with whom my father consorted.

Suddenly I turned on her. "Goddammit," I began, cursing for the first time in front of my mother, whose face immediately evinced the shock of recognition. "Enough is enough. Jesus Christ, this shit has to stop, and stop it will. I've put up with this fucking nonsense long enough. Every goddamned time I come home I have to put up with the same fucking goddamned shit. You don't know your ass from a hole in the ground. Things *will* be different from now on."

My mother's brown eyes blazed. I pressed on with some muddled if less profane declaration about my right to have some say in "things." She pulled me up short. "You've done it now, big boy," she said with a fierceness belying the calm in her voice, that well-chosen appellation that cut to the quick, evincing the knowledge of which she remains secure. "I have a mind to slap the fire out of you." She already had, of course. Then: "I'm through with you, now that you spoke up."

Spoken up I had, though only to my mother, and as I never had before. But I felt none of the expected exhilaration, no sense of the rightness and little of the freedom I had imagined, that in fact had flooded me the night before, what I had fantasized in those almost swooning moments as presaging a new era of maturity and strength. The light of day had only revealed the darkness in which illumination is wrapped and from which it is inseparable.

I had achieved voice—"stolen" may be more accurate. So determined was I to have my say, to vent a voice, having made me, my alleged rights, and my way a side that deserved a hearing, that I set myself in determined opposition to *them,* mother and father alike. In so doing, I obliterated not just the difference between them but also that between my parents and me. I had spoken up, but what I had accomplished was that identity with them they had perhaps all along sought, the doubleness of which René Girard warns us in his exposé of reciprocal violence. Asserting difference had only insured identity.

In reacting impulsively, angrily, moreover, I had failed to say what I had wanted, what I actually felt: I had neglected to fashion and shape my remarks, omitting mention of the love I feel for my parents, which should have prefaced my declaration of independence and difference.

In laying claim to voice, I had forgotten heart, feeling obscured by anger, tenderness sacrificed on the altar of usurped, egoistic opportunity. I should have spoken out, no doubt about that, but I did it badly, and wrong. Subtle are the differences.

My own say, I now realize, is not *my own* say.

My real speaking out is, of course, this essay.

HAVE I FOUND MY VOICE? The overwhelming question. If I *have* found a voice, it is, I would think, less Odysseus's than that of Teiresias, the blind seer who represents quintessentially the both/and vision. The voice I hope can be heard here reflects sympathy. I don't think I will ever be like Odysseus in having the knowledge and the skill to make things right. The best I can hope for, and work toward, is the capacity not only to sympathize (and so to give) but also to control my emotions, my self.

It is not, of course, in the last analysis, simply a matter of voice—it is also a matter of distance, a question of achieving "the right distance." Sympathy respects distance, maintains it in fact, rather than collapsing it into identity. "The right distance" functions as another name for relation, entailing distinction without (so easily) generating into absolute difference. Through writing, one sense of which deconstruction understands as the structure of difference marked by the trace, I wonder if I have come to a more positive relationship with Mama and Daddy?

LESS SUBORDINATE and under another's control than the article, essays allow you your voice. It's a voice impure, contaminated, made up of many others. A both/and creature, amphibious, and not unlike dreaded deconstruction, the critical essay is a combination of commentary on another text and the expression of the critic's voice and personal experience, the capacious product at once of speaking and listening. The essay is, then, not simply protean but also balanced, at one and the same time assertive and respectful. If it speaks out—and to do so is its birthright— the essay has its say responsibly, having earned the right. It opposes indulgence no less than repression. If it steals, it's from the heart.

Notes

Preface

1. George Core, "Stretching the Limits of the Essay," in *Essays on the Essay: Redefining the Genre*, ed. Alexander J. Butrym (Athens: University of Georgia Press, 1989), 217.

2. Core, "Stretching the Limits of the Essay," 207.

3. William H. Gass, "Emerson and the Essay," in *Habitations of the Word* (New York: Simon and Schuster, 1985), 25.

4. Geoffrey H. Hartman, *Criticism in the Wilderness: The Study of Literature Today* (New Haven: Yale University Press, 1980), 4.

5. Georg Lukács, "On the Nature and Form of the Essay," in *Soul and Form*, trans. Anna Bostock (Cambridge: MIT Press, 1974), 14.

6. Lydia Fakundiny, ed., *The Art of the Essay* (Boston: Houghton Mifflin, 1991), 678.

ONE. The Return of/to the Essay

1. As Barbara Lounsberry has written, "The artistry of nonfiction is the great unexplored territory of contemporary criticism. This is ironic, for the second half of the twentieth century has been an age of nonfiction. American book clubs, which began in the 1920s offering primarily fiction, now emphasize nonfiction. Today's *New York Times Book Review* reviews nonfiction over fiction almost three to one. In truth, our age has stopped subscribing to the belief that the novel is the highest form of the literary imagination" (*The Art of Fact: Contemporary Artists of Nonfiction* [Westport, Conn.: Greenwood Press, 1990], xi). The essay is, of course, only one instance of this phenomenon—a distinctive and particularly important one, I would argue.

2. Robert Atwan, Foreword to *The Best American Essays, 1988*, ed. Annie Dillard (New York: Ticknor and Fields, 1988), x; Scott Russell Sanders, "The Singular First Person," *Sewanee Review* 96 (1988): 659.

3. Donald Hall, ed., *The Contemporary Essay* (New York: St. Martin's Press, Bedford Books, 1984), xiii.

4. Annie Dillard, Introduction to *The Best American Essays, 1988*, xvi; Scott Walker, ed., *The Graywolf Annual Three: Essays, Memoirs & Reflections* (Saint Paul, Minn.: Graywolf Press, 1986), vi; Sanders, "The Singular First Person," 660. "In this era of prepackaged thought," claims Sanders, "the essay is the closest thing we have, on paper, to a record of the individual mind at work and play. It is an amateur's raid in a world of specialists. Feeling overwhelmed by data, random information, the flotsam and jetsam of mass culture, we relish the spectacle of a single consciousness making sense of a part of the chaos" (660).

5. John Tallmadge, *New York Times Book Review*, 14 June 1987, 29.

6. Graham Good, *The Observing Self: Rediscovering the Essay* (London: Routledge, 1988), vii. Other books focusing on the essay include Chris Anderson, ed., *Literary Nonfiction: Theory, Criticism, Pedagogy* (Carbondale: Southern Illinois University Press, 1988); John A. McCarthy, *Crossing Boundaries: A Theory and History of Essay Writing in German, 1680–1815* (Philadelphia: University of Pennsylvania Press, 1989); Alexander J. Butrym, ed., *Essays on the Essay: Redefining the Genre* (Athens: University of Georgia Press, 1989); Wilfrid Sheed, *Essays in Disguise* (New York: Knopf, 1990).

7. Edward Hoagland, "What I Think, What I Am," in *The Tugman's Passage* (New York: Penguin, 1983), 25; Joseph Epstein, "Piece Work: Writing the Essay," in *Plausible Prejudices: Essays on American Writing* (New York: Norton, 1985), 400.

8. Réda Bensmaïa, *The Barthes Effect: The Essay as Reflective Text*, trans. Pat Fedkiew, intro. by Michèle Richman, Theory and History of Literature, Vol. 54 (Minneapolis: University of Minnesota Press, 1987), 96.

9. Robert Atwan, Foreword to *The Best American Essays, 1986*, ed. Elizabeth Hardwick (New York: Ticknor and Fields, 1986), ix.

10. Phillip Lopate, "What Happened to the Personal Essay?" in his *Against Joie de Vivre* (New York: Poseidon, 1989), 76.

11. Good, *The Observing Self*, xii.

12. Hoagland, "What I Think," 25.

13. William Howarth, "Itinerant Passages: Recent American Essays," *Sewanee Review* 96 (1988): 642. In praising the essay, Clifford Geertz writes similarly: "For making detours and going by sideroads, nothing is more convenient than the essay form. One can take off in almost any direction, certain that if the thing does not work out one can turn back and start over in some other with only moderate cost in time and disappointment. Midcourse corrections are rather easy, for one does not have a hundred pages of previous argument to sustain, as one does in a monograph or treatise. Wandering into yet smaller sideroads and wider detours does little harm, for progress is not expected to be relentlessly forward anyway, but winding and improvisational, coming out where it comes out. And when there is nothing more to say on the subject at the moment, or perhaps altogether,

the matter can simply be dropped. 'Works are not finished,' as Valéry said, 'they are abandoned'" (*Local Knowledge: Further Essays in Interpretive Anthropology* [New York: Basic Books, 1985], 6).

14. William Zeiger, "The Exploratory Essay: Enfranchising the Spirit of Inquiry in College Composition," *College English* 47 (1985): 460.

15. Ibid., 461.

16. Note Addison's famous distinction: "Among my daily papers which I bestow on the public, there are some which are written with regularity and method and others that run out into the wildness of those compositions which go by the name of *essays*. As for the first, I have the whole scheme of the discourse in my mind, before I set pen to paper. In the other kind of writing, it is sufficient that I have several thoughts on the subject, without troubling myself to range them in such order that they may seem to grow out of one another and be disposed under the proper heads. Seneca and Montaigne are patterns for writing in this last kind, as Tully [Cicero] excels in the other. When I read an author of genius who writes without method, I fancy myself in a wood that abounds with a great many noble objects rising among one another in the greatest confusion and disorder. When I read a methodical discourse, I am in a regular plantation and can place myself in several centers, so as to take a view of all the lines and walks that are struck from them. You may ramble in the one a whole day altogether and every moment discover something or other that is new to you, but when you have done you will have but a confused imperfect notion of the place; in the other, your eye commands the whole prospect and gives you such an idea of it as is not easily worn out of the memory" (Joseph Addison, *Spectator*, no. 476, 4 September 1712).

17. William H. Gass, "Emerson and the Essay," in *Habitations of the Word* (New York: Simon and Schuster, 1985), 25–26.

18. So claims Chris Anderson, "Hearsay Evidence and Second-Class Citizenship," *College English* 50 (1988): 305.

19. Ibid., 300, 303.

20. Ibid., 307.

21. Georg Lukács, "On the Nature and Form of the Essay," in *Soul and Form*, trans. Anna Bostock (Cambridge: MIT Press, 1974), 9; Geoffrey Hartman, *Criticism in the Wilderness: The Study of Literature Today* (New Haven: Yale University Press, 1980), 191.

22. Hartman, *Criticism in the Wilderness*, 157, 155.

23. Anderson, "Hearsay Evidence and Second-Class Citizenship," 305; Gass, "Emerson and the Essay," 25.

24. W. Wolfgang Holdheim, "Introduction: The Essay as Knowledge in Progress," in *The Hermeneutic Mode: Essays on Time in Literature and Literary Theory* (Ithaca: Cornell University Press, 1984), 20.

25. Ibid., 21.

26. Ibid., 30, 28.

27. Good, *The Observing Self*, 180–81.

28. R. Lane Kauffmann, "The Skewed Path: Essaying as Unmethodical Method," in Butrym, *Essays on the Essay*, 224.

29. O. B. Hardison, Jr., "Binding Proteus: An Essay on the Essay," in Butrym, *Essays on the Essay*, 25, 27; Lydia Fakundiny, ed., *The Art of the Essay* (Boston: Houghton Mifflin, 1991), 4, 19.

30. Bensmaïa, *The Barthes Effect*, viii, 96, 90.

31. Anderson, "Hearsay Evidence and Second-Class Citizenship," 305.

32. Geoffrey Hartman, *The Fate of Reading and Other Essays* (Chicago: University of Chicago Press, 1975), 270.

33. Michel Foucault, *The Order of Things: An Archaeology of the Human Sciences* (New York: Pantheon, 1970), 80.

34. In this regard, see Chris Anderson, ed., *The Tyrannies of Virtue: The Cultural Criticism of John P. Sisk* (Norman: University of Oklahoma Press, 1990), esp. xxvii–xxxiv.

35. Paul H. Fry, *The Reach of Criticism: Method and Perception in Literary Theory* (New Haven: Yale University Press, 1983), 200.

TWO. Gardening for Love—The Work of the Essayist

1. Elizabeth Hardwick, Introduction to *The Best American Essays, 1986*, ed. Elizabeth Hardwick (New York: Ticknor and Fields, 1986), xv.

2. Michel Eyquem, Sieur de Montaigne, *The Complete Essays of Montaigne*, trans. Donald Frame (Stanford: Stanford University Press, 1958), 135, 736.

3. William H. Gass, "Emerson and the Essay," in *Habitations of the Word* (New York: Simon and Schuster, 1985), 26–27.

4. Ibid., 27, 28.

5. Graham Good, *The Observing Self: Rediscovering the Essay* (London: Routledge, 1988), xii.

6. William Howarth, "Itinerant Passages: Recent American Essays," *Sewanee Review* 96 (1988): 642.

7. Good, *The Observing Self*, 41.

8. Ibid., 40.

9. Geoffrey Hartman, *The Fate of Reading and Other Essays* (Chicago: University of Chicago Press, 1975), 292.

10. Geoffrey Hartman, *Easy Pieces* (New York: Columbia University Press, 1985), 176–77, 179.

11. John Keats, Letter of 21, 27[?] December 1817 to George and Thomas

Keats, in *Selected Poems and Letters*, ed. Douglas Bush (Boston: Houghton Mifflin, Riverside Press, 1959), 261; George Eliot, *Adam Bede* (New York: New American Library, Signet Books, 1961), 176; Good, *The Observing Self*, 14.

12. *The Prose Works of Alexander Pope*, ed. Norman Ault, vol. 1, *The Earlier Works, 1711–1720* (Oxford: Basil Blackwell, 1936), 148.

13. E. B. White, *Essays of E. B. White* (New York: Harper and Row, 1977), vii.

14. Ibid.

15. Ibid.

16. Ibid., viii.

17. Edward Hoagland, "What I Think, What I Am," in *The Tugman's Passage* (New York: Penguin, 1983), 27.

18. White, *Essays*, viii; Joseph Epstein, "Piece Work: Writing the Essay," in his *Plausible Prejudices: Essays on American Writing* (New York: Norton, 1985), 405.

19. Samuel F. Pickering, Jr., "Being Familiar," *The Right Distance* (Athens: University of Georgia Press, 1987), 9.

20. Susan Allen Toth, *How to Prepare for Your High-School Reunion and Other Midlife Musings* (Boston: Little, Brown, 1988), 160.

21. Quoted in ibid., 160.

22. Samuel F. Pickering, Jr., "These Essays, My Life," *Still Life* (Hanover, N.H.: University Press of New England, 1990), 82–92.

THREE. Critical Writing and the Burden of History

1. Robert Pack and Jay Parini, eds., *The Bread Loaf Anthology of Contemporary American Essays* (Hanover, N.H.: University Press of New England, 1984), v.

2. Geoffrey Hartman, *The Fate of Reading and Other Essays* (Chicago: University of Chicago Press, 1975), 269.

3. Chris Anderson, *Style and Argument: Contemporary American Nonfiction* (Carbondale: Southern Illinois University Press, 1987), 142.

4. Leslie Fiedler, ed., *The Art of the Essay*, 2d ed. (New York: Crowell, 1969), 2.

5. Graham Good, *The Observing Self: Rediscovering the Essay* (London: Routledge, 1988), passim. See also Edward W. Said, *The World, the Text, and the Critic* (Cambridge: Harvard University Press, 1983), esp. 50–53.

6. Theodor Adorno, "The Essay as Form," trans. Bob Hullott-Kentor and Frederic Will, *New German Critique* 32 (Spring 1984): 166; Matthew Arnold, "The Function of Criticism at the Present Time," in *Poetry and Criticism of Matthew Arnold*, ed. A. Dwight Culler (Boston: Houghton Mifflin, Riverside Press, 1961), 246, 244; W. Wolfgang Holdheim, "Introduction: The Essay as Knowledge in Progress," in *The Hermeneutic Mode: Essays on Time in Literature and Theory* (Ithaca: Cornell University Press, 1984), 28; Geoffrey Hartman, *Criticism in the Wilderness: The Study of Literature Today* (New Haven: Yale University Press, 1980), 75.

7. John Keats, Letter of 21, 27[?] December 1817 to George and Thomas Keats, in *Selected Poems and Letters*, ed. Douglas Bush (Boston: Houghton Mifflin, Riverside Press, 1959), 261.

8. Geoffrey Hartman, *Wordsworth's Poetry 1787–1814* (New Haven: Yale University Press, 1964), 290.

FOUR. Criticism, Theory, and the Essay: Strange Bedfellows?

1. Gerald Graff, *Professing Literature: An Institutional History* (Chicago: University of Chicago Press, 1987), 61; Irving Babbitt, *Literature and the American College: Essays in Defense of the Humanities* (Boston: Houghton Mifflin, 1908), 118–19, quoted in Graff, *Professing Literature*, 107; Joseph Epstein, "Piece Work: Writing the Essay," in *Plausible Prejudices: Essays on American Writing* (New York: Norton, 1985), 400.

2. Gerald Graff and Reginald Gibbons, eds., *Criticism in the University* (Evanston, Ill.: Northwestern University Press, 1985), 7, 8.

3. Morris Dickstein, "Criticism and Journalism," in Graff and Gibbons, *Criticism in the University*, 154–55.

4. Ibid., 157.

5. Sandra M. Gilbert, quoted in Gerald Graff, "Feminist Criticism in the University: An Interview with Sandra M. Gilbert," in Graff and Gibbons, *Criticism in the University*, 111, 121. Of course, Bloom has published a novel (1979) and Hartman poetry (a volume, in 1978), facts apparently unknown to Gilbert.

6. James Engell, *Forming the Critical Mind: Dryden to Coleridge* (Cambridge: Harvard University Press, 1989), 257–58.

7. John A. McCarthy, *Crossing Boundaries: A Theory and History of Essay Writing in German, 1680–1815* (Philadelphia: University of Pennsylvania Press, 1989), 88. McCarthy prefers to talk of the essayistic rather than the essay, of the qualities common to more than one genre.

8. Epstein, "Piece Work," 400.

9. Epstein, Introduction to *Plausible Prejudices*, 13–14.

10. Ibid., 18–19.

11. Ibid., 31.

12. Reginald Gibbons, "Academic Criticism and Contemporary Literature," in Graff and Gibbons, *Criticism in the University*, 15, 19.

13. Peter Stitt, "Writers, Theorists, and the Department of English," *Newsletter* (Associated Writing Programs) 19 (September–October 1987): 1.

14. Ibid., 3.

15. Ibid., 19.

16. Quoted in Geoffrey Hartman, "Tea and Totality: The Demand of Theory on Critical Style," in *After Strange Texts: The Role of Theory in the Study of Literature*,

ed. Gregory S. Jay and David L. Miller (University: University of Alabama Press, 1985), 35–36.

17. Graham Good, *The Observing Self: Rediscovering the Essay* (London: Routledge, 1988), 180.

18. Phillip Lopate, *Against Joie de Vivre* (New York: Poseidon, 1989), 84.

19. Walter Benjamin, *The Origin of German Tragic Drama*, trans. John Osborne (London: New Left, 1977), 32, 28.

20. Max Bense, "Über den Essay und seine Prosa," *Merkur* 1, no. 3 (1947): 418, 420; quoted in Theodor Adorno, "The Essay as Form," trans. Bob Hullott-Kentor and Frederic Will, *New German Critique* 32 (Spring 1984): 164, 166.

21. Georg Lukács, "On the Nature and Form of the Essay," in *Soul and Form*, trans. Anna Bostock (Cambridge: MIT Press, 1974), 1, 2, 7.

22. Ibid., 8.

23. Ibid., 9

24. Ibid., 9–10.

25. Ibid., 13.

26. Ibid., 14.

27. Ibid., 16.

28. Geoffrey Hartman, *Criticism in the Wilderness: The Study of Literature Today* (New Haven: Yale University Press, 1980), 195; Lukács, "On the Nature and Form of the Essay," 15.

29. Adorno, "The Essay as Form," 153.

30. Ibid., 165.

31. Ibid., 169–70.

32. Ibid., 164.

33. R. Lane Kauffmann, "The Skewed Path: Essaying as Unmethodical Method," *Essays on the Essay: Redefining the Essay*, ed. Alexander J. Butrym (Athens: University of Georgia Press, 1989), 231.

34. Adorno, "The Essay as Form," 162–63.

35. Ibid., 157.

36. Ibid., 164.

37. Ibid., 158.

38. Ibid., 159.

39. Ibid., 154.

40. Ibid., 160–61.

41. Ibid., 161, 165. And see Martin Jay, *Adorno* (Cambridge: Harvard University Press, 1984), esp. 14–15.

42. Adorno, "The Essay as Form," 168.

43. Kauffmann, "The Skewed Path," 232.

44. Elizabeth W. Bruss, *Beautiful Theories: The Spectacle of Discourse in Contempo-*

rary Criticism (Baltimore: Johns Hopkins University Press, 1982), 116.

45. Ibid., 90.

46. Ibid., 75.

47. Ibid., 78–79.

48. Ibid., 86, 80–81, 86.

49. Ibid., 467.

50. Ibid., 122.

51. Ibid., 123–24.

52. Ibid., 483.

53. Ibid., 132–33.

54. Ibid., 119.

55. Paul H. Fry, *The Reach of Criticism: Method and Perception in Literary Theory* (New Haven: Yale University Press, 1983), 200 (see also G. Douglas Atkins, *Geoffrey Hartman: Criticism as Answerable Style* [London: Routledge, 1990]; Geoffrey H. Hartman, *The Fate of Reading and Other Essays* (Chicago: University of Chicago Press, 1975), 255.

56. Hartman, *Criticism in the Wilderness*, 191; Geoffrey Hartman, "How Creative Should Literary Criticism Be?" *New York Times Book Review*, 5 April 1981, 25; Hartman, *Criticism in the Wilderness*, 195, 191.

57. Hartman, *The Fate of Reading*, 155.

58. Ibid., 9.

59. Ibid., 278–79.

60. Hartman, *Criticism in the Wilderness*, 233.

61. Ibid., 197.

62. Hartman, *The Fate of Reading*, 229; Geoffrey Hartman, *Beyond Formalism* (New Haven: Yale University Press, 1970), 50. I discuss at some length the essayistic nature of his writing in *Geoffrey Hartman: Criticism as Answerable Style*.

63. Hartman, *Criticism in the Wilderness*, 4; Hartman, *The Fate of Reading*, 254, 272.

64. William H. Gass, *On Being Blue* (Boston: Godine, 1976), 44–45.

65. Cynthia Ozick, *Metaphor and Memory* (New York: Knopf, 1989), 109–10.

66. Hartman, *Criticism in the Wilderness*, 1, 11.

67. Ibid., 19.

FIVE. The Return of/to the Personal

1. Jane Tompkins, "Me and My Shadow," *NLH* 19 (1987): 170; Geoffrey Hartman, *Criticism in the Wilderness: The Study of Literature Today* (New Haven: Yale University Press, 1980), 1. Tompkins's essay appears in expanded form in *Gender and Theory: Dialogues on Feminist Criticism*, ed. Linda Kaufman (New York: Basil Blackwell, 1989), 121–39.

2. Tompkins, "Me and My Shadow," 170.

3. Roland Barthes, "Inaugural Lecture, College de France," trans. Richard Howard, in *A Barthes Reader*, ed. Susan Sontag (New York: Hill and Wang, 1982), 457.

4. Scott Walker, ed., *The Graywolf Annual Three: Essays, Memoirs & Reflections* (Saint Paul, Minn.: Graywolf, 1986), vi.

5. John Stone, *In the Country of Hearts: Journeys in the Art of Medicine* (New York: Delacorte, 1990), 7–8.

6. Annie Dillard, Introduction to *The Best American Essays, 1988*, ed. Annie Dillard (New York: Ticknor and Fields, 1988), xvi, xvii.

7. Phyllis Theroux, "Lifelines: Women and Writing," *Lear's*, May 1990, 56, 58.

8. Norman Sims, "The Literary Journalists," in *The Literary Journalists: The Art of Personal Reportage*, ed. Norman Sims (New York: Ballantine, 1984), 5, 17.

9. Ibid., 6, 17.

10. Harvey Cox, *Many Mansions: A Christian's Encounter with Other Faiths* (Boston: Beacon, 1988), 5.

11. Susan A. Handelman, *Fragments of Redemption: Jewish Thought and Literary Theory in Benjamin, Scholem, and Levinas* (Bloomington: Indiana University Press, forthcoming). I am much indebted to this study, which I cite from manuscript. This first quotation appears in 5/13, by which I refer to chapter and page.

12. Emmanuel Levinas, *Otherwise Than Being*, trans. Alphonso Lingis (The Hague: Martinus Nijhoff, 1978), 4.

13. Handelman, *Fragments of Redemption*, 7/1, 7/46.

14. Ibid., 7/47.

15. Ibid., 8/5, 8/34.

16. Ibid., 5/14.

17. Ibid., 6/27.

18. Levinas, *Totality and Infinity: An Essay on Exteriority*, trans. Alphonso Lingis (Pittsburgh: Duquesne University Press, 1969), 245, quoted in Handelman, 6/27.

19. Handelman, *Fragments of Redemption*, 6/27.

20. Levinas, *Otherwise Than Being*, 55, quoted in Handelman, 6/27.

21. Handelman, *Fragments of Redemption*, 7/40. Levinas's similarity to but also difference from Derrida is apparent here.

22. Jim Merod, "Blues and the Art of Critical Thinking," in *Pedagogy Is Politics: Literary Theory and Critical Teaching*, ed. Maria-Regina Kecht (Urbana: University of Illinois Press, 1992), 67–68.

23. John Schilb, "Poststructuralism, Politics, and the Subject of Pedagogy," in *Pedagogy Is Politics*, 53–54.

24. Ibid., 54–55.

25. Stuart Schneiderman, *Jacques Lacan: The Death of an Intellectual Hero* (Cambridge: Harvard University Press, 1983), vi; Shoshana Felman, *Jacques Lacan and*

the Adventure of Insight: Psychoanalysis in Contemporary Culture (Cambridge: Harvard University Press, 1987), 3.

26. Felman, *Jacques Lacan*, 4–5; Jane Gallop, *Reading Lacan* (Ithaca: Cornell University Press, 1985), 18.

27. Tzvetan Todorov, *Literature and Its Theorists: A Personal View of Twentieth-Century Criticism*, trans. Catherine Porter (Ithaca: Cornell University Press, 1987), 161–62, 167.

28. Ibid., 9. From a different perspective there is Michael Ryan's *Politics and Culture: Working Hypotheses for a Post-Revolutionary Society* (Baltimore: Johns Hopkins University Press, 1989), which at the end directly engages the personal.

29. Sandra M. Gilbert, quoted in Gerald Graff, "Feminist Criticism in the University: An Interview with Sandra M. Gilbert," in *Criticism in the University*, ed. Gerald Graff and Reginald Gibbons (Evanston, Ill.: Northwestern University Press, 1985), 113.

30. Frances Murphy Zauhar, "Creative Voices: Women Reading and Women's Voices" (Manuscript), 2, 3. I am indebted to Zauhar for directing me to much of the personal (feminist) criticism briefly discussed below.

31. Rachel M. Brownstein, *Becoming a Heroine: Reading about Women in Novels* (New York: Viking, 1982), xxviii.

32. Blanche Gelfant, *Women Writing in America: Voices in Collage* (Hanover, N.H.: University Press of New England, 1984), 7; Zauhar, "Creative Voices," 8.

33. Zauhar, "Creative Voices," 8–9.

34. Judith Fetterley, *Provisions: A Reader from Nineteenth-Century American Women* (Bloomington: Indiana University Press, 1985), 37.

35. Tompkins, "Me and My Shadow," 169.

36. Ibid., 173.

37. Ursula Le Guin, quoted in ibid., 173–74.

38. Cheryl B. Torsney, "Me and My Essay" (Manuscript), 1.

39. Ibid., 1–2.

40. Ibid., 2–3, 4.

41. Ibid., 8.

42. Ibid., 9–10.

43. Ibid., 11–12.

44. Diane P. Freedman, "Border-crossing as Method and Motif in Contemporary American Writing; or, How Freud Helped Me Case the Joint" (Manuscript), 2, 12; Olivia Frey, "Intimate Criticism: Autobiographical Literary Criticism" (Manuscript), 1. This is an important anthology, in which are included the essays noted by Torsney, Freedman, Zauhar, Brenda Daly, Laurel Smith, Barbara Ryan, and Michelle Johnson, Pam Marshall, and Linnea Stenson. I want to thank Olivia Frey for allowing me to see this work in manuscript. I also want to draw attention to Frey's "Beyond Literary Darwinism: Women's Voices and Critical Discourse,"

College English, 52 (1990): 507–26, as well as to Nicole Ward Jouve's *White Woman Speaks with Forked Tongue: Criticism as Autobiography* (New York: Routledge, 1991).

45. Laurel Smith, "Adrienne Rich, the Tactile Art of Poetry, and Me" (Manuscript), 2; Brenda Daly, "My Friend, Joyce Carol Oates" (Manuscript), 17; Violet Weingarten, *Intimations of Mortality* (New York: Knopf, 1978); Barbara Ryan, "Chrysalis, a Thesis Journal" (Manuscript), 26.

46. Michelle Johnson, Pam Marshall, and Linnea Stenson, "Saturdays, Motorcycles, and Kitchens: 'Life in the Usual Sense'" (Manuscript), 1.

47. Rachel Blau DuPlessis, "For the Etruscans," in *The New Feminist Criticism: Essays on Women, Literature, and Theory*, ed. Elaine Showalter (New York: Pantheon, 1985), 276. After my work was completed, I came across DuPlessis's *The Pink Guitar: Writing as Feminist Practice* (New York: Routledge, 1990), which reprints "For the Etruscans" and makes available other critical experimentation.

48. Annie Dillard, *The Writing Life* (New York: Harper and Row, 1989), 3–4.

49. DuPlessis, "For the Etruscans," 279.

50. Carolyn G. Heilbrun, *Writing a Woman's Life* (New York: Ballantine, 1988), 20; Mary Ann Caws, *Women of Bloomsbury: Virginia, Vanessa, and Carrington* (New York: Routledge, 1990), 2. In some important ways Caws echoes Geoffrey Hartman's notion of the critic as elaborating the text that has called hers or his into being. At any rate, after *Estranging the Familiar* was completed and in press, I received Nancy K. Miller's *Getting Personal: Feminist Occasions and Other Autobiographical Acts* (New York: Routledge, 1991). I regret that I did not have the opportunity to benefit from Miller's arguments and insights or to relate my position here to hers.

51. Caws, *Women of Bloomsbury*, 4–5, 2–3.

52. Ibid., 3.

53. Richard M. Chadbourne, "A Puzzling Literary Genre: Comparative Views of the Essay," *Comparative Literature Studies* 20 (1983): 149.

SIX. Toward an Answerable Style: Critical Experiments and Artful Criticism

1. Geoffrey Hartman, *Criticism in the Wilderness: The Study of Literature Today* (New Haven: Yale University Press, 1980), 26, 155, 113.

2. Geoffrey Hartman, *The Fate of Reading and Other Essays* (Chicago: University of Chicago Press, 1975), 8.

3. Hartman, *Criticism in the Wilderness*, 1, 257.

4. Gillian Rose, *The Melancholy Science: An Introduction to the Thought of Theodor W. Adorno* (New York: Columbia University Press, 1978), 111–12; Hartman, *Criticism in the Wilderness*, 218.

5. Hartman, *Criticism in the Wilderness*, 191. On reader responsibility, see

G. Douglas Atkins, "Reader-Responsibility Criticism: The Recent Work of Geoffrey Hartman," in Atkins, *Reading Deconstruction/Deconstructive Reading* (Lexington: University Press of Kentucky, 1983), and Atkins, *Geoffrey Hartman: Criticism as Answerable Style* (London: Routledge, 1990).

6. Hartman, *The Fate of Reading*, 269.

7. Marianna Torgovnick, "Experimental Critical Writing," *ADE Bulletin* 96 (1990): 10.

8. Samuel F. Pickering, Jr., "Fictive Time and the House of Criticism," *Sewanee Review* 87 (1979): 656; Richard McKeon, "Philosophical Bases of Art Criticism," in *Critics and Criticism: Essays in Method*, ed. R. S. Crane (Chicago: University of Chicago Press, 1957), 193 (I am grateful to my colleague Richard F. Hardin for this reference); H. L. Mencken, quoted in Geoffrey Hartman, "How Creative Should Literary Criticism Be?" *New York Times Book Review*, 5 April 1981: 25.

9. Oscar Wilde, "The Critic as Artist," in *Literary Criticism of Oscar Wilde*, ed. Stanley Weintraub (Lincoln: University of Nebraska Press, 1969), 220.

10. Ibid., 222.

11. Ibid., 220–21.

12. Ibid., 222.

13. Ibid., 222–25; Hartman, *Criticism in the Wilderness*, 259.

14. Wilde, "The Critic as Artist," 225.

15. Ibid., 227.

16. Hartman, *Criticism in the Wilderness*, 256–57, 20.

17. Torgovnick, "Experimental Critical Writing," 9.

18. Ibid., 10.

19. Ibid.

20. John Dryden, Preface to *Ovid's Epistles*, in *Essays of John Dryden*, ed. W. P. Ker (Oxford: Clarendon Press, 1926), 1:237; Ihab Hassan, *Paracriticisms: Seven Speculations of the Times* (Urbana: University of Illinois Press, 1975), 25.

21. Hassan, *Paracriticisms*, xi.

22. Ibid., vii.

23. Ibid., 25.

24. Ibid., xii.

25. Ibid., 122–23.

26. See, esp., Geoffrey Hartman, *The Unmediated Vision: An Interpretation of Wordsworth, Hopkins, Rilke, and Valéry* (1954; New York: Harcourt, Brace, 1966).

27. Hartman, *Criticism in the Wilderness*, 218.

28. Cynthia Ozick, *Metaphor and Memory* (New York: Knopf, 1989), 223.

29. Ozick's essay, included in *Metaphor and Memory*, is "Ruth."

30. Jerome J. McGann, *Swinburne: An Experiment in Criticism* (Chicago: University of Chicago Press, 1972), 1.

31. Ibid., 1–2.

32. Ibid., 3.

33. See the Fall and Winter 1989 issue of *Alaska Quarterly Review*. Robert Pack and Jay Parini, Foreword, *The Bread Loaf Anthology of Contemporary American Essays*, ed. Pack and Parini (Hanover, N.H.: University Press of New England, 1989), vi. Leonard Michaels's *Shuffle* (New York: Farrar, Straus and Giroux, 1990) is billed (on the dustjacket) as "autobiographical fiction in the form of confession, memoir, journal, essay, and short story."

34. "Recalcitrance," by the way, refers not to a person's or persons' opposition but instead to the resistance to formal structures that texts exhibit, a technical, theoretical matter important to Wright, long concerned with form; see, in this regard, Austin M. Wright, *The Formal Principle in the Novel* (Ithaca: Cornell University Press, 1982).

35. Virginia Woolf, *A Room of One's Own* (New York: Harcourt, Brace, 1929), 4–5.

36. Ibid., 80.

37. Ibid., 78.

38. Ibid., 105–6.

39. Ibid., 83.

40. Emir Rodriguez Monegal and Alastair Reid, eds., *Borges: A Reader* (New York: Dutton, 1981), ix.

41. Jorge Luis Borges, "Pierre Menard, Author of *Don Quixote*," trans. Anthony Bonner, in *Ficciones* (New York: Grove Press, 1962), 48–49.

42. Ibid., 54–55.

43. Monegal and Reid, *Borges*, ix.

44. Jorge Luis Borges, "The Enigma of Edward FitzGerald," in *Other Inquisitions, 1937–1952*, trans. Ruth L. C. Simms (Austin: University of Texas Press, 1964), 77–78.

45. Carlos Fuentes, "Borges in Action," in *Myself with Others* (New York: Farrar, Straus and Giroux, 1988), 141.

46. Ibid., 143, 144.

47. Ibid., 146.

48. Ibid., 147, 151–52.

49. Ibid., 156, 157.

50. Ibid., 158, 141.

51. Ibid., 158–59.

52. Hartman, *Criticism in the Wilderness*, 2.

53. Fay Weldon, *Letters to Alice on First Reading Jane Austen* (New York: Carroll and Graf, 1990), 13, 14, 84, 108, 33.

54. Jane Austen, *Emma* (Boston: Houghton Mifflin, Riverside Press, 1957), 192.

55. Weldon, *Letters to Alice*, 93–94.

56. Ibid., 51.

SEVEN. Some Adventures of the Soul: A Journey around Essay

1. Montaigne, *The Complete Essays*, trans. Donald Frame (Stanford: Stanford University Press, 1958), [2].

2. William Howarth, "Itinerant Passages: Recent American Essays," *Sewanee Review* 96 (1988): 633.

3. Tompkins, "Me and My Shadow," *NLH* 19 (1987): 169.

4. John Keats, Letter of 21 April 1819 to George and Georgiana Keats, in *Selected Poems and Letters*, ed. Douglas Bush (Boston: Houghton Mifflin, Riverside Press, 1959), 289.

5. Robert Con Davis, "Critical Introduction: The Discourse of the Father," in *The Fictional Father: Lacanian Readings of the Text*, ed. Robert Con Davis (Amherst: University of Massachusetts Press, 1981), 1–26.

6. Homer, *The Odyssey*, trans. W. H. D. Rouse (1937; New York: New American Library, Mentor Books, 1962), 103, 104. Hereafter, page references are given in the text. I follow Rouse's spelling.

7. Neil Hertz, "Two Extravagant Teachings," in *The Pedagogical Imperative: Teaching as a Literary Genre*, ed. Barbara Johnson, *Yale French Studies*, no. 63 (1982): 60.

EIGHT. Bringing Theory to Life: Crossing the Line

1. Homer, *The Odyssey*, trans. W. H. D. Rouse (New York: New American Library, Mentor Books, 1937), 128.

2. Jacques Derrida, *Of Grammatology*, trans. Gayatri Chakravorty Spivak (Baltimore: Johns Hopkins University Press, 1976), 62; Barbara Johnson, Translator's Introduction, in Jacques Derrida, *Dissemination*, trans. Barbara Johnson (Chicago: University of Chicago Press, 1981), xiii.

3. René Girard, *Violence and the Sacred*, trans. Patrick Gregory (Baltimore: Johns Hopkins University Press, 1977), 29; Andrew J. McKenna, "Biblioclasm: Joycing Jesus and Borges," *Diacritics* 8 (Fall 1978): 29; Paul Tournier, *The Violence Within* (New York: Harper and Row, 1977), 97; Samuel Weber, "After Eight: Remarking Glyph," *Glyph* 8 (1981): 236.

4. Herbert N. Schneidau, *Sacred Discontent: The Bible and Western Tradition* (Baton Rouge: Louisiana State University Press, 1976).

5. Harold S. Kushner, *When Bad Things Happen to Good People* (New York: Schocken Books, 1981), 72.

6. Derrida, *Of Grammatology*, 87; Geoffrey Hartman, *Criticism in the Wilderness: The Study of Literature Today* (New Haven: Yale University Press, 1980), 11, 210, 206.

7. George Eliot, *Adam Bede* (New York: New American Library, Signet Books, 1961), 405. *

8. G. Douglas Atkins, "Going against the Grain: Deconstruction and the Scriblerians," *Scriblerian* 17 (1985): 113–17.

9. Jane Tompkins, "Fighting Words: Unlearning to Write the Critical Essay," *Georgia Review* 42 (1988): 589, 590.

10. Keith Fort, "The Psychopathology of the Everyday Language of the Profession of Literary Studies," *College English* 40 (1979): 751–63. See also his "Form, Authority, and the Critical Essay," rpt. in *Contemporary Rhetoric: A Conceptual Background with Readings*, ed. W. Ross Winterowd (New York: Harcourt, Brace, 1975).

NINE. Finding a Voice

1. Cynthia Ozick, *Metaphor and Memory* (New York: Knopf, 1989), 109–10.

2. Geoffrey Hartman, *Criticism in the Wilderness: The Study of Literature Today* (New Haven: Yale University Press, 1980), 225.

3. William H. Gass, "Emerson and the Essay," in his *Habitations of the Word* (New York: Simon and Schuster, 1985), 28.

4. Pat C. Hoy II, "Mosaics of Southern Masculinity: Small-Scale Mythologies," *Sewanee Review* 97 (1989): 228.

5. Ibid., 220, 229.

6. Samuel F. Pickering, Jr., "Voyages and the Indulgent Self," *Sewanee Review* 97 (1989): 297.

7. This last distinction I know from Donald Hall, Foreword to Ronald Jager, *Eighty Acres: Elegy for a Family Farm* (Boston: Beacon Press, 1990), xii.

8. Samuel F. Pickering, Jr., *The Right Distance* (Athens: University of Georgia Press, 1987), 170.

9. E. B. White, *Essays of E. B. White* (New York: Harper and Row, 1977), viii.

10. Samuel F. Pickering, Jr., *Still Life* (Hanover, N.H.: University Press of New England, 1990), 15; Joseph Epstein, "Piece Work: Writing the Essay," *Plausible Prejudices: Essays on American Writing* (New York: Norton, 1985), 405.

Index